INTERNATIONAL ECONOMIC INTEGRATION

International economic integration is defined as the act of two nations or more agreeing to pursue common aims and policies. Since the world contains numerous schemes of this nature, there is a great need for a book which gives adequate discussion and coverage of *all* significant schemes. The aim of this book is to do precisely that in a brief and concise manner. It is, therefore, a unique book.

The editor, Ali M. El-Agraa, of the University of Leeds, has written widely on the subject and one of his books, *The Economics of the European Community*, has been recognized as the most authoritative work in the field. The contributors are distinguished and international: Drs. Victor G. Bulmer-Thomas of Queen Mary College, M. H. J. Finch and David E. Hojman of the University of Liverpool and Professor Kenneth O. Hall of the University of New York at Oswego, are specialists on Latin America and Caribbean integration; Arthur Hazlewood, Director of the Institute of Commonwealth Studies, University of Oxford, and Professor Peter Robson of the University of St. Andrews have written widely on African integration and disintegration; Professors Paul Marer of Indiana University and John Michael Montias of Yale University, are leading authorities on the CMEA; Professor Victoria Curzon Price of the Institut Universitaire d'Études Européennes, Switzerland, is a specialist on EFTA; and Dr. David G. Mayes, Editor of the *National Institute Economic Review*, is an expert on estimating the quantitative effects of integration.

Also by Ali M. El-Agraa

THE ECONOMICS OF THE EUROPEAN COMMUNITY (*editor*)

THEORY OF CUSTOMS UNIONS (*with A. J. Jones*)

INTERNATIONAL ECONOMIC INTEGRATION

Edited by

Ali M. El-Agraa

St. Martin's Press   New York

ISBN 0–312–42085–4

Library of Congress Cataloging in Publication Data

Main entry under title:

International economic integration.

    Bibliography: p.
    Includes indexes.
    1. International economic integration.
I. El-Agraa, A. M.

HF1411.I51714 1982	337.1	81–21261
ISBN 0–312–42085–4		AACR2

To Diana, Mark
and the Moults

Contents

Preface and Acknowledgements

Those interested in the field of international economic integration probably share my concern regarding the scope of most books under that title: the majority refer to the European Community and some make additional occasional reference to other schemes such as the European Free Trade Association (EFTA), the Council for Mutual Economic Assistance (CMEA, or COMECON as it is generally known in the West) or the Latin-American Free Trade Association (LAFTA). Since international economic integration is defined as the act of two nations or more agreeing to pursue common aims and policies (see Chapter 1) and since the world contains numerous schemes of this nature, it would seem appropriate that such books should give adequate discussion and coverage of *all* significant schemes. My aim with this book is to do precisely that in a brief and concise manner.

The book could not have taken its present form or structure without the cooperation of my distinguished and truly international group of contributors to all of whom I am extremely grateful. Dr Victor Bulmer-Thomas of Queen Mary College, University of London, Dr Henry Finch of the Centre for Latin American Studies, University of Liverpool, and Associate Professor Kenneth Hall of the College of Arts and Science, State University of New York at Oswego are specialists on Latin American and Caribbean integration and contributed the chapters on the Central American Common Market (CACM), LAFTA and the Caribbean Common Market (CARICOM) respectively. Dr David Hojman of the Centre for Latin American Studies, University of Liverpool, collaborated with me in the writing of the chapter on the Andean Pact. The chapter on EFTA was provided by Professor Victoria Curzon Price of the Institut Universitaire d'Études Européennes, a leading authority on the subject. Arthur Hazlewood, Director of the Institute of Commonwealth Studies, University of Oxford, who has written widely on African integration and disintegration, contributed the chapter on

the East African Community (EAC). Associate Professor Paul Marer of
Indiana University and Professor Michael Montias of Yale University,
leading authorities on the CMEA, are the joint authors of the chapter on
that scheme. Dr David Mayes, editor of the *National Institute Economic
Review*, wrote the chapter on his special interest, the quantitative
problems of estimating integration effects. Finally, Professor Peter
Robson of the University of St Andrews, who has written extensively on
integration particularly in Africa, contributed the chapter on the West
African Economic Community.

The analysis of such schemes requires knowledge of the theory of
international economic integration as well as of the problems regarding
the empirical evaluation of integration effects. So as to highlight the
issues involved and to avoid repetition, separate chapters have been
provided on these aspects.

I should like to thank Mrs Margaret Mann of the School of Economic
Studies at the University of Leeds for her typing of the manuscript.

Leeds   A. M. E.-A.

Notes on the Contributors

Dr Victor G. Bulmer-Thomas is Lecturer in Economics, Queen Mary College, University of London. He also lectures to the Public Sector Management Course of the Royal Institute of Public Administration on the role of private enterprise in developing countries. He was VSO Teacher at St Michael's College, Belize City (1966–7), and Research Fellow at Fraser of Allander Institute, Strathclyde University (1975–8). His other activities include involvement in the quarterly review for the Economist Intelligence Unit on the political economy of Central America; being Consultant for the Moroccan government and preparing input–output tables for use in the 1976–8 Development Plan; and preparing of input–output tables for Costa Rica (1974–5). He has written several journal articles and monographs and is author of *Input–Output Analysis: Sources, Methods and Applications for Developing Countries* (1982) and joint author of *Dar-Al-Handasah, Étude d'identification et d'evaluation des possibilités d'investissements industrielles*, 3 vols (1979). He is presently researching on development problems.

Ali M. El-Agraa is Senior Lecturer in Economics, School of Economic Studies, University of Leeds. He was Senior Research Officer (1964–7) and Lecturer in Economics (1967–71), Faculty of Economic and Social Studies, University of Khartoum, and was also Economic Adviser to the Ministry of Finance and Economics, Khartoum, between 1967 and 1968. He has refereed articles for the *Economic Journal, Bulletin of Economic Research* and the *Manchester School*. He has published several journal articles and numerous discussion papers. He is editor of *The Economics of the European Community* (1980), co-author (with A. J. Jones) of *Theory of Customs Unions* (1981) and author of *International Trade* (forthcoming).

M. H. J. Finch is Lecturer in Economic History at the University of Liverpool, having formerly been Lecturer in Economics at the Centre for Latin American Studies at the same university. He has made a number of visits to Latin America since 1967. His publications include *Historia Económica del Uruguay Contemporáneo* (1980) and *A Political Economy of Uruguay since 1870* (1981).

Kenneth O. Hall is an Associate Professor of History at SUNY/Oswego. He was an Instructor at Queen's University, Kingston, Ontario; Adjunct Professor at Hobart and William Smith Colleges, Geneva and New York; and Instructor and Visiting Professor at the University of the West Indies, Mona, Kingston, Jamaica (1966–71). He held administrative and research positions as Chief of the Conference and Documentation Centre and Director of the General Services and Administration Division at the Caribbean Community Secretariat, Guyana (1975–7). Caribbean integration, ACP relations and African history are the three main areas of his research. Some of his consultant work has been with the Third World Forum, Geneva, Switzerland; International Foundation for Development Alternatives, Nyon, Switzerland; ACP Secretariat, Brussels, Belgium; and CARICOM Secretariat, Guyana. He is author of *Imperial Proconsul: Sir Hercules Robinson and South Africa, 1881–1889* (1980) as well as other books and monographs.

Arthur Hazlewood is Warden of Queen Elizabeth House and Director of the Oxford University Institute of Commonwealth Studies. He is a Professorial Fellow of Pembroke College, Oxford. Previously he was Senior Research Officer at the Institute of Economics and Statistics and a Tutorial Fellow of Pembroke College. He has been concerned with African affairs since 1950 and was Director of the Common Market Secretariat in the Office of the President of Kenya during the negotiation of the Treaty for East African Cooperation. His books include *Nyasaland: The Economics of Federation* (co-author 1960), *The Economy of Africa* (1961), *Rail and Road in East Africa* (1964), *African Integration and Disintegration* (editor, 1967), *Economic Integration: The East African Experience* (1975), *Aid and Inequality in Kenya* (co-author, 1976) and *The Economy of Kenya: The Kenyatta Era* (1979).

David E. Hojman is Lecturer in Latin American Economics at the University of Liverpool. He has worked for the University of Chile, the Chilean Corporation of Copper (CODELCO) and the University College of North Wales, Bangor. He is the author of *Regional Development and Planning* (1974) and of contributions to *Resources*

Policy (1980, 1981) and *Commodities, Finance and Trade: Issues in North–South Negotiations* (1980), and joint author of *Unemployment in Wales* (1980). He has presented papers to the Conference of the Association of University Teachers of Economics (AUTE) and to the Conference of the Society for Latin American Studies (SLAS).

Paul Marer is Professor of International Business at the School of Business, Indiana University. He was previously affiliated with the City University of New York and Columbia University. He is co-editor of *East European Integration and East–West Trade* (1980) and *East–West Industrial Cooperation in the 1980s: Findings of a Joint US–Polish Project* (1981), and author of *Soviet and East European Foreign Trade* (1972) and numerous articles and chapters in books on East European integration, centrally planned economies, East–West commercial and financial relations and the role of multinational corporations in Eastern Europe.

David G. Mayes is Editor of the *National Institute Economic Review*, and is currently on leave from the University of Exeter, where he is Senior Lecturer in Economics. He has also held a visiting chair in the Netherlands and is an editor of the *Economic Journal*. He has publications in many journals, and is author of *The Property Boom: The Effects of Building Society Behaviour on House Prices* (1979), *Introductory Economic Statistics* (with A. C. Mayes, (1976), *Projects in Economic and Social Statistics* (editor, 1976, 1978) 2 vols, *Applications of Econometrics* (1981) and *Modern Portfolio Theory and Financial Institutions* (with D. C. Corner, 1982).

John Michael Montias is Professor of Economics at Yale University. He was Chairman of the Council on Russian and East European Studies (1964–74); Consultant in the UN (1972, 1973); Ford Fellow (1956–7); Guggenheim Fellow (1961–2); and Fellow at the Centre for Advanced Study in Behavioural Sciences (1968–9). He went on a study trip to China in 1973. He is a member of many associations including the American Association for the Advancement of Slavic Studies, of which he was Director-at-Large from 1968 to 1970. He is also the editor of the *Journal of Comparative Economics*. He is author of many books including *Central Planning in Poland* (1962), *Economic Development in Communist Russia* (1967) and *The Structure of Economic Systems* (1976).

Victoria Curzon Price is Associate Professor at the Institut Universitaire d'Études Européennes (Graduate Institute of European Studies), University of Geneva, and a faculty member of the Centre d'Études Industrielles (Centre for Education in International Management), Geneva. She is Visiting Lecturer at the Europa Instituut, University of Amsterdam. From 1969 to 1977 she was editor of the *Journal of World Trade Law*. Her publications include *The Essentials of Economic Integration: Lessons of EFTA Experience* (1974), *The Management of Trade Relations in the GATT* (with Gerard Curzon, 1976), *Multinational Enterprise in a Hostile World* (co-editor with Gerard Curzon, 1977), *Unemployment and other Non-Work Issues* (1980) and *Industrial Policies in the European Community* (1981).

Peter Robson has occupied the Chair of Economics at St Andrews University since 1968. He was previously Professor of Economics at the University of Nairobi. International economic integration has been one of his major interests for a number of years. He has undertaken empirical studies of several groupings and written numerous articles. He is the author of *Economic Integration in Africa* (1968) and *The Economics of International Integration* (1980). He has also edited *International Economic Integration* (1971), has written a monograph on fiscal compensation in economic groupings and is co-author of *The Economies of Africa* (1969).

1 General Introduction

Ali M. El-Agraa

INTERNATIONAL ECONOMIC INTEGRATION

'International economic integration' is one aspect of 'international economics' which has been growing in importance in the past two decades or so. The term itself has a rather short history; indeed, Machlup (1977) was unable to find a single instance of its use prior to 1942. Since then the term has been used at various times to refer to practically any area of international economic relations. By 1950, however, the term had been given a specific definition by economists specialising in international trade to denote a state of affairs or a process which involves the amalgamation of separate economies into larger regions, and it is in this more limited sense that the term is used today. More specifically, international economic integration is concerned with the discriminatory removal of all trade impediments between the participating nations and with the establishment of certain elements of cooperation and coordination between them. The latter depends entirely on the actual form that integration takes. Different forms of international integration can be envisaged and some have actually been implemented:

(i) *free trade areas*, where the member nations remove all trade impediments among themselves but retain their freedom with regard to the determination of their policies *vis-à-vis* the outside world (the non-participants) – for example, the European Free Trade Association (EFTA) and the Latin American Free Trade Area (LAFTA);

(ii) *customs unions*, which are very similar to free trade areas except that member nations must conduct and pursue common external commercial relations – for instance, they must adopt common external tariffs on imports from the non-participants as is the case

1

in the European Community (EC); the EC is in this particular sense a customs union, but, as we shall presently see, it is more than that;

(iii) *common markets*, which are customs unions that also allow for free factor mobility across national member frontiers, i.e. capital, labour, enterprise should move unhindered between the partici-pating countries – for example, the East African Community (EAC), the EC (but again it is more complex);

(iv) *complete economic unions*, which are common markets that ask for complete unification of monetary and fiscal policies, i.e. a central authority is introduced to exercise control over these matters so that existing member nations effectively become regions of one nation;

(v) *complete political integration*, where the participants become liter-ally one nation, i.e. the central authority needed in (iv) not only controls monetary and fiscal policies but is also responsible to a central parliament with the sovereignty of a nation's government.

It should be stressed that each of these forms of economic integration can be introduced in its own right: they should not be confused with *stages* in a *process* which eventually leads to complete political integration. It should also be noted that within each scheme there may be sectoral integration, as distinct from general across-the-board integration, in particular areas of the economy, for example in agriculture as is the case in the EC – hence the Common Agricultural Policy. Of course, sectoral integration can be introduced as an aim in itself as was the case in the European Coal and Steel Community (ECSC), but sectoral integration is a form of 'cooperation' since it is not consistent with the accepted definition of international economic integration.

In concluding this section one should point out that international economic integration can be *positive* or *negative*. The term 'negative integration' was coined by Tinbergen (1954) to refer to the removal of impediments on trade between the participating nations or to the elimination of any restrictions on the process of trade liberalisation. The term 'positive integration' relates to the modification of existing instruments and institutions and, more importantly, to the creation of new ones so as to enable the market of the integrated area to function properly and effectively and also to promote other broader policy aims of the union. Hence, at the risk of oversimplification, it can be stated that sectoral integration and free trade areas are forms of international economic integration which require only 'negative integration', while the remaining types require 'positive integration' since, as a minimum, they all require the positive act of adopting common external relations. However, in reality, this distinction is unfair since practically all existing types of international economic integration have found it necessary to introduce some elements of 'positive integration'.

THE GLOBAL EXPERIENCE

Since the end of the Second World War various forms of international economic integration have been proposed and numerous ones have actually been implemented. Even though some of those introduced were later discontinued or completely reformulated, the number adopted during the decade commencing in 1957 was so impressive as to prompt Haberler (1964) to describe that period as 'the age of integration'.

The EC is the most significant and influential of these arrangements since it comprises some of the most advanced nations of Western Europe: Belgium, Denmark, France, Ireland, Italy, Luxembourg, the Netherlands, the United Kingdom (UK) and West Germany. The EC was founded by six (usually referred to as the Original Six) of the nine present member countries under the Treaty of Rome in 1957, with the remaining three (Denmark, Ireland and the UK) joining later in 1973. Greece became a full member in January 1981 and Portugal, Spain and Turkey have already submitted applications for membership. Although the Treaty of Rome relates simply to the formation of a customs union and the basis for a common market in terms of factor mobility, many of the originators of the EC saw it as a phase in a process culminating in complete economic and political integration. Thus the present efforts to achieve harmonisation in member countries' monetary, fiscal and social policies and to accomplish a monetary union can be seen as positive steps towards the attainment of the desired goals.

EFTA is the other major scheme of international economic integration in Western Europe. To understand its membership one has to learn something about its history. In the mid-1950s when a European Community comprising the whole of Western Europe was being contemplated, the UK was unprepared to commit itself to some of the economic and political aims envisaged for that Community. For example, the adoption of a common agricultural policy and the eventual political unity of Western Europe were seen as aims which were in direct conflict with the UK's interests in the Commonwealth, particularly with regard to 'imperial preference' which granted preferential access to the markets of members of the Commonwealth. Hence the UK favoured the idea of a Western Europe which adopted free trade in industrial products only, thus securing the advantages of 'Commonwealth preference' as well as opening up Western Europe as a free market for her industrial goods. In short, the UK sought to achieve the best of both worlds for herself, which is of course quite understandable. However, it is equally understandable that such an arrangement was not acceptable to those seriously contemplating the formation of the European Community. As a result the UK approached those Western European nations who had similar interests with the purpose of forming an alternative scheme of international economic integration. The outcome was EFTA which was established in 1960 by the Stockholm Convention with the object of creating a free market for industrial products only; there were some agreements on non-manufactures but these were relatively unimportant. The membership consisted of: Austria, Denmark, Norway, Sweden, Switzerland (and Liechtenstein) and the UK. Finland became an associate member in 1961; Iceland joined in 1970 as a full member. But, as already stated, Denmark and the UK, together with Ireland, joined the EC in 1973. This left EFTA with a membership consisting mainly of the relatively smaller nations of Western Europe. However, in 1972 the EC and EFTA entered into a series of free trade agreements which have in effect resulted in virtual free trade in industrial products in a market which includes their joint membership. This outcome has of course provided the cynical observer of British attitudes towards Western Europe with a great deal to reflect upon!

International economic integration is not confined to the so-called 'free' nations of the world. Indeed, the socialist planned economies of Eastern Europe have their own arrangement which operates under the Council for Mutual Economic Assistance (CMEA), or COMECON as it is generally known in the West. CMEA was formed in 1949 by Bulgaria, Czechoslovakia, the German Democratic Republic, Hungary, Poland, Romania and the USSR; they were later joined by three non-European countries: Mongolia (1962), Cuba (1972) and Vietnam (1978). In its earlier days, before the death of Stalin, the activities of the CMEA were confined to the collation of the plans of the member states, the development of a uniform system of reporting statistical data and the recording of foreign trade statistics. However, during the 1970s a series of measures was adopted by the CMEA to implement the 'Comprehensive Programme of Socialist Integration', hence indicating that the organisation is moving towards a form of integration based principally on methods of plan coordination and joint planning activity, rather than on market levers (Smith, 1977). Finally, attention should be drawn to the fact that the CMEA comprises a group of relatively small countries and one 'super power' and that the long-term aim of the organisation is to achieve a highly organised and integrated economic bloc, without any agreement having yet been made on how and when this will be accomplished.

Before leaving Europe it should be stated that another scheme exists in the form of regional cooperation between the five Nordic countries (the Nordic Community): Denmark, Finland, Iceland, Norway and Sweden. However, in spite of claims to the contrary (Sundelius and Wiklund 1979), the Nordic scheme is one of cooperation rather than international economic integration since Denmark is a full member of the EC while the other countries are full members of EFTA; hence a substantial group of economists would argue that the Nordic Community has little practical relevance.

In Africa, there are several schemes of international economic integration (Hazlewood, 1967 and Robson, 1968). The *Union Douanière et Économique de l'Afrique Centrale* (UDEAC) comprises the People's Republic of the Congo, Gabon, Cameroon and the Central African Republic. Member nations of UDEAC plus Chad, a former member, constitute a monetary union. The *Communauté Economique de l'Afrique de l'Ouest* (CEAO) which was formed under the Treaty of Abidjan in 1973 consists of the Ivory Coast, Mali, Mauretania, Niger, Senegal and Upper Volta. Member countries of CEAO, except for Mauretania plus Benin and Togo, are participants in a monetary union. In 1973 the Mano River Union (MRU) was established between Liberia and Sierra Leone. The MRU is a customs union which involves a certain degree of cooperation particularly in the industrial sector. The Economic Community of West African States (ECOWAS) was formed in 1975 with fifteen signatories: its membership consists of all those countries who participate in UDEAC, CEAO, MRU plus some other West African States. In 1969 the Southern African Customs Union (SACU) was established between Botswana, Lesotho, Swaziland and the Republic of South Africa. The Economic Community of the Countries of the Great Lakes (CEPGL) was created in 1976 by Rwanda, Burundi and Zaire. Until its collapse in 1977, there was the East African Community (EAC) between Kenya, Tanzania and Uganda. Several other schemes were in existence in the past but have been discontinued while others never got off the ground.

There are four schemes of international economic integration in Latin America and the Caribbean. Under the 1960 Treaty of Montevideo, the

Latin American Free Trade Association (LAFTA) was formed between Mexico and all the countries of South America except for Guyana and Surinam. The Managua Treaty of 1960 established the Central American Common Market (CACM) between Costa Rica, El Salvador, Guatemala, Honduras and Nicaragua. In 1969, the Andean Group was established under the Cartagena Agreement between Bolivia, Chile, Colombia, Ecuador, Peru and Venezuela; the Andean Group forms a closer link between some of the least developed nations of LAFTA. In 1973 the Caribbean Community (CARICOM) was formed between Antigua, Barbados, Belize, Dominica, Grenada, Guyana, Jamaica, Montserrat, St Kitts–Nevis–Anguilla, St Lucia, St Vincent, Trinidad and Tobago – CARICOM replaced the Caribbean Free Trade Association (CARIFTA).

Asia does not figure very prominently in the league of international economic integration but this is not surprising given the existence of such large countries as China, India and Japan. The Regional Cooperation for Development (RCD) is a very limited arrangement for sectoral integration between Iran, Pakistan and Turkey. The Association of South-East Asian Nations (ASEAN) comprises five nations: Indonesia, Malaysia, the Philippines, Singapore and Thailand. ASEAN was founded in 1967 in the shadow of the Vietnam War. After almost a decade of inactivity 'it was galvanized into renewed vigour in 1976 by the security problems which the reunification of Vietnam seemed to present to its membership' (Arndt and Garnaut, 1979). The drive for the establishment of ASEAN and for its vigorous reactivation in 1976 was both political and strategic. However, right from the start, economic cooperation was one of the most important aims of ASEAN, indeed most of the vigorous activities of the group between 1976 and 1978 were predominantly in the economic field (Arndt and Garnaut, 1979). Recently a Free Trade Agreement was signed by Australia and New Zealand but the term 'free trade' is interesting in this context!

There are two schemes of international economic integration which are not based on geographical proximity. The first of these is the Organisation of Petroleum Exporting Countries (OPEC), founded in 1960 with a truly international membership. Its aim is to protect the main interest of its member nations: petroleum. The second is the Organisation of Arab Petroleum Exporting Countries (OAPEC), established in January 1968 by Kuwait, Libya and Saudi Arabia. These were joined in May 1970 by Algeria and the four Arab Gulf Emirates (Qatar, Abu Dhabi, Bahrain, and Dubai). In March 1972 Egypt, Iraq and Syria became members. OAPEC was temporarily liquidated in June

1971 and Dubai is no longer a member. The agreement establishing the organisation states:

> The principal objective of the Organization is the cooperation of the members in various forms of economic activity . . . the realization of the closest ties among them . . . the determination of ways and means of safeguarding the legitimate interests of its members . . . the unification of efforts to ensure the flow of petroleum to its consumption markets on equitable and reasonable terms and the creation of a suitable climate for the capital and expertise invested in the petroleum industry in the member countries. (*Middle East Economic Survey*, 1968)

OAPEC was originally conceived as an example of sectoral integration with the political objective of using petroleum as a weapon for international bargaining against the Israeli occupation of certain Arab areas. Recently, however, the organisation has undertaken a number of projects both internally and externally – see Mingst (1977/78).

Finally, there are also the North Atlantic Treaty Organisation (NATO), the OECD, the Organisation for African Unity (OAU) and the Council of Arab Economic Unity (CAEU) – four members of which formed the Arab Common Market in 1971 but which practically never got off the ground – but these are strictly speaking for political and economic cooperation only.

THE MOTIVES FOR INTERNATIONAL ECONOMIC INTEGRATION

In reality, almost all existing schemes of economic integration were either proposed or formed for political reasons even though the arguments popularly put forward in their favour were expressed in terms of possible economic gains. However, no matter what the motives for economic integration are, it is still necessary to analyse the economic implications of such geographically discriminatory groupings.

At the customs union (and free trade area) level, the possible sources of economic gain can be attributed to:

(i) enhanced efficiency in production made possible by increased specialisation in accordance with the law of comparative advantage;

(ii) increased production levels due to better exploitation of economies of scale made possible by the increased size of the market;

(iii) an improved international bargaining position, made possible by the larger size, leading to better terms of trade;

(iv) enforced changes in economic efficiency brought about by enhanced competition; and

(v) changes affecting both the amount and quality of the factors of production due to technological advances.

If the level of economic integration is to proceed beyond the customs union level, to the economic union level, then further sources of gain become possible due to:

(vi) factor mobility across the borders of member nations;

(vii) the coordination of monetary and fiscal policies; and

(viii) the goals of near full employment, higher rates of economic growth and better income distribution becoming unified targets.

It should be apparent that some of these considerations relate to static resource reallocation effects while the rest relate to long-term or dynamic effects. The possible attainment of the benefits of these effects must be considered with great caution:

> . . . Membership of an economic grouping cannot of itself guarantee to a member state or the group a satisfactory economic performance, or even a better performance than in the past. The static gains from integration, although significant, can be – and often are – swamped by the influence of factors of domestic or international origin that have nothing to do with integration. The more fundamental factors influencing a country's economic performance (the dynamic factors) are unlikely to be affected by integration except in the long run. It is clearly not a necessary condition for economic success that a country should be a member of an economic community as the experience of several small countries confirms, although such countries might have done even better as members of a suitable group. Equally, a large integrated market is in itself no guarantee of performance, as the experience of India suggests. However, although integration is clearly no panacea for all economic ills, nor indispensable to success, there are many convincing reasons for supposing that significant economic benefits may be derived from properly conceived arrangements for economic integration. (Robson, 1980)

PLAN OF THE BOOK

This book is concerned with international economic integration defined in the limited sense of a state of affairs or a process which involves the amalgamation of separate economies into larger regions. Hence schemes of sectoral integration or international cooperation do not constitute a part of this book. This does not mean that OPEC, OAPEC, RCD, NATO, OECD, the Nordic Community, the CAEU and OAU are not important, but simply that they are different in both nature and scope, and space limitations do not permit an adequate consideration of every conceivable scheme. Moreover, of the schemes which qualify according to this limited definition, the book contains chapters only on those which have a fair degree of firm experience behind them or whose experience has given valuable insights into integration problems: EC, EFTA, CMEA, EAC, the West African Economic Community, CARICOM, LAFTA, Andean Pact and CACM. The remaining African schemes have had to be omitted given the specific purpose of the book. There is no specific single chapter on ASEAN for reasons given in the concluding chapter.

The reader will also find two chapters on the theory of international economic integration and the problems of the quantitative estimation of integration effects. The methodological aspects and the difficulties of statistical estimation are common to all schemes: it would therefore seem wise to tackle these problems separately in order that the chapters on actual cases of integration should be relieved of this task.

2 The Theory of Economic Integration

Ali M. El-Agraa

INTRODUCTION

In reality, almost all existing cases of economic integration were either proposed or formed for political reasons even though the arguments popularly put forward in their favour were expressed in terms of possible economic gains. However, no matter what the motives for economic integration are, it is still necessary to analyse the economic implications of such geographically discriminatory groupings.

As mentioned in the Introduction, at the customs union (and free trade area) level, the possible sources of economic gain can be attributed to:

   (i) enhanced efficiency in production made possible by increased specialisation in accordance with the law of comparative advantage;

 (ii) increased production levels due to better exploitation of economies of scale made possible by the increased size of the market;

(iii) an improved international bargaining position, made possible by the larger size, leading to better terms of trade;

 (iv) enforced changes in economic efficiency brought about by enhanced competition; and

  (v) changes affecting both the amount and quality of the factors of production due to technological advances.

If the level of economic integration is to proceed beyond the customs union level, to the economic union level, then further sources of gain become possible due to:

 (vi) factor mobility across the borders of member nations;

(vii) the coordination of monetary and fiscal policies; and

(viii) the goals of near full employment, higher rates of economic growth and better income distribution becoming unified targets.

I shall now discuss these considerations in some detail.

THE CUSTOMS UNION ASPECTS

THE BASIC CONCEPTS

Before the theory of second-best was introduced, it used to be the accepted tradition that customs union formation should be encouraged. The rationale for this was that since free trade maximised world welfare and since customs union formation was a move towards free trade, customs unions increased welfare even though they did not maximise it. This rationale certainly lies behind the guidelines of the GATT articles which permit the formation of customs unions and free trade areas as the special exceptions to the rules against international discrimination.

Viner (1950) challenged this proposition by stressing the point that customs union formation is by no means equivalent to a move to free trade since it amounts to free trade *between* the members and *protection vis-à-vis* the outside world. This combination of free trade and protectionism could result in 'trade creation' and/or 'trade diversion'. Trade creation is the replacement of expensive domestic production by cheaper imports from a partner and trade diversion is the replacement of cheaper *initial* imports from the outside world by more expensive imports from a partner. Viner stressed the point that trade creation is beneficial since it does not affect the rest of the world while trade diversion is harmful and it is therefore the relative strength of these two effects which determines whether or not customs union formation should be advocated. It is therefore important to understand the implications of these concepts.

Assuming perfect competition in both the commodity and factor markets, automatic full employment of all resources, costless adjustment procedures, perfect factor mobility nationally but perfect immobility across national boundaries, prices determined by cost, three countries H (the home country), P (the potential customs union partner) and W (the outside world), plus all the traditional assumptions employed in tariff theory, we can use a simple diagram to illustrate these two concepts.

In Figure 2.1 I am using partial-equilibrium diagrams because it has

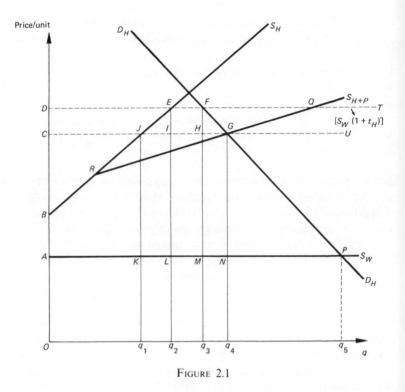

FIGURE 2.1

been demonstrated that partial- and general-equilibrium analyses are, under certain circumstances, equivalent – see El-Agraa and Jones 1981. S_W is W's perfectly elastic tariff free supply curve for this commodity; S_H is H's supply curve while S_{H+P} is the joint H and P tariff free supply curve. With a non-discriminatory tariff imposition by H of AD (t_H), the effective supply curve facing H is $BREFQT$, i.e. its own supply curve up to E and W's, subject to the tariff $[S_W(1+t_H)]$ after that. The domestic price is therefore OD which gives domestic production of Oq_2, domestic consumption of Oq_3 and imports of $q_2 \, q_3$. H pays $q_2 LMq_3$ for these imports while the domestic consumer pays $q_2 EFq_3$ with the difference ($LEFM$) being the tariff revenue which accrues to the H government. This government revenue can be viewed as a transfer from the consumers to the government with the implication that when the government spends it, the marginal valuation of that expenditure should be exactly equal to its valuation by the private consumers so that no distortions should occur.

If H and W form a customs union, the free trade position will be restored so that Oq_5 will be consumed in H and this amount will be imported from W. Hence free trade is obviously the ideal situation. But if H and P form a customs union, the tariff imposition will still apply to W while it is removed from P. The effective supply curve in this case is $BRGQT$. The union price falls to OC resulting in a fall in domestic production to Oq_1, an increase in consumption to Oq_4 and an increase in imports to q_1q_4. These imports now come from P.

The welfare implications of these changes can be examined by employing the concepts of consumers' and producers' surpluses. As a result of increased consumption, consumers' surplus rises by $CDFG$. Part of this ($CDEJ$) is a fall in producers' surplus due to the decline in domestic production and another part ($IEFH$) is a portion of the tariff revenue now transferred back to the consumer subject to the same condition of equal marginal valuation. This leaves the triangles JEI and HFG as gains from customs union formation. However, before we conclude whether or not these triangles represent *net* gains we need to consider the overall effects more carefully.

The fall in domestic production from Oq_2 to Oq_1 leads to increased imports of q_1q_2. These cost q_1JIq_2 to import from P while they originally cost q_1JEq_2 to produce domestically. (Note that these resources are assumed to be employed elsewhere in the economy without any adjustment costs or redundancies!) There is therefore a saving of JEI. The increase in consumption from Oq_3 to Oq_4 leads to new imports of q_3q_4 which cost q_3HGq_4 to import from P. These give a welfare satisfaction to the consumers equal to q_3FGq_4. There is therefore an increase in satisfaction of HFG. However, the *initial* imports of q_2q_3 cost the country q_2LMq_3 but these imports now come from P costing q_2IHq_3. Therefore these imports lead to a loss equal to the loss in government revenue of $LIHM$ ($IEFH$ being a re-transfer). It follows that the triangle gains ($JEI + HFG$) have to be compared with the loss of tariff revenue ($LIHM$) before a definite conclusion can be made regarding whether or not the net effect of customs union formation has been one of gain or loss.

It should be apparent that q_2q_3 represents, in terms of our definition, trade diversion, and $q_1q_2 + q_3q_4$ represent trade creation, or alternatively that areas JEI plus HFG are trade creation (benefits) while area $LIHM$ is trade diversion (loss). (The reader should note that I am using Johnson's 1974 definition so as to avoid the unnecessary literature relating to a trade-diverting welfare-improving customs union promoted by Lipsey, 1960, Gehrels, 1956–7 and Bhagwati, 1971.) It is then obvious that trade creation is economically desirable while trade diversion is undesirable. Hence Viner's conclusion that it is the relative strength of these two effects which should determine whether or not customs union formation is beneficial or harmful.

The reader should note that if the initial price is that given by the intersection of D_H and S_H (due to a higher tariff rate), the customs union would result in pure trade creation since the tariff rate is prohibitive. If the price is initially OC (due to a lower tariff rate), then customs union formation would result in pure trade diversion. It should also be apparent that the size of the gains and losses depends on the price elasticities of S_H, and S_{H+P} and D_H and on the divergence between S_W and S_{H+P}, i.e. cost differences.

THE COOPER/MASSELL CRITICISM

Viner's conclusion was challenged by Cooper and Massell (1965a). They suggested that the reduction in price from OD to OC should be considered in two stages: firstly, reduce the tariff level indiscriminately (i.e. for both W and P) to AC which gives the same union price and production, consumption and import changes; secondly, introduce the customs union starting from the new price OC. The effect of these two steps is that the gains from trade creation ($JEI + HFG$) still accrue while the losses from trade diversion ($LIHM$) no longer apply since the new effective supply curve facing H is $BJGU$ which ensures that imports continue to come from W at the cost of $q_2 LMq_3$. In addition, the new imports due to trade creation ($q_1 q_2 + q_3 q_4$) now cost less leading to a further gain of $AJIL$ plus $MHGN$. Cooper and Massell then conclude that *a policy of unilateral tariff reduction is superior to customs union formation.*

FURTHER CONTRIBUTIONS

Following the Cooper/Massell criticism have come two independent but somewhat similar contributions to the theory of customs unions. The first development is by Cooper and Massell (1965b) themselves, the essence of which is that two countries acting together can do better than each acting in isolation. The second is by Johnson (1965) which is a private plus social costs and benefits analysis expressed in political economy terms. Both contributions utilise a 'public good' argument with Cooper and Massell's expressed in practical terms and Johnson's in theoretical terms. However, since the Johnson approach is expressed in familiar terms this section is devoted to it – space limitations do not permit a consideration of both.

Johnson's method is based on four major assumptions:

(i) governments use tariffs to achieve certain non-economic (political, etc.) objectives;
(ii) actions taken by governments are aimed at offsetting differences between private and social costs. They are, therefore, rational efforts;
(iii) government policy is a rational response to the demands of the electorate;
(iv) countries have a preference for industrial production.

In addition to these assumptions, Johnson makes a distinction between private and public consumption goods, real income (utility enjoyed from both private and public consumption, where consumption is the sum of planned consumption expenditure and planned investment expenditure) and real product (defined as total production of privately appropriable goods and services).

These assumptions have important implications. Firstly, competition among political parties will make the government adopt policies that will tend to maximise consumer satisfaction from both 'private' and 'collective' consumption goods. Satisfaction is obviously maximised when the *rate of satisfaction per unit of resources is the same in both types of consumption goods*. Secondly, 'collective preference' for industrial production implies that consumers are willing to expand industrial production (and industrial employment) beyond what it would be under free international trade.

Tariffs are the main source of financing this policy simply because GATT regulations rule out the use of export subsidies and domestic political considerations make tariffs, rather than the more efficient production subsidies, the usual instruments of protection.

Protection will be carried to the point where *the value of the marginal utility derived from collective consumption of domestic and industrial activity is just equal to the marginal excess private cost of protected industrial production*.

The marginal excess cost of protected industrial production consists of two parts: the marginal production cost and the marginal private consumption cost. The marginal production cost is equal to the proportion by which domestic cost exceeds world market cost. In a very simple model this is equal to the tariff rate. The marginal private

consumption cost is equal to the loss of consumer surplus due to the fall
in consumption brought about by the tariff rate which is necessary to
induce the marginal unit of domestic production. This depends on the
tariff rate and the price elasticities of supply and demand.

In equilibrium, the proportional marginal excess private cost of
protected production measures the marginal 'degree of preference' for
industrial production. This is illustrated in Figure 2.2 where: S_W is the
world supply curve at world market prices; D_H is the constant-utility
demand curve (at free trade private utility level); S_H is the domestic
supply curve; S_{H+u} is the marginal private cost curve of protected

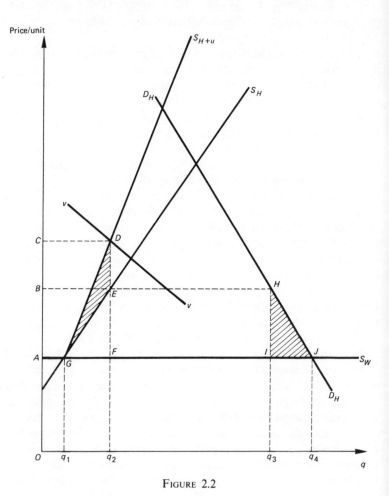

FIGURE 2.2

industrial production, including the excess private consumption cost [*FE* is the first component of marginal excess cost – determined by the excess marginal cost of domestic production in relation to the free trade situation due to the tariff imposition (*AB*) – and the area *GEF* (= *IHJ*) is the second component which is the dead loss in consumer surplus due to the tariff imposition]; the height of *vv* above S_W represents the marginal value of industrial production in collective consumption and *vv* represents the preference for industrial production which is assumed to yield a diminishing marginal rate of satisfaction.

The maximisation of *real* income is achieved at the intersection of *vv* with S_{H+u} requiring the use of tariff rate *AB/OA* to increase industrial production from Oq_1 to Oq_2 and involving the marginal degree of preference for industrial production *v*.

Note that the higher the value of *v*, the higher the tariff rate, and that the degree of protection will tend to vary inversely with the ability to compete with foreign industrial producers.

It is also important to note that, in equilibrium, the government is maximising real income, not real product: maximisation of real income makes it necessary to sacrifice real product in order to gratify the preference for collective consumption of industrial production.

It is also important to note that this analysis is not confined to net importing countries. It is equally applicable to net exporters, but lack of space prevents such elaboration.

The above model helps to explain the significance of Johnson's assumptions. It does not, however, throw any light on the customs union issue. To make the model useful for this purpose it is necessary to alter some of the assumptions. Let us assume that industrial production is not one aggregate but a variety of products in which countries have varying degrees of comparative advantage; that countries differ in their overall comparative advantage in industry as compared with non-industrial production; that no country has monopoly/monopsony power (conditions for optimum tariffs do not exist); and that no export subsidies are allowed (GATT).

The variety of industrial production allows countries to be both importers and exporters of industrial products. This, in combination with the 'preference for industrial production', will motivate each country to practise some degree of protection.

Given the third assumption, a country can gratify its preference for industrial production only by protecting the domestic producers of the commodities it imports (import-competing industries). Hence the condition for equilibrium remains the same: $vv = S_{H+u}$. The condition must now be reckoned differently, however: S_{H+u} is slightly different because, firstly, the protection of import-competing industries will reduce exports of both industrial and non-industrial products (for balance of payments purposes!). Hence, in order to increase total industrial production by one unit it will be necessary to increase protected industrial production by more than one unit so as to compensate for the induced loss of industrial exports. Secondly, the protection of import-competing industries reduces industrial exports by raising their production costs (due to perfect factor mobility!). The stronger this effect, *ceteris paribus*, the higher the marginal excess cost of industrial production.

These will be greater, the larger the industrial sector compared with the non-industrial sector and the larger the protected industrial sector relative to the exporting industrial sector.

If the world consists of two countries, one must be a net exporter and the other necessarily a net importer of industrial products and the balance of payments is settled in terms of the non-industrial sector. Hence both countries can expand industrial production at the expense of the non-industrial sector. Therefore for each country the prospective gain from reciprocal tariff reduction must lie in the expansion of exports of industrial products. The reduction of a country's own tariff rate is therefore a source of loss which can only be compensated for by a reduction of the other country's tariff rate (for an alternative, orthodox, explanation see El-Agraa 1979b).

What if there are more than two countries? If reciprocal tariff reductions are arrived at on a 'most-favoured nation' basis, then the reduction of a country's tariff rate will increase imports from *all* the other countries. If the tariff rate reduction is, however, discriminatory (starting from a position of non-discrimination), then there are two advantages: firstly, a country can offer its partner an increase in exports of industrial products without any loss of its own industrial production by diverting imports from third countries (trade diversion); secondly, when trade diversion is exhausted any increase in partner industrial exports to this country is exactly equal to the reduction in industrial production in the same country (trade creation), hence eliminating the gain to third countries.

Therefore, discriminatory reciprocal tariff reduction costs each partner country less, in terms of the reduction in domestic industrial production (if any) incurred per unit increase in partner industrial production, than does non-discriminatory reciprocal tariff reduction. On the other hand, preferential tariff reduction imposes an additional cost on the tariff reducing country: the excess of the costs of imports from the partner country over their cost in the world market.

The implications of this analysis are:

(i)   both trade creation and trade diversion yield a gain to the customs union partners;

(ii) trade diversion is preferable to trade creation for the preference granting country since a sacrifice of domestic industrial production is not required;

(iii) both trade creation and trade diversion may lead to increased efficiency due to economies of scale.

Johnson's contribution has not achieved the popularity it deserves because of the alleged nature of his assumptions. However, a careful consideration of these assumptions indicates that they are neither extreme nor unique: they are the kind of assumptions that are adopted in any analysis dealing with differences between social and private costs and benefits! It can, of course, be claimed that an

> . . . economic rationale for customs unions on public goods grounds can only be established if for political or some such reasons governments are denied the use of direct production subsidies – and while this may be the case in certain countries at certain periods in their economic evolution, there would appear to be no acceptable reason why this should generally be true. Johnson's analysis demonstrates that customs union and other acts of commercial policy may make economic sense under certain restricted conditions, but in no way does it establish or seek to establish a general argument for these acts. (Krauss, 1972.)

While this is a legitimate criticism it is of no relevance to the world we live in: subsidies are superior to tariffs, yet all countries prefer the use of tariffs to subsidies! It is a criticism related to a first-best view of the world. Therefore, it seems unfair to criticise an analysis on grounds which do not portray what actually exists; it is what prevails in practice that matters. That is what Johnson's approach is all about and that is what the theory of second-best tries to tackle. In short, the lack of belief in this approach is tantamount to a lack of belief in the validity of the distinction between social and private costs and benefits.

DYNAMIC EFFECTS

The so-called dynamic effects (Balassa, 1962) relate to the numerous means by which economic integration may influence the rate of growth of GNP of the participating nations. These ways include the following:

(i) scale economies made possible by the increased size of the market for both firms and industries operating below optimum capacity before integration occurs;

(ii) economies external to the firm and industry which may have a downward influence on both specific and general cost structures;

(iii) the polarisation effect, by which is meant the cumulative decline either in relative or absolute terms of the economic situation of a particular participating nation or of a specific region within it due either to the benefits of trade creation becoming concentrated in one region or to the fact that an area may develop a tendency to attract factors of production;

(iv) the influence on the location and volume of real investment; and

(v) the effect on economic efficiency and the smoothness with which trade transactions are carried out due to enhanced competition and changes in uncertainty.

Hence these dynamic effects include various and completely different phenomena. Apart from economies of scale, the possible gains are extremely long term in nature and cannot be tackled in orthodox economic terms: for example, intensified competition leading to the adoption of best business practices and to an American-type of attitude, etc. (Scitovsky, 1958) seems like a naive socio-psychological abstraction that has no solid foundation with regard to both the aspirations of those countries contemplating economic integration and to its actually materialising!

Economies of scale can, however, be analysed in orthodox economic terms. In a highly simplistic model, like that depicted in Figure 2.3 where scale economies are internal to the industry, their effects can easily be demonstrated. $D_{H,P}$ is the identical demand curve for this commodity in both H and P and D_{H+P} is their joint demand curve; S_W is the world supply curve; AC_P and AC_H are the average cost curves for this commodity in P and H respectively. Note that the diagram is drawn in such a manner that W has constant average costs and that it is the most efficient supplier of this commodity. Hence free trade is the best policy resulting in price OA with consumption which is satisfied entirely by imports of Oq_4 in each of H and P giving a total of Oq_6.

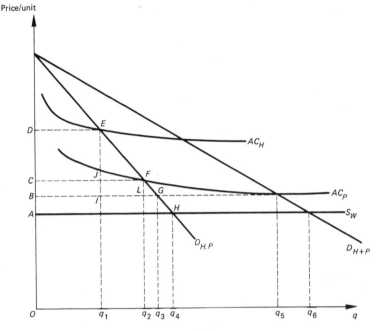

FIGURE 2.3

If *H* and *P* impose tariffs, the only justification for this is that uncorrected distortions exist between the privately and socially valued costs in these countries – see Jones (1979) and El-Agraa and Jones (1981). The best tariff rates to impose are Corden's (1972b) made-to-measure tariffs which can be defined as those which encourage domestic production to a level that just satisfies domestic consumption without giving rise to monopoly profits. These tariffs are equal to AD and AC for *H* and *P* respectively, resulting in Oq_1 and Oq_2 production in *H* and *P* respectively.

When *H* and *P* enter into a customs union, *P*, being the cheaper producer, will produce the entire union output – Oq_5 at a price OB. This gives rise to consumption in each of *H* and *P* of Oq_3 with gains of $BDEG$ and $BCFG$ for *H* and *P* respectively. Parts of these gains, $BDEI$ for *H* and $BCFL$ for *P*, are 'cost-reduction' effects. There also results a production gain for *P* and a production loss in *H* due to abandoning production altogether.

Whether or not customs union formation can be justified in terms of the existence of economies of scale will depend on whether or not the net effect is a gain or a loss, since in this example *P* gains and *H* loses, as the loss from abandoning production in *H* must outweigh the consumption gain in order for the tariff to have been imposed in the first place. If the overall result is net gain, then the distribution of these gains becomes an important consideration. Alternatively, if economies of scale accrue to an integrated industry, then the locational distribution of the production units becomes an essential issue.

TERMS OF TRADE EFFECTS

So far the analysis has been conducted on the assumption that customs union formation has no effect on the terms of trade. This implies that the countries concerned are too insignificant to have any appreciable influence on the international economy. Particularly in the context of the EC and groupings of a similar size, this is a very unrealistic assumption.

The analysis of the effects of customs union formation on the terms of trade is extremely complicated – see Mundell (1964) and Arndt (1968). At this level of generality, however, it suffices to state that nations acting in consort or in unison are more likely to exert an influence than each acting alone. It could also be argued that the bigger the group the stronger its bargaining position *vis-à-vis* the outside world. Indeed, Petith (1977) found evidence of improved terms of trade for the EC.

It should be stressed, however, that possible gains from improved terms of trade can be achieved only if the outside world does not retaliate. Indeed, the gains found by Petith for the EC could be attributed entirely to this factor. Hence, larger groupings do not necessarily automatically guarantee favourable changes in the terms of trade since such groupings may also encourage joint action by those nations excluded from them.

CUSTOMS UNIONS v. FREE TRADE AREAS

The analysis so far has been conducted on the premise that differences between customs unions and free trade areas can be ignored. However, the ability of the member nations of free trade areas to decide their own commercial policies *vis-à-vis* the outside world raises certain issues. Balassa (1962) pointed out that free trade areas may result in deflection of trade, production and investment. Deflection of trade occurs when imports from *W* (the cheapest source of supply) come via the member country with the lower tariff rate, assuming that transport and administrative costs do not outweigh the tariff differential. Deflection of production and investment occur in commodities whose production requires a substantial quantity of raw materials imported from W – the tariff differential regarding these materials might distort the true comparative advantage in domestic materials therefore resulting in resource allocations according to overall comparative disadvantage.

If deflection of trade does occur, then the free trade area effectively becomes a customs union with a CET equal to the lowest tariff rate which is obviously beneficial for the world – see Price (1974). However, most free trade areas seem to adopt 'rules of origin' so that only those commodities which originate in a member state are exempt from tariff imposition. If deflection of production and investment does take place, we have the case of the so-called 'tariff factories' but the necessary conditions for this to occur are extremely limited – see El-Agraa in El-Agraa and Jones (1981, Chapter 3).

ECONOMIC UNIONS

The analysis of customs unions needs drastic extension when applied to economic unions. Firstly, the introduction of free factor mobility may enhance efficiency through a more efficient allocation of resources but it may also lead to depressed areas and therefore create, or aggravate, regional problems and imbalances. Secondly, fiscal harmonisation may also improve efficiency by eliminating non-tariff trade distortions and by subjecting factors of production to equal treatment hence encouraging their mobility. Thirdly, the coordination of monetary and fiscal policies implied by monetary integration will ease unnecessarily severe imbalances hence promoting the right atmosphere for stability in the economies of member nations.

These 'economic union' elements must be considered *simultaneously* with trade creation and trade diversion. However, such interactions are too complicated to consider here; the interested reader should consult El-Agraa (1980).

MACROECONOMICS OF INTEGRATION

We have seen that trade creation and trade diversion are the two concepts most widely used in international economic integration. We have also seen that their economic implications for resource reallocation are usually tackled in terms of particular commodities under conditions of global full employment. However, the economic consequences for the outside world and their repercussions on the integrated area are usually left to intuition. Moreover, their implications for employment are usually ruled out by assumption.

In an effort to rectify these serious shortcomings, I have used a macroeconomic model (see Chapters 6–8 of El-Agraa and Jones, 1981) with the purpose of investigating these aspects. The model is still in its infancy and a sophisticated model is now being constructed. However, even the crude model so far published indicates that the advantages of using a macro model are that it clearly demonstrates the once-and-for-all nature of trade creation and trade diversion. It also shows the insignificance of their overall impact given realistic values of the relevant coefficients: marginal propensities to import; marginal propensities to consume; tariff rates, etc. The model also demonstrates that trade creation is beneficial for the partner gaining the new output and exports but is detrimental to the other partner and the outside world. Also that trade diversion is beneficial for the partner now exporting the commodity but is detrimental for the other partner and the outside world. The author feels that a sophisticated model will corroborate these conclusions.

ECONOMIC INTEGRATION IN DEVELOPING COUNTRIES

It has been claimed that the body of economic integration theory as so far developed has no relevance for the Third World. This is due to the fact that the theory suggested that there would be more scope for trade creation if the countries concerned were initially very competitive in production but potentially very complementary and that a customs union would be more likely to be trade creating if the partners conducted most of their foreign trade amongst themselves – see Lipsey (1960) and Meade (1955). These conditions are unlikely to be satisfied in the majority of the developing nations. Moreover, most of the effects of integration are initially bound to be trade diverting, particularly since most of the Third World seeks to industrialise.

On the other hand, it was also realised that an important obstacle to the development of industry in these countries is the inadequate size of their individual markets – see Brown (1961), Hazlewood (1967, 1975) and Robson (1980). It is therefore necessary to increase the market size so as to encourage optimum plant installations – hence the need for economic integration. This would, however, result in industries clustering together in the relatively more advanced of these nations – those that have already commenced the process of industrialisation.

I have demonstrated elsewhere (El-Agraa, 1979a) that there is essentially *no theoretical difference* between economic integration in the Advanced World and the Third World but that there is a major difference in terms of the *type* of economic integration that is politically feasible: the need for an equitable distribution of the gains from industrialisation and the location of industries is an important issue (see above). This suggests that any type of economic integration that is being contemplated must incorporate as an essential element a common fiscal authority and some coordination of economic policies. But then one could equally well argue that *some degree* of these elements is necessary in *any* type of integration – see the Raisman Committee recommendations for the EAC (1961).

ECONOMIC INTEGRATION AMONG COMMUNIST COUNTRIES

The only example up to now of economic integration among communist countries is the CMEA. However, here the economic system perpetuates a fundamental lack of interest of domestic producers in becoming integrated with both consumers and producers in other member countries. As Marer and Montias emphasise in Chapter 6, the integration policies of member nations must focus on the mechanism of state-to-state relations rather than on domestic economic policies which would make CMEA integration more attractive to producers and consumers alike. That is, integration must be planned by the state at the highest possible level and imposed on ministries, trusts and enterprises. It should also be stated that the CMEA operates different pricing mechanisms for intra- and extra-area trade. Moreover, the attitude of the USSR is extremely important since the policies of the East European members of the CMEA are somewhat constrained by the policies adopted by the organisation's most powerful member, for economic as well as political reasons. CMEA integration, therefore, has to be approached within an entirely different framework; the appropriate place for discussing it is Chapter 6.

CONCLUSIONS

The conclusions reached here are consistent with my 1979 conclusions and with those of Jones in El-Agraa and Jones (1981). They are:

Firstly, that the rationale for regional economic integration rests upon the existence of constraints on the use of first-best policy instruments. Economic analysis has had little to say about the nature of these constraints, and presumably the evaluation of any regional scheme of economic integration should incorporate a consideration of the validity of the view that such constraints do exist to justify the pursuit of second- rather than first-best solutions.

Secondly, that even when the existence of constraints on superior policy instruments is acknowledged, it is misleading to identify the results of regional economic integration by comparing an arbitrarily chosen common policy with an arbitrarily chosen national policy. Of course ignorance and inertia provide sufficient reasons why existing policies may be non-optimal but it is clearly wrong to attribute gains which would have been achieved by appropriate unilateral action to a policy of regional integration. Equally, although it is appropriate to use the optimal common policy as a point of reference, it must be recognised that this may overstate the gains to be achieved if, as seems highly likely, constraints and inefficiencies in the political processes by which policies are agreed prove to be greater among a group of countries than within any individual country.

Although the first two conclusions raise doubts about the case for regional economic integration, in principle at least, a strong general case for economic integration does exist. In unions where economies of scale may be in part external to national industries, the rationale for unions rests essentially upon the recognition of the externalities and market imperfections which extend beyond the boundaries of national states. In such circumstances, unilateral national action will not be optimal whilst integrated action offers the scope for potential gain.

As with the solution to most problems of externalities and market imperfections, however, customs union theory frequently illustrates the proposition that a major stumbling block to obtaining the gains from joint optimal action lies in agreeing an acceptable distribution of such gains. Thus the fourth conclusion is that the achievement of the potential gains from economic integration will be limited to countries able and willing to cooperate to distribute the gains from integration so that all partners may benefit compared to the results achieved by independent action. It is easy to argue from this that regional economic integration may be more readily achieved than global solutions but, as the debate about monetary integration in the EC illustrates (see Chapter 4), the chances of obtaining potential mutual gain may well founder in the presence of disparate views about the distribution of such gains and weak arrangements for redistribution.

3 The Problems of the Quantitative Estimation of Integration Effects[1]

David G. Mayes

INTRODUCTION

It is a common finding in economics that the development of the theory on a particular topic and the development of empirical research have pursued rather different courses. It is, however, difficult to think of a better example of this divergence than the study of the effects of economic integration. Not only that, but while one can discuss *the* theory of economic integration as if it were a unified body of ideas it too has two rather separate strands. On the one hand there is what can be described as customs union theory developing through the work of Viner (1950), Meade (1955), Lipsey (1957), Johnson (1965) and many others while on the other there are the works of Balassa (1962), *inter alia*, and El-Agraa (1980), developing aspects of integration beyond those purely relating to trade. In the previous chapter this second category of integration effects are described under the heading of 'economic union'. The relative development of the theory in its two parts is reflected in the balance of that chapter where by far the larger part is devoted to customs unions. Yet as El-Agraa makes clear the two aspects 'must be considered *simultaneously*' (his italics).

The general path of empirical work on economic integration has been to look at various particular aspects of integration, primarily the effects on trading patterns, and to treat them separately. The most crucial distinction which is made in practice is between 'price' effects and 'income' effects. This occurs largely for the trivial reason that the main initial instruments in economic integration are tariffs and quotas and other obstacles to trade between countries which act primarily on relative prices in the first instance. All eight sources of possible economic gain, set out in the previous chapter, however, include income effects as well as those of price changes alone.

However, rather than survey the characteristics and drawbacks of existing models, thereby extending and updating Mayes (1978), I shall set out the problems of estimating the full range of economic effects of integration from tariff reductions to coordinated policies and common currencies. This approach will thus relate the quantitative evidence and empirical verification to the theory set out in the previous chapter. The discussion will be divided into four sections, the first dealing with the effects on trade of customs unions and free trade areas, the second with the measurement of the 'dynamic' effects of integration, the third with the movement of factors rather than goods and the last with the consequences of the implementation of common policies.

This last section can be regarded as a treatment of the problem of measuring the effects of 'positive' integration in the sense developed by Pinder (1968) from the suggestion of Tinbergen (1954) – see Chapter 1. The initial stages of integration usually proceed by the dismantling of barriers to the free exchange of goods, factors and payments and are thus in a sense 'negative', whereas the later stages involved the 'positive' commitment to organise common demand management, monetary control, regional policy, etc. These definitions are not comprehensive as there are many barriers in the form of language, social customs and habits, standards, taxation and others whose removal or circumvention while not necessarily constituting positive integration is certainly 'non negative'. The positive/negative distinction is an important behavioural categorisation and the two parts present different problems in quantification.

CUSTOMS UNIONS, FREE TRADE AREAS AND THE EFFECTS ON TRADE

Customs unions and free trade areas are usually conceived of as involving merely the progressive removal of tariffs between partner countries and, in the former case, the forming of a common external tariff with respect to the rest of the world. The removal of quotas and other barriers to trade are usually subsumed within the tariff changes for the purpose of estimation. These tariff changes are thought to result in a series of relative price changes. The price of imports from partner countries falls, for commodities where the tariff is cut, relative to the price of the same commodity produced in the domestic country. In third countries which are excluded from the union relative prices may change for more than one reason. They will change differently if the tariff with respect to third countries is shifted from its pre-integration level or it may change if producers in third countries have different pricing reactions to the change in price competition. Some third country producers may decide to absorb rather more of the potential change by reducing profits rather than by increasing prices relatively compared with domestic producers. Relative prices are also likely to change with respect to different commodities and hence there is a complex set of interrelated income and substitution effects to be explained.

The immediate difficulty is thus the translation of tariff changes and other agreed measures in the customs union treaty into changes in prices and other variables which are known to have an impact on economic behaviour. Such evidence as there is suggests that there are wide discrepancies among the reactions of importers benefiting from tariff cuts and also among competitors adversely affected by them (EFTA, 1968) and that reactions of trade to tariff changes are different from those to price changes (Kreinin, 1961). Two routes would appear to be open, one is to estimate the effect of tariff changes on prices and then estimate the effects of these derived price changes on trade patterns and the other is to operate directly with observed relative price movements. This latter course exemplifies a problem which runs right through the estimation of the effects of economic integration and makes the obtaining of generally satisfactory results almost impossible. It is that to measure the effect of integration one must decide what would have happened if integration had not occurred. Thus, if in the present instance any observed change in relative prices were assumed to be the result of the adjustment to tariff changes, all other sources of variation in prices would be ignored, which is clearly an exaggeration and could be subject to important biases if other factors were affecting trade at the same time.

THE IDEAL PROCEDURE

If economic integration could be treated like any other change in exogenous or policy variables in a model the correct econometric procedure would be to estimate a model which was large enough to reflect all the influences in the economy which we thought were important. Having estimated the model one would then fit it over the data of the period of integration and then rerun inserting the values of the appropriate variables as they would have been without integration. The difference between the two estimates is then the identifiable effects of integration according to our model of behaviour.

Unfortunately, this is no mean task and can only be approached by use of large models of the international economy such as those of the IMF (Deppler and Ripley, 1978) or the OECD (1979) or perhaps the COMET model of Barten *et al.* (1976). The main problems are: (a) the size of model required (b) the constancy of parameters over time. The normal response in practice (see Mayes, 1978) is to estimate a highly simplified model and make a further simple assumption about changes in parameters. Furthermore, one of the stages in the argument is usually left out and instead of comparing what the model predicts with integration to what it predicts without integration authors tend to compare actual behaviour with what would have happened without integration attributing all the difference to the effects of integration. Given the simplicity of the models and the assumptions about changes in parameters this can result in substantial biases in the estimates.

THE SIZE OF THE MODEL

There are two basic issues over the size of model: the first is one of aggregation and the second of how many relations are necessary to capture the effects of integration throughout the economy and not just the initial impact on trade flows. The aggregation issue is well known (see Barker, 1970 for a very clear example relating to the United Kingdom) and occurs, first because the direct price and substitution elasticities of demand for imports vary very considerably over different commodities, running from direct price elasticities near zero for essential commodities which cannot be produced locally to quite substantial values for finished manufactures such as consumer durables for which there are many close substitutes. It is secondly emphasised by the changing commodity composition of trade which tends to result in a downward bias in the estimates (see Orcutt, 1950 for the original exposition and Morgan, 1970 for a more recent example)! A more trivial reason for disaggregation can be advanced as in the case of EFTA Secretariat (1969), which looked at the effects of integration on a 36-commodity breakdown of trade for its member states. One wants to know the results in some detail otherwise it is difficult to assess which are important, especially in so far as one is interested in examining whether *inter*-industry specialisation has taken place rather than the *intra*-industry specialisation which took place in the EC (see inter alia, Grubel and Lloyd, 1975; Kreinin, 1979).

The second issue regarding which influences to incorporate is a much harsher problem. Using a simple logarithmic import function in prices and incomes, like Houthakker and Magee (1969) for example,

$$\ln M = a + b \ln RP + c \ln Y + e \tag{1}$$

where M is imports, $RP = PM/PD$, the relative price of imports to the domestic product and Y is a measure of income, a, b and c are parameters and e an unobservable residual, one could estimate the direct price effect of integration by multiplying our estimate of the price elasticity, b, by the calculated change in relative prices due to integration (Kreinin, 1973; Mayes, 1971). [A more complex RP term can allow for substitution between imports from partners and non-members as well as substitution between imports and domestic prices to be incorporated (Verdoorn and Schwartz, 1972).] However, the relative fall in the price of imports will have other consequences in the economy. If output prices are a mark-up on costs then they will tend to be lower as some of the imports are inputs to domestic output. Imports going both to final and intermediate demand will tend to lower the rate of price inflation and this in turn will have consequences for the wage rate through the usual inflationary spiral and the price of exports and hence export demand.

Exports will in any case be affected by the change in tariffs in partner countries. In so far as the increased export demand is met by increased output, demand will also increase both at the intermediate and final levels creating the usual multiplier process in the economy. The model must also be able to take account of the effects of increased imports on domestic output which will have a deflationary influence on demand. At the very least it is also necessary to have some balance of payments/exchange rate relation.

Therefore without disaggregating over commodities or countries we are considering a model of at least ten equations for each identified country that we need to examine. It is thus immediately clear why this route is avoided in practice as it would require an immense amount of data collection and work on estimation.

Whatever model is adopted we do need to be able to explain imports and exports disaggregated at the very least by trading area and usually by country as well if we are to obtain estimates of trade creation, trade diversion, and the effects on the balance of payments and welfare.

CONSTANCY OF PARAMETERS

If some of the expected effects of integration take place, such as the exploitation of economies of scale and the changes in economic efficiency, it will not be just the variables in the model which change with integration, but also the parameters. Thus it would not be possible to use a model estimated in a period with integration to suggest what would have happened without integration by changing the variables alone or vice-versa. Furthermore, if we take periods such as the formation of EFTA and the EC during the 1960s, or the enlargement in the EC in 1973 there is a good argument that general economic conditions were not similar in the periods before and after integration. Certainly the years after the oil crisis of 1973/4 and the period of floating exchange rates are not readily comparable with preceding periods. Balassa (1967, 1974) actually uses changes in the income elasticity of demand for imports as a means of estimating the effects of the formation of the EC.

THE DISADVANTAGES OF SIMPLE MODELS

The advantages of simple models are clear as is shown in Kreinin (1979). Even with a more sophisticated model we can only get an idea of an order of magnitude not an accurate single number, hence if it is possible to use only a relatively limited amount of readily available information to estimate that magnitude we can make much more efficient use of our resources by adopting the simple model. In Mayes (1978) I showed in a survey of the estimates of trade creation and trade diversion in the EC that the approximate bounds for the likely size of trade creation where, in the view of the authors surveyed, 8–15 billion US dollars, or to put it differently between approximately 9 and 17 per cent of total EC trade in that year. If that degree of accuracy is acceptable then it might be possible to stop there and merely advise that, providing appropriate bounds are set by varying the assumptions behind the simple model, this is sufficient.

However, I would argue that this is not the case and that these orders of magnitude could easily be substantially incorrect. On the whole these simplified models work by projecting either shares of trade or shares in total consumption from the pre-integration period into the post-integration period, perhaps 'normalised' by the behaviour of third countries during the post-integration period or by the share of member countries in the market of third countries in the post-integration period. Normalisation in this context means, for example, that if imports in the rest of the world increased their share in total consumption by a certain percentage, then, without integration, import shares in the integrating countries would also have increased by that amount.

Normalisation of some form is certainly necessary otherwise all differences in the general level of world trade and activity which lead to differences in activity and trade among the integrating countries will be attributed to integration. Thus in the period up to 1969/70 trade creation in the EC is approximately halved by appropriate normalisation (Kreinin, 1972) whereas in the post-enlargement period since 1973, trade creation is increased by normalisation, world trade and activity having grown more slowly than formerly. However, there is no means of deciding what portion of the increase in activity in the integrating countries is due to integration or separating changes due to relative price changes stemming from tariff changes, from changes due to technology, movement of factors rather than goods, changes in consumption patterns, etc. Thus the final figure is an amalgam of effects. It shows us how trade patterns have changed in the integrating countries compared to normalisation. This is certainly interesting and useful information, but whether it is a measure of trade creation or trade diversion as described in the last chapter is another matter. Because it has no explicit explanation of how changes in trade from integration take place, all changes from whatever source (after normalisation) are included in measured trade creation and diversion; they might be positive or negative, but we have no information about their sign or size.

It is worth noting before leaving this section that the main emphasis of quantitative work on these static effects on trade is largely in the context of the exploitation of comparative advantage, yet the work of Petith (1977) suggests that the effects from the change in the terms of trade on the EC and EFTA may have been between two and six times as important at 0.34 to 0.93 per cent of GDP as that from trade creation.

THE DYNAMIC EFFECTS

While the discussion of the exploitation of comparative advantage, the gains from a favourable movement in the terms of trade and often those from economies of scale is expressed in terms of comparative statics, as we explained in the previous section, it is difficult to disentangle them from feedback onto incomes and activity. The essence of the gains from increased efficiency and technological change is that the economy should reap dynamic gains. In other words integration should enhance the rate of growth of GDP rather than just giving a step up in welfare. Again it is necessary to explain how this might come about explicitly.

There are two generalised ways in which this can take place, first through increased productivity growth at a given investment ratio or secondly through increased investment itself. This is true whether the increased sales are generated internally or through the pressures of demand for exports from abroad through integration. Growth gains can, of course, occur temporarily in so far as there are slack resources in the economy. Again it is possible to observe whether the rate of growth has changed but it is much more difficult to decide whether that is attributable to integration.

Krause (1968) attempted to apply a version of Denison's (1967) method of identifying the causes of economic growth but suggested that *all* changes in the rate of business investment were due to the formation of the EC (or EFTA in the case of those countries). In Mayes (1978) I showed that if the same contrast between business investment before and after the formation of the EC (EFTA) were applied to Japan there was a bigger effect observed than in any of the integrating countries! Clearly changes in the rate of business investment can occur for reasons other than integration.

THE MOVEMENT OF FACTORS

Unlike the study of trade flows the theory of factor movements is relatively underdeveloped. This makes the quantification of the effects difficult right from the outset. It is possible to measure the flows of labour and of direct and portfolio investment, although data on the latter are sometimes rather inaccurate and definitions vary widely from one country to another. However, it is much more difficult to decide what proportion of any change which takes place after integration is due to that integration. This is the same problem as in the case of the trade flows and with a lack of suitable well-determined models of factor movements reliance is likely to have to be placed on an analysis of trends.

The assumption at the outset of the present discussion is that economic integration reduces or possibly eliminates the barriers to factor movements. This assumption is not a necessary condition for factor movements to take place and is not applicable in the case of some free trade areas which refer only to products. It is used to simplify the analysis. Changes in factor movements may still take place even if barriers remain unchanged (provided, naturally, that they are not prohibitive) because of the changes in trade and activity stemming from the free trade area.

Increased trade may require increased distribution networks or complementary production – greater familiarity with some countries may increase both capital and labour migration. As in all such cases there are incentives for capital and labour to leave one country and incentives for them to enter specific other countries (often described as push and pull factors).

There are clear relations between the movement of labour and the movement of capital: relatively low wages in one country compared with another encourage labour to move from the lower wage to the higher wage country to obtain higher incomes and capital to move in the opposite direction to exploit lower costs, although, of course, many other considerations, marginal tax rates for example, will tend to modify these decisions. Nevertheless we shall treat the labour and capital movements separately for ease of exposition. In the limit, movements of capital will increase the number of jobs available in the destination country and in relative terms, decrease it in the source country to such an extent that coupled with the movement of labour in the opposite direction factor prices will tend towards equalisation in the absence of other distortions. This, however, is sufficiently far from reality that we only need consider it as a means of determining the theoretical signs of the changes rather than the likely magnitude. The degree to which factor prices move towards equalisation will, of course, in itself be a measure of the movement towards integration.

The labour movement decision is perhaps the easier to consider as it reflects household behaviour in the light of the push and pull factors. While the nature of the relative wage incentive and the relative employment opportunities may be clear and measurable, the effects of other determinants, such as language, division of the family if only the worker concerned is permitted to move, the availability of housing – which certainly acts as a barrier to internal labour movements in the UK – and similar social considerations are immensely difficult to quantify. Reactions are different as the behaviour shown in Table 3.1 suggests. Labour movements from the three largest EC countries are all $\frac{1}{2}$ per cent of the domestic working population or less. Italy had about $3\frac{1}{2}$ per cent working abroad, reflecting perhaps its greater income differential from the other members and Luxembourg also showed a higher figure possibly reflecting its small land area. It is the Irish Republic which stands out. Although it had the lowest income per head of the nine countries, the figure of nearly half as many again as the domestic working population being employed in other member countries is of course grossly distorted in relative terms by the relation with the UK. What it does show is that labour migration can be very large indeed if countries are closely integrated. The second half of Table 3.1 indicates that labour migration can be very substantial even if the countries are not closely integrated as in the case of Portugal, where, despite language barriers, no common frontier with the EC and not having the advantages of membership, $17\frac{1}{2}$ per cent of the working population were employed in EC countries in 1976. Shifts of this size have important implications for the likely effects of membership of Greece, Portugal, Spain and even Turkey in the Communities.

TABLE 3.1   *Foreign employees in the European Communities, 1976*

	Nationals working in other member states (thousands) (1)	Domestic working population (thousands) (2)	(1) as a percentage of (2) (3)
Belgium	68	3 713	1.8
Denmark	7	2 293	0.2
Germany	137	24 556	0.5
France	114	20 836	0.5
Irish Republic	455	1 021	44.6
Italy	694	18 930	3.6
Luxembourg	6	148	4.1
Netherlands	83	4 542	1.8
United Kingdom	61	24 425	0.2
Total EC	**1 625**	**100 568**	**1.6**
Spain	447	12 535	3.5
Greece	239	3 230	7.4
Portugal	569	3 279	17.4
Turkey	587	14 710	4.0
Yugoslavia	458		
Algeria	447		
Morocco	183		
Tunisia	85		
Others	1 392		
Total non-EC	**4 407**		
Total	**6 032**		

SOURCE   M. Emerson, 'The European Monetary System in the broader setting of the Community's economic and political development', in P. H. Trezie (ed.), *The European Monetary System: Its Promise and Prospects* (Washington, DC: Brookings Institution, 1979).

Although the need for an integrated theory of trade and investment has been stated on many occasions, actual steps to implement it have been limited. Such attempts as there have been, Casson (1980) and Grey (1980), for example, have not been applied to actual data, let alone to the quantification of the effects of integration. Although portfolio capital can be invested abroad by the personal sector and the government largely in response to relative expected yields (assessed through relative interest rates, expected inflation and exchange rates) and risks, as explained in Cuthbertson *et al.* (1980), the interesting decision lies in the choice by firms whether to export to a particular country, buy participation in the activity of other companies already operating there through portfolio investment or invest directly in that country themselves.

The interaction of possible effects under the formation of a customs union which also eases restrictions on the movement of factors is complex. In so far as direct investment in a particular market has taken place to enable operation inside a market which has tariffs restricting trade, one might expect that trade might be used as a substitute for direct investment if that country is included in a customs union. If one thought of equivalent concepts to trade creation and trade diversion as investment creation and investment diversion, on this argument they might both have opposite signs to their trade counterparts. The freeing of trade would tend to make trade relatively attractive compared with investment hence leading to an overall reduction in direct investment in partner countries. Secondly direct investment in non-member countries would become relatively attractive thus diverting investment away from the member countries.

Against these influences there are three sets of offsetting factors. In the first place the removal of controls on factor movements within the customs union will encourage direct investment as well as trade. Secondly any increased growth occurring within the member countries will attract investment relative to that in third countries and thirdly trade and investment have a large measure of complementarity as well as substitutability. According to Panić (1980) a UK Department of Trade enquiry in 1976 revealed that 'about 29 per cent of the exports covered . . . went to related enterprises'. It may be easier to transport goods at some stages of production rather than others thus requiring both direct investment and trade. In addition, other distortions, such as internal tax systems, which are not specifically related to trade may encourage multinational operation.

The overall picture is thus confused and it is not surprising that there has been a tendency to develop an eclectic explanation of the phenomenon, such as Dunning (1980) who suggests that perceived advantages to the firm of direct investment abroad can be classified under the three headings of ownership, internalisation and location. The empirical evidence, such as is available, is also difficult to interpret. Figures for the UK shown in Table 3.2 suggest that direct investment in both directions with Western Europe increased rapidly before the UK joined the EC as well as subsequently. To some extent this is also explicable by Dunning's theory of the development of direct investment: countries with very low per capita incomes have a low capacity to absorb direct investment, but as the country grows the inflow of capital builds up until it reaches a maximum somewhere in the range of incomes between Singapore and New Zealand. Beyond that point domestic industrial and financial activity is such that the country can support an increasing outflow of direct investment. At some point the net movement of capital moves from an inflow to an outflow and for the EC countries (other than the UK) this tended to be reached during the period 1967 to 1975. Clearly the nature of countries' financial institutions themselves affects the exact timing.

Such a loose form of quantification is clearly unsatisfactory if one wants to explain not just the approximate level of capital flows but the

TABLE 3.2   *Distribution of UK assets abroad and foreign assets in the UK (as percentage of total)*

	Western Europe	North America	Other developed	Rest of world	Total (£m)
(a) UK assets					
1962	13.4	23.1	27.1	36.5	3 405.0
1965	15.4	21.8	29.9	32.9	4 210.0
1968	17.6	23.0	30.8	28.5	5 585.3
1971	21.9	20.0	29.8	26.3	6 666.9
1974	27.5	22.0	29.3	21.3	10 117.8
(b) Foreign assets in UK					
1962	20.9	75.9	2.3	0.9	1 429.7
1965	19.9	77.3	1.0	1.8	1 999.9
1968	21.8	75.3	1.8	1.1	2 728.0
1971	23.4	71.2	4.1	1.3	3 817.0
1974	28.1	62.1	4.6	5.2	6 585.3

SOURCE M. Panić, 'Some longer term effects of short-run adjustment policies: behaviour of UK direct investment since the 1960s', International Economics Study Group, *Conference Proceedings* (University of Sussex).

effects of changes in their determinants as is necessary in the case of integration. However, at least some important steps have been made in this direction, rather more than can be said for the quantification of the effects of positive integration which is considered in the final section.

POSITIVE INTEGRATION AND THE QUANTIFICATION OF THE EFFECTS OF COMMON POLICIES

The emphasis on the effects of positive integration, within the EC at any rate, has been on agriculture. As the Common Agricultural Policy (CAP) takes over three quarters of the total EC budget this is to be expected. However, the issues which it raises can be applied to the other areas of common policies which occur as integration develops, whether they apply to fisheries, regional or monetary and economic policies. The essential feature is that positive integration will normally entail the transfer of resources between member states. These transfers may occur either through direct payments from one country to another (or to a central authority) or through the need to maintain relative price levels which are different from those which would obtain under free trade and payments.

Thus, for example, the CAP imposes two costs on the UK, the first because it contributes more than it receives under the European Agricultural Guidance and Guarantee Fund, EAGGF or FEOGA, and secondly because it has to pay higher prices for its food than would otherwise be the case. Clearly, producers gain from this second form of resource adjustment, and as can be seen from Table 3.3 these effects tend to amplify those from the net receipts from the EAGGF.

If these resource flows result in a deficit on the balance of payments, a country has three solutions to the problem. The first is to depreciate its rate of exchange in the hope that the balance of payments will be improved through the relative price effect, the second is to deflate and attempt to improve the balance through the relative income effect and the third is to obtain a continuing capital inflow. Without integration this last course is not usually open (countries such as Australia and New Zealand are of course exceptions), but with integration this is no different from the continuing regional deficits and surpluses which exist within countries virtually indefinitely. The existence of a common currency precludes depreciation and deflation is likely to be the exact opposite of the intentions of regional policy because the deficit region tends to be relatively depressed already (as in the case of Scotland,

TABLE 3.3   *Resource costs in the European Communities Common Agricultural Policy, 1978 (£m)*

	Net receipts from EAGGF (1)	Benefit from higher export prices (2)	Cost from higher import prices (3)	Net benefit (2)−(3) (4)	Total cost/ benefit (1)+(4) (5)
Belgium– Luxembourg	33	287	382	−95	−62
Denmark	408	222	9	213	621
West Germany	−122	366	648	−282	−404
France	41	801	321	480	521
Irish Republic	343	211	48	163	506
Italy	−344	45	487	−442	−786
Netherlands	241	653	266	387	628
United Kingdom	−673	283	428	−145	−818

SOURCE   C. N. Morris, 'The Common Agricultural Policy', *Fiscal Studies*, vol. 1, no. 2, March (1980).

Northern Ireland, Wales and parts of the North of England in the case of the UK).

The assessment of the costs of common policies depends on the route which is chosen for adjustment to the required resource flows. Under a common currency system or a managed adjustable set of aligned parities as in the European Monetary System (EMS) the pressure tends to be on the deficit rather than the surplus countries to adjust. In this way, *on balance*, the adjustment to the costs of the common policies is deflationary and welfare is foregone in the community as a whole. Similarly if depreciation is chosen as the method under fully employed resources it is necessary to reduce domestic demands in order to release resources for increased exporting. Furthermore, Kaldor (1971) points out that if a country tries to resist the pressure to depreciate it may enter a vicious circle of low competitiveness, deflation, reduced investment and hence even lower competitiveness and so on.

A second cost must also be considered, namely that of inflation. The greater the weight placed on adjustment by surplus countries the greater the likely overall rate of inflation within the EC. It is clear, therefore, that positive integration through the implementation of common policies tends to lead to the search for common solutions to the effects on member countries. The EMS will not be more than a means of smoothing exchange rate fluctuations between member countries if it does not result in agreed fiscal and monetary measures between the members to solve imbalances and to use the European Monetary Cooperation Fund to permit enduring deficits in some countries in the way that these are permitted within single countries.

CONCLUDING REMARKS

It is clear from the preceding discussion that quantification of the effects of integration is relatively rudimentary partly due to the lack of consideration of the many problems involved, but more importantly due to the inherent complexity of the effects. While changes in tariffs may exert straightforward static effects on trading patterns, these effects are observed in a dynamic context of evolving trade, payments and activity. That evolution must be explained to attempt to measure the effects of integration. The use of the difference between actual behaviour and some hypothetical 'anti-monde', which might have occurred without integration, based on the extrapolation of previous trends and concurrent behaviour in other countries and markets is bound to result in biases because all residual changes in behaviour are attributed to integration, not just those which can be directly explained by it. Furthermore such analyses often exclude the feedback of reactions to tariff and relative price changes on incomes and efficiency. Given the very small size of the static effects on trade and payments compared with a change in the rate of economic growth by half of 1 per cent, it would be very easy to draw totally erroneous conclusions over the size or even the sign of the aggregate effect.

As soon as the analysis is extended to include changes in economic growth, efficiency and the movement of factors rather than just trade in goods and services the problems of quantification become immense. There is no well developed theory of the interrelated movements of trade, payments, incomes and factors, let alone one which can be clearly applied and estimated to calculate the effects of integration.

Many of the barriers to integration such as language and customs are inherently difficult to quantify so the overwhelming tendency is to try to use generalised methods which can at least determine the order of magnitude of the effects. However it is not just the pressures which are placed upon countries which matter. The responses of an economic community to the resource costs of common policies as well as that from tariff reduction affects their overall consequence. In particular the less coordinated the response the more likely it is to be deflationary. It is difficult enough to measure the effects of integration where the result depends upon the aggregated reactions of firms and households, but where it also depends on the hypothetical reactions of government policy to different economic pressures it is only possible to attempt to quantify the results of different policy choices and no single conclusion can be reached.

Research on the quantification of the effects of economic integration has been muted in recent years both in response to its difficulty and to its lack of topicality in the face of more pressing world economic problems. The challenge for further work is considerable as many problems remain to be resolved particularly when attention is directed beyond the mere static effects of the removal of tariff barriers towards the assessment of dynamic consequences and movements to closer integration.

NOTES

1. I am grateful for helpful comments from Fred Meyer and Ann Morgan.

4 The European Community

Ali M. El-Agraa

NATURE AND AIMS OF THE COMMUNITY

The European Community (EC or the Community) consists of six original member states, namely, Belgium, France, West Germany, Italy, Luxembourg and the Netherlands, and three members who joined in 1973: Denmark, Ireland and the United Kingdom. Greece joined the EC as a full member in January 1981 and Portugal, Spain and Turkey have already submitted applications for full membership.

The EC is in reality an amalgamation of three separate communities: the European Coal and Steel Community (ECSC), established by the Treaty of Paris in 1951 and valid for fifty years; the European Economic Community (EEC), created under the Treaty of Rome in 1957 for an unlimited period; and the European Atomic Energy Community (Euratom), formed by another Treaty of Rome in 1957 and also of unlimited duration. Subsequently, other texts have added to, or have amended, these three basic documents and any significant changes are incorporated in treaties which must be ratified by each member state in accordance with its own legal processes. Hence for example, changes in the budget procedures and the agreements to admit Denmark, Ireland and the UK to the EC constitute the subject of special treaty instruments and the *totality* of these documents, *together* with the legislative acts to which they give rise and the case law of the Court of Justice (see below), can be considered as the constitution of the EC – see Collins (1980).

It follows that the aims of the EC extend beyond those stated in this constitution to include other objectives which the EC may deem necessary in the future. Moreover, uppermost in the minds of the original instigators of the EC was the eventual political union of its member nations and recent developments seem to indicate a revival of this notion. Therefore, it can be stated that the EC has an evolving (dynamic) set of aims and aspirations, hence it is far from static in nature.

The initial objectives of the EC can be summarised as:

(i) The establishment of free trade between the member nations such that *all* impediments on intra-EC trade are eliminated. The Treaty does not simply ask for the elimination of tariffs, import quota restrictions and export subsidies, but of all measures which have an equivalent or similar effect (non-tariff trade distortions). Moreover, the Treaty calls for the establishment of *genuine* free trade and therefore specifies rudiments of common competition and industrial policies;

(ii) The creation of an intra-EC free market for all factors of production by providing the necessary prerequisites for ensuring perfect factor mobility. These include taxes on, and subsidies to, capital, labour, enterprise, etc;

(iii) The formation of common policies with regard to particular industries which the EC deemed it necessary to single out for special treatment, namely, agriculture (hence the Common Agricultural Policy – CAP) and transport (hence the Common Transport Policy – CTP);

(iv) The establishment of a common commercial policy *vis-à-vis* the outside world, i.e. the creation and management of the common external tariff rates (CETs), the adoption of a common stance in multinational and multilateral trade negotiations and a common attitude towards the association of other countries and the consideration of new membership.

These initial aims should be supplemented by those pertaining to (v) a common market for, and equitable access to, steel and coal as expressed in the treaty establishing the ECSC and (vi) a common approach to energy as expressed in the treaty creating Euratom. One must also add the aim of achieving (vii) monetary integration as expressed in the Werner Report (1970), with the European Monetary System (EMS), established in 1979, being its latest manifestation.

It is obvious that these aims cannot be achieved without the provision of some institutional arrangements to facilitate them. On the administrative side (see Shanks, 1977 and Collins, 1980), the main executive body is the *Commission* whose work is harmonised and increasingly directed by the *Council* which is a body of ministerial representatives. The Commission is ultimately responsible to the *European Parliament* which hopes eventually to become the main legislative body but, at this stage, even though it has the power of sacking the Commission in its totality, it is a platform for public comment and is therefore largely advisory in nature, although it possesses certain budgetary powers some of which it has actually used. The *Court of Justice* is responsible for the settling of all legal matters concerning the EC regulations and procedures. However, the administrative structure is not as rigid as is suggested by this brief, and inevitably generalised description, since it includes regular consultations between the governments of member nations at both the ministerial and head of state levels and also allows for representations by various lobbying groups, particularly farmers. On the financial side, the arrangements include the creation of a European Social Fund, with the aim of improving employment prospects and raising living standards, and the European Investment Bank (EIB), with the object of exploring new avenues for the promotion of economic expansion within the EC.

In the light of the general discussion of Chapter 1 it can therefore be categorically stated that the EC is *a common market with definite aspirations for complete economic and political unity.*

OBJECTIVES OF CERTAIN POLICIES

Before attempting an assessment of the progress made by the EC in terms of its principal stated objectives (the overall aim being the establishment of free intra-EC trade), it would be helpful to the reader to state the aims of some of the special policies mentioned in the previous section which relate to a *common approach* rather than to free trade – a common approach because 'perfect competition' does not exist in the real world hence 'imperfections' have to be tackled in a common way, i.e. distortions have to be harmonised.

The CAP aims at protecting the farm sector from a decline in incomes *relative* to the national (EC) average by:

(i) increasing agricultural incomes not only by a system of transfers from the non-farm population through a price support policy, but also by the encouragement of rural industrialisation to promote alternative employment opportunities to agricultural labour;

(ii) increasing agricultural productivity through specialisation promoted by eliminating artificial market distortions; and

(iii) preserving the family farm and ensuring that structural and price policies go together.

The CAP, therefore, has both *structural* and *price support* elements.

The objectives of the CTP are to ensure that transport rates are not used to discriminate between goods of different intra-EC origin (i.e. to eliminate the use of transport rates as non-tariff trade distortions), but also to ensure that transport as an 'industry' operates under equal competitive conditions within the EC. The latter is due to the fact that the transport sector has been operated not simply with efficiency in mind: social, safety and environmental considerations vary in importance from one country to another.

Industrial policy comprises all acts and policies of the country in relation to industry. Such policy can be either positive (relating to state participation in, or control of, industry) or negative (by minimising intervention in industry). The positive elements include: the allocation of resources between industries (e.g. energy, pricing, monopolies, restrictive practices); the structure of industry (e.g. degree of concentration, industrial location, state aids to declining and expanding industries, the public sector); industry and the environment; conditions of employment; and fiscal and monetary policy. In short, industrial policy embraces all aspects of state attitudes towards industry in its economic, social and environmental setting. Competition policy within the EC covers a wide range of industrial activities including price setting, monopoly control, public sector industries, state aids, multinationals and restrictions on imports and exports. Hence competition policy is one wide aspect of industrial policy.

STATISTICAL BACKGROUND

Table 4.1 and Figure 4.1 together give adequate coverage of the necessary statistical background to the EC. These are self-explanatory.

TABLE 4.1(a)   *EC population and employment*

	Population (thousands)	*Area (000 km²)*	*Density (per km²)*	*Civilian employment (% of total population)*
Belgium	9 840	30.5	323	40.5*
Denmark	5 104	43.1	118	50.8
France	53 277	544.0	98	42.0
Greece	9 361	132.0	71	35.8
Ireland	3 311	70.0	47	33.9
Italy	56 714	301.3	188	38.8
Luxembourg	358	2.6	138	43.0
Netherlands	13 942	41.2	338	36.4
United Kingdom	55 902	244.1	229	46.6
West Germany	61 327	248.6	247	42.2

* 1978

TABLE 4.1(b) *EC GDP, government and consumer prices*

	GDP (billion US $)	GDP per capita (US $)	Consumer prices: average annual increase 1974–9 (% p. a.)	Current government expenditure (% of GDP)	Current government revenue (% of GDP)
Belgium	111.5	9 850	7.5	45.1	42.7
Denmark	65.6	10 950	9.8	42.8	46.5
France	566.9	8 850	10.1	42.1	42.3
Greece	37.5	3 370	14.1	30.0	30.2
Ireland	14.9	3 780	14.5	41.5	38.4
Italy	318.6	4 590	15.8	42.5	37.4
Luxembourg	4.1	9 800	6.9	45.2	53.9
Netherlands	151.8	9 380	6.7	53.1	54.4
United Kingdom	391.2	5 530	15.5	40.5	38.8
West Germany	755.8	10 420	4.2	41.3	43.3

TABLE 4.1(c) *EC trade and official reserves*

	Imports (% of world imports)	Exports (% of world exports)	Balance of trade (million ECU)	Total official reserves (million SPR)	Intra-EC trade (% of EC trade) Imports	Intra-EC trade (% of EC trade) Exports
Belgium	3.9*	3.7*	− 3 022*	5 307*	67.3*	72.8*
Denmark	1.2	1.0	− 2 806	2 514	50.0	49.0
France	6.9	6.4	− 6 490	16 212	50.1	52.8
Greece	0.6	0.3	− 4 220	863	44.2	49.1
Ireland	0.6	0.5	− 1 955	1 693	75.4	77.6
Italy	5.0	4.7	− 4 149	16 122	44.2	49.4
Luxembourg	3.9*	3.7*	− 3 022*	5 307*	67.3*	72.8*
Netherlands	4.4	4.1	− 2 619	7 302	56.4	72.6
United Kingdom	6.6	5.9	− 8 695	15 719	40.8	41.8
West Germany	10.3	11.2	+ 8 933	43 197	49.3	48.3

* BLEU

SOURCES Eurostat, *Basic Statistics of the EEC*; OECD *Observer.*

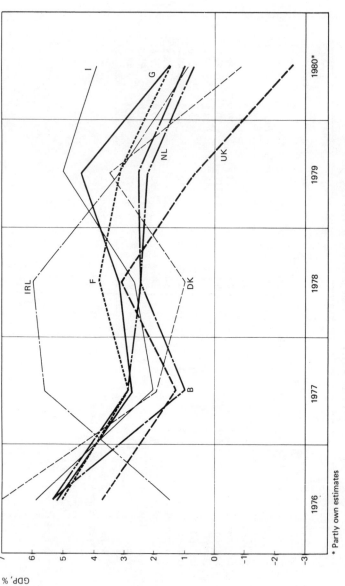

FIGURE 4.1(a)   *Real gross domestic product in EC countries**

* Change over previous year.
SOURCE Kommission der Europäischen Gemeinschaften, *Generaldirektion Wirtschaft und Finanzen, Europäische Wirtschaft*, no. 6 (July 1980) p. 106.

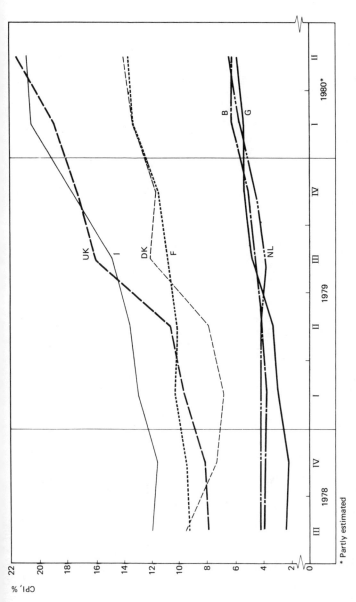

FIGURE 4.1(b) *Inflation rates in EC countries (consumer prices, % change of previous year, quarterly averages)*

SOURCE *International Financial Statistics* (Jan 1980) p. 45; (Oct 1980) p. 45.

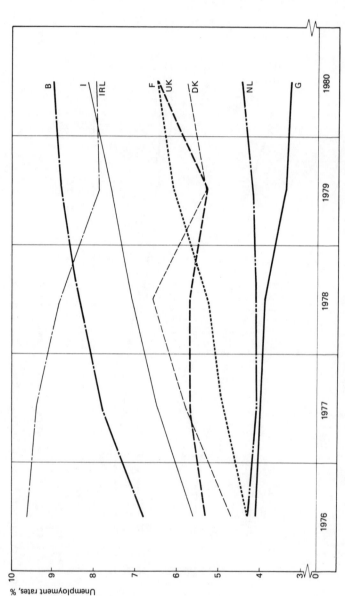

FIGURE 4.1(c)   *Unemployment rates in EC countries (annual averages)*

SOURCE Kommission der Europäischen Gemeinschaften, *Generaldirektion Wirtschaft und Finanzen, Europäische Wirtschaft,* no. 6 (July 1980) p. 106.

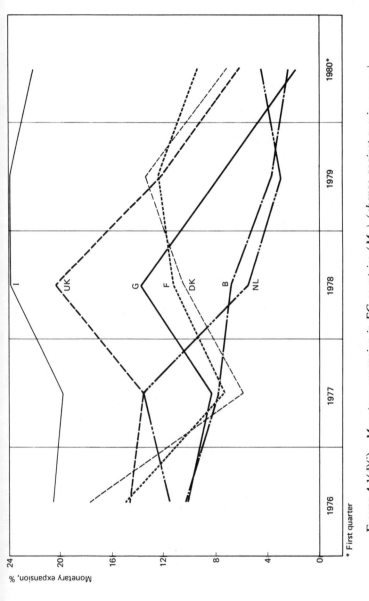

FIGURE 4.1(d)(i) *Monetary expansion in EC countries* (M_1) *(change against previous year)*

SOURCE *International Financial Statistics* (Aug 1980) pp. 44–5.

* First quarter

Monetary expansion, %

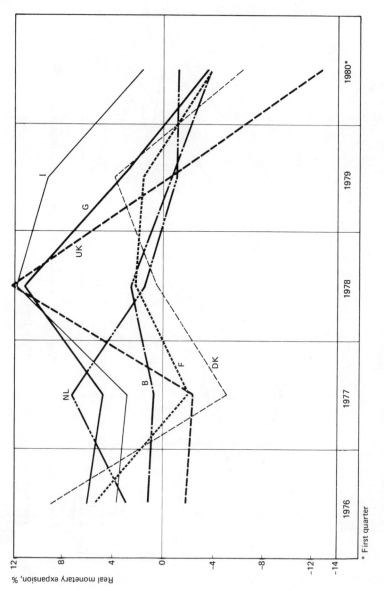

FIGURE 4.1(d)(ii)   *Real monetary expansion in EC countries* (*change against previous year*)

* First quarter

SOURCE   *International Financial Statistics* (Aug 1980) pp. 44–5.

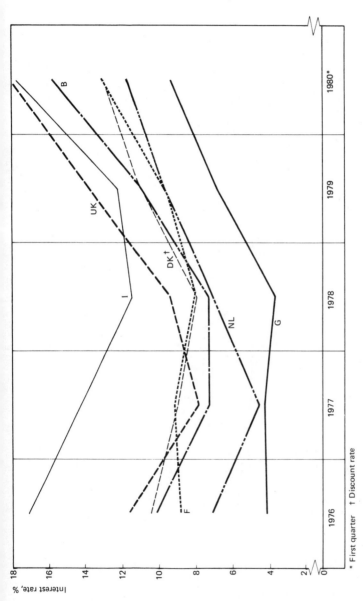

FIGURE 4.1(e)(i) *Monetary market rates in EC countries (three months)*

* First quarter † Discount rate

SOURCE *International Financial Statistics* (Aug 1980) p. 45; *Weltwirtschaft*, no. 1 (1980) Table 5.

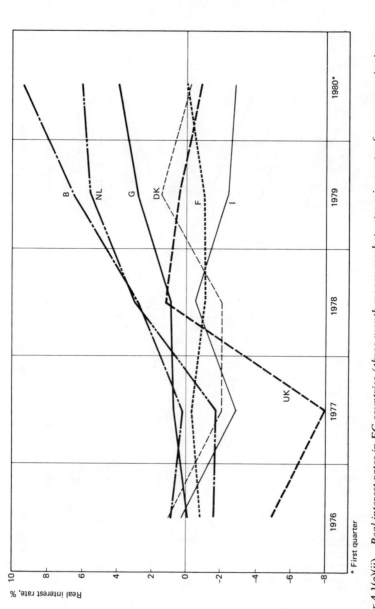

FIGURE 4.1(e)(ii) *Real interest rates in EC countries (three-month money market rates minus rate of consumer price increase, year over year)*

SOURCE *International Financial Statistics* (Aug 1980) p. 45; *Weltwirtschaft*, no. 1 (1980) Table 5.

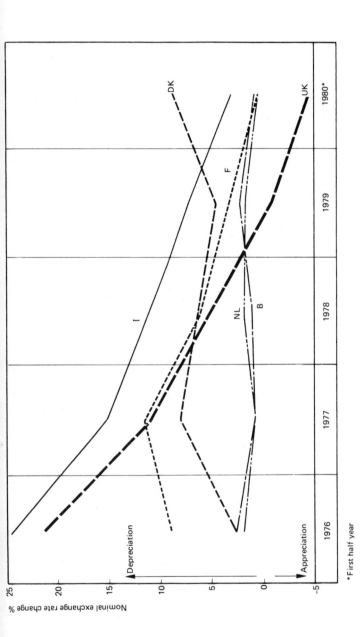

FIGURE 4.1(f)(i) *Nominal exchange rate changes of EC currencies against the D-Mark (change of annual averages for calendar years)*

SOURCE N. Walter, 'The European Monetary System – Performance and Prospects', paper to Salford Conference, 1980, p. 15.

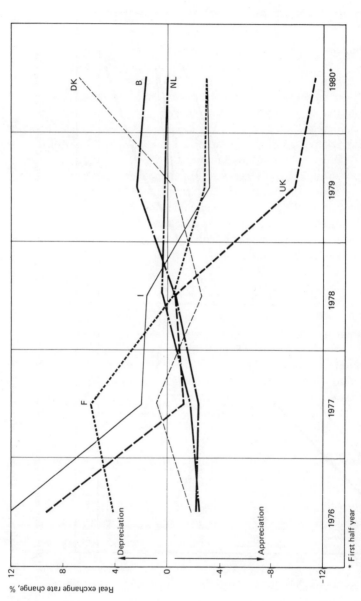

FIGURE 4.1(f)(ii)   *Real exchange rate changes of EC currencies against the D-Mark (change of annual averages for calendar years)*

SOURCE   Shadow European Economic Policy Committee, *Policy Statement and Position Papers* (Paris, 1979) p. 51.

PROGRESS AND ASSESSMENT

TRADE AND SPECIALISATION

Bearing in mind the reservations expressed in Chapter 2 and in El-Agraa and Jones (1981) and taking into consideration the severe limitations stated in Chapter 3 and in El-Agraa (1980, Chapter 5), it is possible to conclude, *for what it is worth*, that the formation of the EC has resulted in a substantial increase (over 50 per cent) in intra-EC trade and in a modest change in specialisation – see Balassa (1974, 1975) and Table 4.2. To single out the UK as an example, the change in specialisation in Britain has been detrimental to its interests in the manufacturing sector. (For a substantial statement to this effect the reader should consult the various publications on the work carried out by the Cambridge Economic Policy Group at the Department of Applied Economics.) Those interested in the particular case of the UK should also consult Pinder (1971) and Wallace (1980). Moreover, both intra-EC trade and specialisation have been at the expense of the outside world, particularly in the agricultural sector, as the discussion in El-Agraa (1980, Chapter 7) clearly demonstrates.

The formation of the EC has resulted in some improvement in its terms of trade with the outside world (Petith, 1977), but, of course, this has been due to the lack of retaliation by the latter. Moreover, there has been no evidence of increased foreign investment in the EC, particularly with regard to investment coming from the USA – it had generally been believed that discrimination against the outside world would attract more investment from abroad, i.e. foreign firms were expected to avoid the discriminatory trade impediments erected against them by working within the Community (Scaperlanda, 1967; Bergesten and Krause, 1975, Chapter 3 and Corner and Stafford, 1977). Of course, the Japanese have made successful investments but the overall picture is far from clear.

Therefore, it would appear that the only indisputable conclusion that can be made with respect to the customs union aspect of the EC is that its formal achievement (the removal of intra-EC mutual tariffs and quota restrictions on trade and the establishment of common external trade barriers) was, as Table 4.3(a) shows, accomplished ahead of schedule (in July 1968, one and a half years ahead of the original target date) and that the new partners, as Table 4.3(b) shows, have had no great difficulties in accommodating themselves to it within the periods of transition that were mutually agreed.

TABLE 4.2(a) *EC extra-area imports (million US $)*

| | Actual imports 1959 (1) | Hypothetical imports in 1970 calculated at growth rates of extra-area imports for the period: | | Actual imports 1970 | | Differences between actual and hypothetical imports, 1970 (5) – (2) (6) |
		1953–59 (in 1959 prices) (2)	1959–70 (in 1959 prices) (3)	In 1959 prices (4)	In 1970 prices (5)	
US	2 448 (100.0)	6 625 (270.6)	7 024 (286.9)	7 791 (318.3)	8 718 (356.1)	+ 2 093
UK	1 298 (100.0)	4 100 (315.9)	4 389 (338.1)	3 442 (265.2)	3 944 (303.9)	– 156
Continental EFTA	2 448 (100.0)	6 887 (281.3)	6 794 (277.5)	5 805 (237.1)	6 565 (268.2)	– 322

Other developed countries*	1866 (100.0)	4284 (229.6)	3844 (206.0)	5502 (294.9)	6100 (326.9)	+1816
Centrally planned economies	942 (100.0)	2538 (269.4)	2422 (257.1)	2851 (302.7)	3016 (320.2)	+478
Associated developing countries	1344 (100.0)	3155 (234.7)	2729 (203.1)	3330 (247.8)	3521 (262.0)	+366
Other less-developed countries	5770 (100.0)	14660 (254.1)	14464 (250.7)	12945 (224.4)	13160 (228.1)	−1500
Extra-area imports, total	16166 (100.0)	42249 (262.2)	41666 (258.5)	41666 (258.5)	45024 (279.4)	2775

* Australia, Canada, Japan, New Zealand, South Africa and those European countries that were not members of either the EC or EFTA during the period under consideration (Finland, Greece, Iceland, Ireland, Spain and Turkey).

SOURCE Balassa, *European Economic Integration* (Amsterdam: North-Holland, 1975) p. 88.

TABLE 4.2(b) EC extra-area total imports (million US $)

| | Actual Imports 1959 (1) | Hypothetical imports in 1970 calculated at growth rates of extra-area imports for the period: | | Actual imports 1970 | | Differences between actual and hypothetical imports, 1970 (5)−(2) (6) |
		1953–59 (In 1959 prices) (2)	1959–70 (3)	In 1959 prices (4)	In 1970 prices (5)	
Extra-area imports, total						
0+1−07 Food, beverages, tobacco	3 193	7 219	5 876	5 876	6 172	− 1 047
2+4 Raw materials	4 729	8 347	8 123	8 123	9 001	+ 654
3 Fuels	2 460	6 950	8 343	8 343	7 766	+ 816
5 Chemicals	682	3 490	2 982	2 982	2 532	− 958
71+72 Machinery	1 031	1 849	4 147	4 147	5 716	+ 3 867
73 Transport equipment	319	1 121	1 341	1 341	1 644	+ 523
6+8 Other manufactures	2 873	11 794	9 691	9 691	10 878	− 916
0−8−07 All of above	15 337	40 770	40 503	40 503	43 709	+ 2 939
07 Tropical beverages	779	1 479	1 163	1 163	1 315	− 164
0−8 All commodities	16 116	42 249	41 666	41 666	45 024	+ 2 775

SOURCE B. Balassa, *European Econmic Integration* (Amsterdam: North-Holland, 1975) p. 399.

TABLE 4.3(a) *EC intra-area tariff reductions (per cent)*

	Acceleration of:									
	1.1. 1959	1.7. 1960	1.1. 1961	1.1. 1962	1.7. 1962	1.6. 1963	1.1. 1965	1.1. 1966	1.7. 1967	1.7. 1968
Individual reductions made on 1.1.57 level	10	10	10	10	10	10	10	10	5	15
Cumulative reduction	10	20	30	40	50	60	70	80	85	100

The establishment of the CET (per cent)

	Acceleration of:				
	1.1.61	1.1.62	1.7.63	1.1.66	1.7.68
Industrial products adjustment	30		30		40
Cumulative adjustment	30		60		100
Agricultural products adjustment		30		30	40
Cumulative adjustment		30		60	100

TABLE 4.3(b) *New members intra-tariff reductions (per cent)*

	1.4.1973	1.1.74	1.1.1975	1.1.1976	1.7.1977
Individual reductions made on 1.1.1972 level	20	20	20	20	20
Cumulative reduction	20	40	60	80	100

Approaching the CET (for products which differ by more than 15 % from CET) (per cent)

	1.1.1974	1.1.1975	1.1.1976	1.7.1977
Individual adjustment made on 1.1.1972 level	40	20	20	20
Cumulative adjustment	40	60	80	100

SOURCES EC Commission, *First General Report on the Activities of the Communities* (Brussels) p. 34; HMSO. Cmnd. 4862-I.

NON-TARIFF DISTORTIONS

As far as non-tariff barriers are concerned, there are virtually no successes and certain commentators would argue that in some instances there has been a degree of retreat. More specifically, however, having adopted the VAT system and having accepted a unified method of calculating it, the EC has also acceded to the destination principle which is consistent with free intra-EC trade. It has been agreed by all member states that the coverage of VAT should be the same and should include the retail stage (now the normal practice), that crude raw materials, bought-in elements and similar components are to be deductible from the tax computation and that investment in stock and inventories should be given similar treatment by all member nations. There is agreement about the general principal of VAT exemptions but the precise nature of these seems to vary from one member country to another thus giving rise to problems with regard to the tax base – see El-Agraa (1980, Chapter 11) and Prest (1979). However, this similarity of principles is, in practice, contradicted by a number of differences. The tax coverage varies from one member country to another since most seem to have different kinds as well as different levels of exemptions. There is a wide variation in rate structure.

With regard to corporation tax, all systems (Split-Rate, Separate, Imputation) have been entertained at some time or another and all that can be categorically stated is that the EC has, at this stage, limited its choice to the Separate and Imputation Systems.

As far as excise duties are concerned, progress has been rather slow and this can be partially attributed to the large extent of the differences between the rates on the commodities under consideration in the different member countries. This is a partial explanation, however, because these taxes are important for government revenue purposes and it would therefore be naive to suggest that rate uniformity can be achieved without giving consideration to the political implications of such a move. The greatest progress here has been in tobacco and stamp duties.

Very little has been achieved regarding the harmonisation of 'official standards', state subsidies, export subsidies, and regional aid; and the problems of 'state monopolies', and 'public purchasing' have not yet been tackled.

INDUSTRIAL AND COMPETITION POLICIES

In the field of industrial policy (mainly to enable industry to cope with structural changes, to collaborate in science and technology and to protect the consumer), the EC has achieved very little – see Bayliss (1980), El-Agraa (1980), and Nevin (1980). This can be attributed to the fact that the EC does not specifically ask for an overall industrial policy and that there have been very fundamental national differences of attitude with regard to the appropriate form the common policy should take. With regard to scientific and technological collaboration, the policy is still in its very early stages. The common policy for consumer protection has not had time to develop.

The EC competition policy is an exception to the other EC policies (which have their origins in national policies and EC compromise) in that it has developed as a result of case law promulgated by the Commission and the Court of Justice. Competition policy has therefore been specifically developed for a certain purpose and it can therefore be assumed that it should be free of many of the problems that have arisen in other areas through attempts to modify existing policies to deal with EC problems.

It should be noted, however, that EC competition regulations only apply to those situations where intra-EC trade is affected. Thus actions having purely domestic effect in a member country or having effect outside the EC are excluded. On the other hand, actions occurring outside the EC but having effect within it are included. This latter interpretation, Professor Bayliss (1980) argues, has consequently had important implications for multinational companies; for instance, actions in terms of 'restrictive practices', by subsidiaries of firms incorporated outside the EC, are the responsibility of parent companies and in cases of 'dominant market positions', the global position of the parent company is to be taken into consideration.

One of the most important successes of the competition policy has been the development by the EC of a policy to deal with cartels and concentrations. It is an achievement simply because a large number of commentators doubted the ability of the EC to take a strict line here due to the political sensitivity of the issue. In fact the Community has created a fairly effective machinery for dealing with anti-trust phenomena.

This success should be qualified, however. Article 86, which tackles the question of abuse of dominance, has not been extensively applied – of course, it could be argued that this is due to the relatively ineffective size (contrary to popular belief – see Collins, 1980) of the EC

Commission. Also a situation of deadlock on the question of mergers still obtains.

The nature of the EC as more than just a customs union is explained in the first section of this chapter. In this section I shall consider the 'common market' aspects of the EC: the establishment of the necessary prerequisites for the free mobility of factors of production.

Articles 92–4 were introduced by the original Six during the transitional period to provide regulations for the free movement of labour. In theory complete and free labour mobility was achieved in 1968. Much to the surprise of the Commissioners, actual mobility did not materialise, so attempts were made to encourage it: the progressive development of a vacancy clearing system (Article 49) and the creation of a system of transferability of social security rights (Article 51) – see Collins (1980) and El-Agraa and Goodrich (1980).

It should, of course, not be surprising that labour mobility is not forthcoming. Professor Brown, writing in the context of regional labour mobility within the UK, states:

> . . . mobility in the sense of propensity to change address is quite high; households move, on the average, more than once in ten years, making about six million changes of address by individuals annually. Three-quarters of all moves within the country are, however, over distances of *less than ten miles, and only about one-eighth of the total, involving in England and Wales about 1½ per cent of the population (three-quarters of a million) each year, are interregional.* The Labour Mobility Survey shows most short-distance moves to be motivated by housing considerations, long-range moves to be connected mostly with change of employment, or, to a smaller extent, with retirement. (Brown, 1972, p. 253, emphasis added)

If labour mobility is so insignificant within the regions of one nation, at this early stage (despite deliberate policy encouragement) it is hardly surprising that it is even less so between nations of the EC.

The mobility of capital is even more complicated than that of labour, particularly since it is very much interconnected with the questions of monetary integration (El-Agraa 1980, Chapters 9 and 10) and the common regional policy (Nevin, 1980), subjects that I shall turn to in a later section. Here it can be pointed out that capital mobility (the technical problems of which were discussed in the Segré Report which was presented to the Council in January 1967) has been inhibited by the fluctuations in the rates of exchange of the member countries. In addition, the practice of controlling the convertibility of domestic currencies into foreign currencies for international transactions (for short run balance of payments equilibrating purposes and for protecting job-creating investments) and the imposition of restrictions (for the purposes of effective control of the money supply and inflation) on non-member nationals seeking to acquire short-term securities have been further inhibiting and distorting factors.

SPECIFIC POLICIES

The EC calls for certain common policies some of which are specifically stated in the Treaty and others which have been incorporated since then.

The CAP has been a success as far as the adoption of a common system and common prices is concerned. [This is not, however, strictly correct in the case of the latter since the MCA (monetary compensatory amounts which are payments made to offset discrepancies in costs of agricultural products from different nations of the EC arising from changes in their cross-rates of exchange) system works against common prices and has proved beneficial to the country least expected to gain from it, namely West Germany (Hu, 1979).] That is all that can be stated in favour of the CAP apart from the fact that it was the result of hard bargaining and compromises (Swann, 1978). However, the system adopted is the most inefficient possible (El-Agraa, 1980, Chapter 7) since by setting prices at a high level it encourages excessive production, discourages consumption and therefore creates unwanted surpluses which make nonsense of the mechanism of financing the policy. Moreover, it is a system which works against the interests of the outside world, particularly the developing world, and is therefore one of the causes of the tense external relationships of the EC – see below.

With regard to the common transport policy, Professor Gwilliam's 1980 conclusion should be stressed: in total it is difficult to escape the prognostication that the inertia which has hitherto characterised the development of the common transport policy will continue, and even be accentuated. Infrastructure appears to be the sole exceptional area where new initiatives are proposed. But even here the initiatives may turn out to be modest in content and effect, coordinating national investment activities and attempting to iron out the more obvious deficiencies in international infrastructure provision. The more contentious matter of common infrastructure pricing, despite all the efforts devoted to it in the last eight years, still seems a long way from resolution. Thus, in the short term the common transport policy will have little effect on the existing national entry controls and rate controls of the individual member states. Nor does it seem likely that the fiscal system under which the transport system operates will come under any effective supranational control. Of course, that is not to say there are no problems in transport policy but merely that the problems that do exist are predominantly domestic and must be approached primarily in the context of domestic policies.

The EC has a common energy policy (not specified in the Treaty), the need for which has been particularly apparent since the world oil price upheavals. The success of this policy is very limited: the EC has been able to devise methods of estimating the growth in its total energy demand, and it has agreed to alter its demand pattern for energy so as to be less dependent on world supplies (Hu, 1980). The arguably vital decisions regarding the development of national coal industries, the enhancement of atomic energy programmes and their financing remain the responsibility of the individual member nations. However, the EC has succeeded in establishing some procedures for energy: in 1968 a minimum stockholding of oil was agreed; methods for sharing oil supplies and for discouraging the consumption of oil in times of crisis have been introduced (Swann, 1978).

Dr Hu argues, an argument worth stating in detail since it has general applicability to all EC policies, that if by a policy one means a combination of a clear vision of the future, a coherent set of principles, a range of policy instruments adequate to the objectives that are set, and the existence of sufficient legitimacy and authority to carry the measures through, it follows by definition that Europe does not have an energy policy. But is this surprising, when even a full political union and a real common market, the US, with its vast resources, does not have an energy policy in this sense? If one adopts the supranational or integrationist view of what constitutes a common policy, it is clear there is no common policy, since much of the conception and implementation of energy policy remains with the member states. Again this is not surprising in view of the importance and sensitiveness of the issues involved. Nor is the Community entirely devoid of 'own' policy instruments (e.g. the EIB) but the coal crisis of 1958–60 clearly showed that, even where such dispositions exist legally, it would be difficult to activate them without the consent of the member states. If one abandons the Procrustean mould of integration theory and recognises the reality of national policies, the question is no longer one of a common policy but of a convergence of national policies towards the common good. Such a convergence is facilitated or made difficult by the environment, but it also presupposes a convergence of national interests, which depends on perceptions, material circumstances, mutual trust, and the arrangement of package deals. In any case, negative integration (the common market in oil) is not viable without positive integration (effective oil-sharing in times of crisis).

Why should the EC have a common energy policy? If this question is accepted, the answer must be sought in economies of scale, increased bargaining strength, decreased vulnerability, or the need to maintain certain other common policies regarding, for example, conservation and R and D. In fact, however, the justification for a common energy policy depends on the vision that one has of the Community and of what it should become. If one believes in the ever closer working together of the peoples of Europe, the question becomes: why should the Community not work together in this vital area? It becomes a question, not of a strict separation of powers, but of combining national and Community initiatives towards common goals.

The EC has a common fisheries policy, agreement on which was reached in October 1970, and it came into force in February 1971 – a very opportune time considering the imminent membership of Denmark, Ireland and the UK. The policy has two elements: market organisation and structural aspects. The market organisation covers fresh fish and frozen and preserved products and its main aim is to apply common marketing standards and to facilitate trading between the member nations of the EC. The structural aspects are basically concerned with equal access to fishing grounds for all EC nationals, with provisos for certain kinds of offshore fishing. Overall, it can fairly be stated that this policy is far from common since so far it has been based on *ad hoc* compromises and concessions for *individual* member nations.

HARMONISATION OF LIVING CONDITIONS

The Community budget, the regional policy, and the social policy should be considered together since all three relate in some way to improved and harmonised living conditions.

An influential Community budget would play an effective role in narrowing income disparities, as Brown (1980) clearly argues. Moreover, it could be reformed in a manner which replaced the existing inadequate financing system which consists of the revenue collected from the CET, levies on agricultural imports and a maximum of 1 per cent of the VAT base, and therefore relieve the pressure exerted by the CAP on the budget (El-Agraa 1980, Chapter 7). However, the present size of the budget is too small (0.7 per cent of the GDP of the whole EC as compared with about 40 per cent for individual states – see the MacDougall Report 1977) to exert any substantial distributive influences. This is a particularly important point since the net contributions of the individual member states have not been consistent with their relative income position within the EC – see Figure 4.2.

Nevin (1980) argues that some progress has been made in the common regional policy but that a genuinely independent Community regional policy is still far distant. This can be attributed to the inadequate size of the EC budget and to the implications of monetary integration (see below) for the management of regional imbalance. Moreover the prospects for the British regional policy, which is the best established within the EC, are mixed since there are EC elements which both enhance and undermine it.

As far as the social policy is concerned, Collins (1980) argues that the main lesson of developments so far seems to be that the Community is likely to edge forward very slowly in the social field, dependent on occasions when, for their own reasons, member states see it as

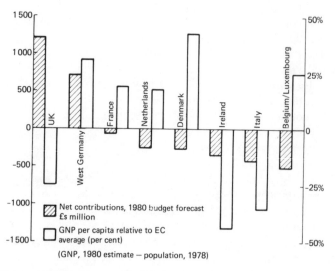

FIGURE 4.2(a)   *Net contributions to EC budget and GNP per capita*

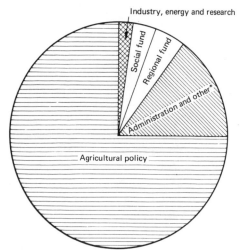

Industry, energy and research

Social fund

Regional fund

Administration and other*

Agricultural policy

*Including the European Parliament, the Council, the Court of Justice,
the Court of Auditors and the administrative part of the ECSC Budget

FIGURE 4.2(b)   *EC expenditure average 1973–80, as a percentage of total*

SOURCE   *Economic Progress Report*, February 1980.

opportune to allow a new initiative. The history of attempts to develop a social policy shows member states as reluctant to allow changes which cost money and this makes any Commission proposal very vulnerable in the absence of a Community social budget. States have shown that they dislike too many direct contacts to grow between the Commission and non-governmental agencies and have managed to retain their grasp of channels of communication as in the case of social fund grant aid. There remains a dormant conflict between the Commission and the Council concerning how far collaboration under Article 118 can be insisted upon and whether the Council has an obligation to activate Article 235 to ensure action when no other means exist. At the present time, specific, concrete initiatives making for an incremental social policy seem more likely than grand policies.

A reflection on how far social policy has developed since 1951, or even since 1957, leads to a realisation that there is now a Community dimension to be considered on matters of health, social security and working conditions. Change does occur, albeit slowly. Broad social issues such as the migration of workers, the pollution of the environment, industrial welfare and democracy, issues of competitive cost, consumer protection and regional subsidy have all now to be considered on a wider than national basis. Issues such as lower, or more flexible retirement ages, a shorter working week and job creation schemes as means of alleviating unemployment are now freely discussed at the highest EC level. When it is remembered, however, that the next major political act of the Community is the enlargement of the group, with countries whose per capita income is lower than the existing average, then member states will doubtless consider that any necessary aids to make enlargement possible constitute the maximum they are prepared to offer to make possible new initiatives in the social field. Thus the main theme of social policy in the near future is likely to be the contribution that can be made to the support of national policies.

There is a curious duality about Community social policy which makes it hard to assess. It contains large, inspirational goals along with work of the utmost detail and highly specialised content. It is difficult to trace the path towards the former by immersion in the latter and the lack of instant appeal from which so much of the work suffers can lead to the assumption that the detail is insignificant.

The Community institutions, and particularly the Commission, can however claim a great advantage for they are in a better position than governmental institutions to identify the broad processes of social and economic change occurring in Western Europe and to consider the extent to which the social policy response must be one which is taken in concert rather than independently. It is clearer today than was once the case that there are indeed such issues but their consideration only requires a standardisation of policy in discrete circumstances.

MONETARY INTEGRATION

The question of monetary integration is a very tricky and sensitive one. The aspirations of the EC are for complete monetary integration and the Werner Report (1970) suggested its achievement, by stages, in 1980. When the Six became nine in 1973 and the world monetary system was in complete disarray, it was inevitable that the 1980 date should be waived – see the Marjolin Report, 1975. However, in 1978 the Bremen Conference affirmed its commitment to achieving monetary union in the near future by adopting the EMS.

Before one proceeds further one needs to define monetary integration. Monetary integration has two essential components: an exchange rate union and capital market integration. An exchange rate union is established when member countries have what is *de facto* one currency.

The actual existence of one currency is not necessary, however, (one could of course argue that the adoption of a single currency would guarantee the irreversibility of undertaking membership of a monetary union, which would have vast repercussions for the discussion of the EMU as an actual union), because if member countries have *permanently* fixed exhange rates amongst themselves, the result is effectively the same even though the member currencies may vary in unison relative to non-member currencies.

Capital market integration is concerned with convertibility. Convertibility refers to the *permanent* absence of all exchange controls for both current and capital transactions including interest and dividend payments (and the harmonisation of *all* relevant taxes and measures affecting the capital market) within the union. It is of course absolutely necessary to have complete convertibility for trade transactions, otherwise an important requirement of the customs union aspect of the EC is threatened, namely the promotion of free trade between members of the union. Convertibility for capital transactions is related to free factor mobility and is therefore an important aspect of capital market integration which is necessary for the common market element of the EC.

Monetary union, therefore, takes place when an exchange rate union is accompanied by capital market integration. However, it has now been recognised that, in practice, the definition should include:

(i) an explicit harmonisation of monetary policies;
(ii) a common pool of foreign exchange reserves;
(iii) a single central bank.

Due to space limitations one cannot go into the reasons for the inclusion of these elements; those interested should consult Corden (1972a and 1977) and El-Agraa (1980). One only needs to stress that these elements hint at the advantages of adopting a single currency.

True monetary integration has many advantages – all the advantages of having one EC currency and one authority to manage it: the promotion of trade and investment; economy in the use of foreign exchange reserves; a commitment on the part of those member nations in temporary surplus to help those with temporary deficits; a common policy towards structural regional imbalance, etc. These advantages outweigh (see El-Agraa 1980, Chapter 9) any conceivable disadvantages which, according to Corden (1972a, 1977) are the extra deflation/inflation which is induced by forgoing the rate of exchange as a policy instrument.

However, the process of actually achieving these aspirations is an extremely difficult one (see Cairncross, 1974, Corden, 1972a and 1977 and El-Agraa 1980, Chapter 10) and some commentators would therefore advocate that it should be postponed for as long as possible. The EMS is arguably a step in the right direction but it is not complete monetary integration since it relates to areas of monetary stability, rather than complete fixity of exchange rates, the common pooling of foreign exchange reserves, the creation of a Community central bank and the coordination of monetary and economic policies. That is why most economists would agree that, 'however indispensable to full economic integration, monetary union could prove disastrous by itself if it was not accompanied by the political and other conditions inseparable from full integration and collective economic mangement' (Cairncross 1974, p. 34). That political will, at least as far as Britain is concerned, seems not to be forthcoming, although the present Conservative government seems set in that direction.

EXTERNAL RELATIONS

The EC has made some attempts at establishing some form of external relations with the outside world (El-Agraa 1980, Chapter 17) so that its own development should not appear to be entirely inward looking, for example the first round of tariff cuts was applied globally as agreed in the Kennedy Round of tariff negotiations. More specifically, however, the EC has proved capable of acting as a unit in international trade negotiations and has negotiated with the US on equal terms; it has pursued and has succeeded in concluding association treaties (although some of these were designed to secure French interests in Africa); and it has succeeded in attracting new membership. These successes should be viewed with considerable caution, particularly since the results of the international negotiations have strengthened the protectionist elements in the EC (El-Agraa 1980, Chapter 17); the association treaties have had a very marginal impact and it could be argued that they were detrimental to the Third World; the EC does not only seem reluctant to have a clear policy on aid to the Third World but, in spite of conceding to the *generalised system of preferences*, it has remained basically selective and this selective nature has been essentially for its own benefit; and the terms negotiated for new membership have been, albeit marginally, at the expense of the newly contracting parties.

CONCLUSIONS

The EC has been very successful in achieving negative integration (defined as the removal of mutual tariff barriers between member nations – see Chapter 1, Pinder, 1971 and El-Agraa, 1980, Chapter 1) and in adopting some elements of positive integration (defined as the act of adopting new policies and of introducing common external relations, policy harmonisation, etc.), for instance the introduction of common external tariff rates, the Common Agricultural Policy and the progress towards monetary integration. However, in the latter area, and that is where true integration is really tested, progress has been very slow and in some instances altogether lacking. This is, of course, not meant to suggest that there have been no apparent signs of strength in the forces pushing the EC towards more integration. Indeed, the opposite is the case; it is only that progress has been slow because true positive integration is very much connected with the sensitive issue of sovereignty. Moreover, *lest it be forgotton, the EC stands for the harmonised integration of some of the oldest countries in the world with very diverse cultures and extremely complicated economic systems.*

On the face of it, it seems that the EC is set to take either of two alternative courses: to become a more diluted arrangement (the implications of which are discussed in El-Agraa and Jones (1981), Chapter 3, so as to accommodate more members who are jealously guarding their sovereignty, or to take a 'quantum leap' (Ingram, 1973) in terms of a political commitment to a United States of Western Europe. There does not seem to be a middle ground (though some commentators have predicted that the EC will become a two-tier organisation with the original Six minus Italy going ahead with complete political integration and the remaining four plus new members forming a diluted and less committed second tier) because that is the area where principles are diluted and temporary disadvantages become a permanent reality. However, one cannot help feeling, despite the quarrels between the British government and the rest of the EC over the British net contribution to the Community budget, that political commitment is on the way. This feeling is justified by the recent progress towards the European Monetary System; all member nations except Britain are now full participants and the UK has taken two steps that indicate imminent membership: it exchanged 20 per cent of its dollar and gold reserves against European units of account (which is an indication of positive participation in the European Monetary Cooperation Fund) and in October 1979 it abolished all foreign exchange restrictions. Of course, it could be argued that these measures were sensible for budgetary purposes and that the Labour Party is seriously committed to British withdrawal from the EC, but unless future events prove the contrary neither proposition can be taken seriously.

5 The European Free Trade Association

Victoria Curzon Price

The European Free Trade Association [(EFTA)-(II)] celebrated its 20th anniversary in 1980. It was smaller and leaner than the EFTA of 1960, but doubtless more viable. The nature and aims of EFTA-(I) (1960–72) – see Price (1974) and EFTA Secretariat 1980a and 1980b – form the first part of this chapter, while EFTA-(II) and its members' relationship with the European Communities (EC) occupy the remainder.

EFTA-(I): THE FREE TRADE AREA PROTOTYPE

EFTA-(I) was founded in 1960 by seven countries which, at the time, did not wish to join the EC. (These countries were Austria and Switzerland in the centre of Europe, Denmark, Norway and Sweden in the north, Portugal to the south and the UK to the west; Finland joined as an Associate Member in 1961 – a more geographically dispersed group of countries would have been difficult to find!) From the point of view of 'games theory', this was a classical reaction on the part of a set of countries severely threatened with the prospect of trade diversion caused by the newly created EC. However, because EFTA was much smaller than the EC, and its individual members smaller still and extremely dependent on their relationship with the nascent Common Market, this retaliatory aspect was played down. In fact, from the start the basic objective of EFTA's members, hence of EFTA itself, was to reach a mutually satisfactory understanding with the EC. The history of EFTA-(I) is essentially about how they managed to do this, and the history of EFTA-(II) is about how this mutually satisfactory arrangement, negotiated in 1972, turned out in practice.

Barely twelve months after EFTA-(I) began functioning, its largest member, the UK, decided to apply for full membership of the EC. It was followed by Denmark and Norway, two EFTA members which had already decided that they would follow their principal export market wherever it went. EFTA looked dead before it was born. The remaining members considered the British move to be a severe blow to their prospects of reaching a satisfactory agreement with the EC. Interestingly enough, however, they managed to extract from a reluctant UK, (which thought it had signed a mere free trade area – FTA – treaty, with no limits on its right to conduct an independent foreign policy) the then-famous 'London Declaration' of June 1961. By this, the British government bound itself with a solemn promise not to join the EC until 'satisfactory arrangements' had been worked out to 'meet the various legitimate interests of all members of EFTA' (EFTA Secretariat 1966, pp. 22–3). In the event, General de Gaulle's January 1963 veto cut short the negotiations, but the feeling lingered that the London Declaration had helped the General to reach his decision, confirming the worst suspicions of the smaller EFTA countries, namely, that the EC was not prepared to meet their 'various legitimate interests'.

These small neutral countries – Austria, Finland, Sweden and Switzerland – all had overriding political reasons for not joining the EC, the most obvious being that the Soviet Union would no longer have recognised at best their neutrality or at worst their very right to existence as sovereign states (which could have led to the re-occupation of Austria and Finland by Soviet troops). Switzerland, in addition, had strong domestic political reasons for abstaining from membership of the EC, connected with its finely balanced federal structure designed to accommodate a multi-cultural society. In summary, one might say that in the early 1960s, the small neutral countries were prepared to pay the cost, in terms of trade diversion, of keeping their neutrality credible in the eyes of the only military power that mattered, while the members of the EC saw no reason to reduce that cost for their sake.

EFTA-(II) AND THE FREE TRADE AREA ARRANGEMENTS: FROM PROTOTYPE TO MASS PRODUCTION

For the rest of the decade EFTA and the EC trod separate paths. EFTA's members concentrated on demonstrating that intra-area tariffs could be dismantled, that non-tariff barriers could be kept under control, that origin rules could be devised and administered satisfactorily and that both sides of industry could shoulder the inevitable burden of structural adjustment without difficulty.

This they did, and when General de Gaulle's departure from the centre of Europe's political stage reopened the question of Britain's accession to the EC in December 1969, the FTA as a model of economic integration was no longer a disputed blueprint, but a successful operational prototype. This time, the EC Council of Ministers itself announced that the interests of the non-applicant neutral countries would be taken into account during the process of enlargement, and that, in particular, existing free trade would not be compromised in the process. This made it unnecessary to extract a second London Declaration from the UK, which, once bitten, twice shy, would probably have refused to give such a pledge in any event.

The form in which the EC was to honour its promise was, however, left undefined. A customs union, a FTA, partial preference zone or what? In view of the very sceptical attitude of the EC towards FTAs, it is interesting that this formula should have been chosen for the EFTA–EC trade links.

That the FTA formula should suit the neutrals' purposes is self-evident. They obtain access to the EC for their industrial products in exchange for eliminating their own already low tariffs on manufactured goods. They do not have to participate in the costly Common Agricultural Policy (CAP), and they remain free to determine their own commercial policy *vis-à-vis*, for example, developing countries, Japan, Eastern Europe and Hong Kong. On the other hand, they must forego the privilege of helping to shape EC policies with respect to industrial policy, free movement of labour, transport, energy, fisheries, competition, monetary cooperation, and a host of other areas where EC member states are moving slowly and often painfully towards a 'common' position – see Chapter 4. This is the price that the neutrals must pay for their neutrality, and some of the following pages will be devoted to discussing just how high it is.

But what of the EC? Right up to and during the 1971–72 negotiations, both the EC Commission and France viewed the FTA formula with deep distaste. On the straightforward technical level there was the problem of policing the origin system. Surely origin rules would be avoided by hordes of unscrupulous traders, requiring equally large armies of zealous customs officials to track them down? EFTA's empirical demonstration to the contrary was partly discounted on the grounds that in such a geographically dispersed grouping, the incentive for circumventing origin rules was much diminished by high intra-area transport costs. This would no longer be the case if, say, France and Switzerland were linked in a FTA. This scepticism has not died with time and lies behind the very much stricter origin rules established for the EC – EFTA links than within the old EFTA-(I) system (see Binswanger and Mayrzedt (1972) pp. 63–6, and Price (1974) pp. 234–9), an issue to which I shall shortly turn.

On the more complex and elevated level of policy and principle the European hawks (proponents of 'l'Europe pure et dure') were very worried that FTAs represented a soft option – integration without tears – which might prove an attractive alternative to some faint-hearted European doves *within* the EC, as well as to potential members, such as Greece or Spain. In fact, the FTA option *did* provide an alternative to Norway which, after vacillating, took it up in preference to joining the EC, in 1972. In short, the European hawks were loath to relinquish the use of the economic threat of trade diversion to further their longer range political objectives. Having done so, of course, they may be sure now that the countries which choose to join are doing so for political reasons: but exactly what political reasons is anybody's guess!

Upon reflection, however, the advantages of the FTA formula began to dawn on even its sternest opponents. Indeed, how could the EC agree to tie its own hands in a stronger link (say via a customs union) with a non-member? This would be tantamount to giving Sweden, for instance, veto power over any changes in the EC's common external tariff (CET), a privilege which only fully paid-up members ought to enjoy. A weaker link, for instance via a preferential trading zone stopping short of full free trade, would not only fall foul of GATT's Article 24, but would also renege on the European Summit's promise not to allow trade barriers to reappear between the new EC members and their old EFTA partners. It has to be admitted that this possibility was in fact briefly entertained (Price, 1974, p. 228) but it did not win much support among most EC members and was dismissed indignantly by the neutrals. In the end, the FTA formula proved to be the only one which satisfied everybody's interests at minimal cost and without transgressing international obligations. Negotiations were brought to a successful conclusion in July 1972 with the signature of six bilateral Free Trade Agreements (AFTs) between the EC and the neutrals (plus Portugal and – a relative newcomer to the European integration scene – Iceland). The picture was completed with the signature of the Norway–EC AFT in May 1973, making seven in all.

COVERAGE

One of the reasons why the EFTA-(I) prototype proved so successful was that it made no attempt to cover agriculture. This sector has not been exposed to market forces for at least a century in most European countries, including those of EFTA, and any attempt to free trade on a regional basis would either have been meaningless (public policy would have continued to govern trade, prices and production) or highly distorting unless a 'common' policy could be developed (à la CAP). Neither the original EFTA members, nor today's, ever wished to make this effort in the EFTA context – the payoff was too obviously unattractive: little or no likelihood of specialisation, nor indeed a good reason for anything so trade-diverting, in exchange for superhuman efforts to achieve consensus on a sensitive political issue, and – with the wisdom of hindsight – the mortgaging of the entire fund of integrative goodwill in the population at large for years to come.

On the other hand, by concentrating their efforts in the industrial field alone the members of EFTA achieved a maximum of real integration, in terms of intra-area specialisation, for a minimum of integrative effort, in terms of achieving a public policy consensus among several countries. The reason for this high payoff is that the mere act of removing tariffs (slightingly referred to as 'negative integration' by some authors – see Chapter 1) in sectors of industry governed by market forces is enough to bring about intra-area specialisation, without the need for further government action. In particular, it is not necessary to achieve painful, delicate and unstable consensi at government level, admiringly termed 'positive integration' by those who tend to confuse effort with results. Because EFTA governments sit back and let market forces do the job of integrating, the EFTA Secretariat functions with no more than seventy people; for the same reason, EFTA's history appears to be remarkably uneventful because the really important things (namely market-induced specialisation) happen at such a micro-economic level that they escape the commentator's eye.

IMPACT OF INTEGRATION, DISINTEGRATION AND RE-INTEGRATION

Doubts that mere 'negative' integration can have startling effects on patterns of trade and production, even in such a dispersed FTA as EFTA, can be laid to rest by consulting the evidence – see Table 5.1.

TABLE 5.1   *EFTA exports by areas 1959–78 (% shares in total)*

	1959	1967	1972	1978
Intra-EFTA*	11.1	16.6	19.0	15.1
Denmark/UK	16.2	18.2	18.4	16.9
EC 6	34.0	29.7	29.3	31.5
EC 9	50.5	48.2	48.1	48.8
USA	8.7	7.8	7.3	5.9
Japan	0.6	1.2	1.4	1.7
Communist countries	7.7	7.2	6.0	7.5
OPEC	2.4	1.9	2.1	5.4
NICs†	4.9	6.4	7.2	6.2

* Figures refer to EFTA-(II): Austria, Finland, Iceland, Norway, Portugal, Sweden and Switzerland.
† Newly industrialising countries.
SOURCE   EFTA Secretariat (1980a). *EFTA – Past and Future* (Geneva: EFTA Secretariat, 1980a).

From 1959 to 1972 intra-EFTA trade as a proportion of total trade rose from 11 to 19 per cent, and the annual rate of growth of intra-area trade was consistently higher than the rate of growth of EFTA's trade in general: 15 per cent (as compared with 9.2 per cent) from 1959 to 1967, and 17.4 per cent (as compared with 14.3 per cent) from 1967 to 1972 – see EFTA Secretariat 1980a. Whether this substantial degree of intra-area specialisation was on balance trade-creating or trade-diverting is, of course, another matter – see Chapter 3. On the EFTA secretariat's own estimate, trade creation amounted to 721 million US dollars by 1967, and trade diversion to 592 million US dollars (EFTA Secretariat 1980a, – the figures refer to those countries given in Table 5.1 minus Iceland). Most of the trade diversion, however, was thought to have arisen within Europe, as EFTA-based industrialists, as a result of the area preference, sought to replace marginally cheaper EC sources of supply by slightly more expensive EFTA ones.[1] The 1972 AFTs have since removed this source of trade diversion, besides establishing conditions for further trade creation and trade diversion in their own right. Only the roughest estimates of the effects of the AFTs will be made here, but trade figures suggest that the principal impact has been to eliminate the intra-European trade diversion inherent in the preceding integration arrangements. Thus, the original six members of the EC took 29 per cent of EFTA's exports in 1972, the last year before the AFTs came into effect, and 31.5 per cent in 1978, one year after the principal tariffs were finally abolished. This compares with a share of 34 per cent in 1959 (EFTA Secretariat 1980a, p. 44).

If one were to assume (simplistically) that this 1959 ratio would have continued unchaged at 34 per cent in the absence of the chequered history of European integration, distintegration and re-integration of the 1950s, 1960s and 1970s, then one could say that the EC's share in EFTA exports was about 4 per cent lower by 1972, and still 2.5 per cent lower by 1978, than it would otherwise have been, the more significant shift having taken place before 1972 under the impact of the division of Europe.

Interestingly, however, most of this change took place *at the expense of intra-EFTA trade*, whose share fell from 19 per cent in 1972 to 15 per cent in 1978, and *at the expense of EFTA–UK/Denmark* trade, whose share fell from 18 per cent in 1972 to 17 per cent in 1978, and which together still account for a quarter of EFTA's total exports. In the meantime, EFTA also *increased* its share of exports going to Japan, Eastern Europe and OPEC. In a word, the AFTs appear to have been undoing the harm caused by the division of Europe during the 1960s without having a noticeable detrimental effect on third parties.

Looking at the reverse side of the coin – the change in the EC's share in EFTA imports (see Table 5.2) – we can see that it is less dramatic, but equally revealing. The EC supplied 45.6 per cent of EFTA's imports in 1959, and 41.8 per cent in 1967 (indicating a loss due to trade diversion caused jointly by the EC and EFTA); the share then rose slightly to 42.8

TABLE 5.2   *EFTA imports by areas 1959–78 (% shares in total)*

	1959	1967	1972	1978
Intra-EFTA	9.3	13.8	16.6	13.8
Denmark/UK	13.4	15.4	14.1	12.0
EC 6	45.6	41.8	42.8	43.7
EC 9	58.9	57.3	57.0	55.9
USA	8.7	7.3	6.2	6.6
Japan	0.8	2.4	2.8	3.2
Communist countries	6.9	5.6	5.2	6.6
OPEC	2.5	2.6	2.5	4.5
NICs	2.9	3.6	4.1	4.1

SOURCE   *EFTA – Past and Future*   (Geneva: EFTA Secretariat, 1980a).

per cent in 1972 and to 43.7 per cent in 1978 (EFTA Secretariat 1980a, pp. 42–3). Small though the change was, it took place entirely at the expense of intra-EFTA and EFTA–UK/Denmark trade, and left room for the expansion of Japanese, Eastern European, OPEC and even US trade shares.

There appear to be two broad reasons why the EC's share in EFTA imports has not changed much under the AFTs. Firstly, the share is already very large, not only because EFTA countries are much smaller than those of the EC, but also because they tend to have lower levels of protection. Thus the CET of the EC averaged out at 7.4 per cent in 1972, as compared with the 4.7 per cent for EFTA (derived from EFTA Secretariat 1980a, Table 12, p. 47). In other words, the EFTA countries were already fairly well integrated into the EC economy via their own low-tariff policies and the AFTs changed little in the accessibility of their markets to EC entrepreneurs. On the other hand, the rather more protectionist policies of the EC meant that the AFTs *did* improve the ability of EFTA firms to export to the EC rather more substantially, and possibly provided them with a meaningful preference over third-country suppliers.

Secondly, these figures relate to total trade, hiding some substantial sectoral changes. They include, in particular, the impact of the oil price increase on the share of OPEC countries in EFTA imports. This has had the effect of masking, for the time being, the steady shift towards ever greater intra-European specialisation due to integration, a matter to which we now turn in order to determine whether the AFTs on balance, have been trade-creating or trade-diverting.

We know, without always grasping its full significance, that wealth is based on specialisation (Smith, 1776), both within and between countries. In fact, countries are cultural and political creations that follow no particular economic logic. We call the specialisation that occurs between countries 'international trade', but it is no different in nature from the specialisation that occurs within countries between individual firms. The more specialised an individual becomes, the more he will trade with others – and the richer he will be,[2] thanks mainly to the fact that he no longer has to bear the high opportunity cost of making for himself what others (who are also specialised and therefore highly skilled) can do at a lower opportunity cost. It has long been recognised that *groups* of people can improve their standard of living by specialising and trading with other groups of people through 'trade liberalisation'. This enlarges the ratio of imports to total consumption of a given product. We also know that if trade liberalisation is conducted on a discriminatory basis, it does not necessarily enlarge the ratio of imports to total consumption, but may simply shift their source – trade diversion (see Chapter 2). However, *if* a given customs union can be shown to have produced an increase in the ratio of imports to total consumption, this is evidence that the degree of specialisation has increased – trade creation (see Chapter 2). Indeed, an increase in the ratio of imports to apparent consumption (production plus exports minus imports) implies the existence of *net trade creation*, that is, trade creation in excess of trade diversion.[3]

The EFTA Secretariat has very thoughtfully calculated such specialis-ation ratios (ratio of imports to apparent consumption on a value-added basis for manufactured goods for several areas over an extended time period 1954/1976).[4] This allows one to reach some tentative conclusions as to the trade-creating impact of the history of discriminatory and non-discriminatory trade liberalisation during these years.

Table 5.3 shows, for instance, that the degree of EFTA's specialis-ation as measured by this ratio almost doubled – rising from 40 per cent in 1954 to 68 per cent in 1976. This suggests that imports displaced domestic production to a very considerable extent, and appear to have accounted for almost all the growth in demand during those years. The rate of specialisation, however, was not constant (see third column of Table 5.3). It was more rapid from 1954 to 1960, at an annual average rate of 3 per cent, than from 1960 to 1967, where it fell to 1.8 per cent per annum, to rise again to 3 per cent from 1972 onwards. The big surges coincide, in the first period, with the dismantling of quantitative restrictions and exchange controls under OEEC auspices, and in the second period, with the combined effect of the AFTs and the post-

TABLE 5.3   *EFTA: total import ratios, 1954–76*

	Import ratio (%)	*Change* (% points)	*Annual average rate of change of import ratio* (%)
1954	39.9		
1960	47.8	7.9	3.0
1967	54.1	6.3	1.8
1972	60.7	6.6	2.3
1976	68.3	7.6	3.0

SOURCE   *EFTA – Past and Future*   (Geneva: Secretariat, 1980a) p. 64.

implementation of the Kennedy Round tariff cuts. The 1960–67 period emerges as comparatively barren, since it was marked by the division of Europe, and the rather disappointing Dillon Round. But it does suggest that the implementation of EFTA-(I) *inter alia* helped to fight off the impact of trade diversion from the EC, since trade creation effects were still highly visible (imports rising from 48 per cent to 54 per cent of apparent consumption). Over the 20-year period, however, EFTA has an uninterrupted history of trade creation, since the ratio of imports to apparent consumption has grown in every period. But how much of this is due to MFN tariff reduction, and how much to preferential trade liberalisation?

TABLE 5.4   *EFTA: import ratios from the EC, 1954–76*

	Import ratio from EC (%)	Change in share (% points)	Annual average rate of change in import ratios (% p.a.)
1954	18.8		
1960	24.5	5.7	4.5
1967	23.5	− 1	− 0.6
1972	26.3	2.8	2.1
1976	31.1	4.8	4.3

SOURCE   *EFTA – Past and Future*   (Geneva: EFTA Secretariat, 1980a) p. 64.

This question can be answered if we look at the evolution of EFTA's import ratios *from the EC* (see Table 5.4). From 1954 to 1960 specialisation between the future EFTA and EC groups forged ahead at a rate (for EFTA) of 4.5 per cent per annum: the ratio of EC imports to domestic EFTA consumption rose from 18.8 per cent to 24.5 per cent during that period. This trend was abruptly stopped in its tracks after 1960, and by 1967 the share of imports from the EC in total EFTA consumption had dropped back to 23.5 per cent. *Here* is the evidence of net trade diversion caused by the *combined effect* of two parallel integration systems on *one* of them, namely EFTA. (This trade diversion loss, however, was more than outweighed by a trade creation gain on intra-EFTA trade, as measured by an increase in the EFTA import/consumption ratio from 6.7 to 10.4 per cent during these years.) From 1967 to 1972 the EC import ratio edged up again, but not very fast – presumably the result, among other things, of Kennedy Round tariff cuts. Finally, the ratio rose very rapidly again from 1972 to 1976, suggesting that the strong general trade creation effect noted in Table 5.3 (jump of 7.6 percentage points from 1972 to 1976) was in great measure due to increased specialisation with the EC (jump of 4.8 percentage points), hence was in substantial measure the work of the AFTs.[5]

TABLE 5.5   *Share in total EFTA manufactured imports, 1973–9 (per cent)*

	1973	1978	1979
USA	5.6	6.6	6.7
Japan	4.4	4.5	3.9
Developing countries	2.4	3.2	3.2
Communist countries	2.8	2.5	2.7
Other Europe	1.5	1.3	1.5

SOURCE   GATT, *International Trade* (Annual Review) 1980 volume, EFTA – *Past and Future* (Geneva: EFTA Secretariat, 1980a) Table A.20.

Evidence of trade diversion would have to be sought in a decline in the share of third-party suppliers to EFTA markets since 1972. Trade figures supplied in Table 5.2 show, on the contrary, that non-members either held their share steady (NICs, USA) or actually increased them (Communist countries, Japan and, not surprisingly, OPEC). Taking a longer view (since 1959) we note that the USA is the only third country supplier to have suffered a decline in its share of EFTA imports, but this should be less attributed to the existence of preferential trading arrangements in Europe than to the relative loss of US competitiveness *vis-à-vis* Japan and NICs. If we look at the evolution of *manufactured goods only* from 1973 to 1979 (Table 5.5) the picture is slightly different – the USA and developing countries have increased their shares, the Communist countries have held theirs steady, while Japan suffered a sharp decline from 1978 to 1979. Whether this is due to (a) generally restrictive policies towards trade with Japan or (b) trade diversion affecting Japanese goods more than others or (c) Japanese goods losing competitiveness *vis-à-vis* newly industrialising countries, and hitting higher levels of effective protection (EP) in the more advanced sectors, cannot be determined within the scope of this chapter.

For the remaining countries there is virtually no indication of trade diversion, although the aggregates may well hide individual cases in specific sectors, as we shall see later.

THE DISCREET CHARM OF FREE TRADE AREAS

From a theoretical point of view, FTAs produce roughly the same effects as customs unions (Balassa, 1962, Shibata, 1971, Price, 1974 and El-Agraa in El-Agraa and Jones, 1981). However, they do differ in detail, and in particular, tend to cause rather more trade creation and less trade diversion than a tariff-averaging customs union – a detail which has not received much attention in the literature.

In order to demonstrate this point, we must start by making all the conventional assumptions of micro-economic analysis (perfect competition, no transport costs, short-run rising marginal cost curves, free entry and exit, and constant or gently rising long-term costs as inter-factoral substitution and technological advance permit escape from diminishing returns in the long run). We must add the assumptions common to trade theory (perfectly elastic world supply, tariffs being the only instrument of trade policy) and an extra assumption particular to free trade area theory, namely, the frictionless operation of a 'perfect' origin system which prevents trade deflection (i.e. goods manufactured outside the FTA entering at the lowest point in the non-harmonised tariff wall, and proceeding free of duty to more protected markets), without distorting side-effects.

Using the notation of Shibata (*H* for the high-tariff, relatively inefficient producer, *L* for the low-tariff, relatively efficient producer) and a simple partial equilibrium model, we can proceed as in Figure 5.1, which illustrates the position before union. With tariff *TH* in operation,

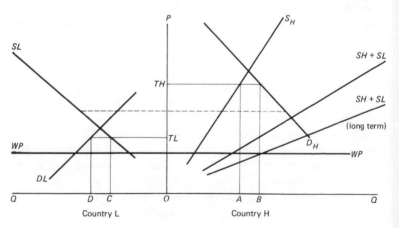

FIGURE 5.1

country *H* produces *OA*, consumes *OB* and imports *AB* from the lowest-cost world supplier at world prices (*WP*). Turning to the left-hand side of Figure 5.1, with tariff *TL* in use, country *L* produces *OC*, consumes *OD* and imports *CD*.

After the FTA is established, producers in *L* gain access to the high-price market in *H* and will serve that market in preference to their own, gradually bringing down the price in *H*. Consumers in *L* need not fear for supplies, however, for world producers will always be prepared to export to *L* at *WP* plus the tariff *TL*, in infinite quantities if need be. Theoretically, the entire production of *L* could be freed for export to *H*. This is the 'shifting' effect described by Shibata: it is supposedly a unique feature of FTAs (for a fundamental and cryptic criticism of this notion see El-Agraa in El-Agraa and Jones, 1981, Chapter 3).

It is important to ask: in this situation what happens to country *H*? According to Shibata, if we accept his analysis, the final price in country *H* is indeterminate, and depends on (a) the relative size and/or elasticity of supply in *L* and (b) on the size and/or elasticity of demand in *H*. In the gloomiest of cases, if *L*'s supply is relatively small and inelastic, and *H*'s demand relatively large and elastic, it is clear that the price in *H* will not fall much, if at all. In this case, the FTA would cause less trade creation and more trade diversion than a tariff-averaging customs union. The reverse holds true in the most optimistic case, the price in *H* falling to or close to the level in *L*. Shibata accordingly concludes that 'there are no a priori grounds for making a general statement as to which of these two systems (a customs union or a FTA is better, even from the point of view of the world as a whole' (Shibata 1971, p. 83).

In my view, a more positive conclusion can be reached. The analysis must be carried further, out of the short-term span, in which producers cannot increase production significantly without incurring rapidly increasing marginal costs, and into the longer term, during which they can increase or decrease capacity according to whether the price they face in the market covers their long-term average costs or not.

Returning to Figure 5.1, it is clear that it represents a short-run situation. If the two supply curves are added together on the right-hand side (*SH* + *SL*), and applied to *H*'s demand curve, the short-run equilibrium price turns out to be higher than the long-run equilibrium price in *L*(*TL*). However, as long as this situation persists, entrepreneurs in *L* will be encouraged to expand capacity, since they were presumably meeting their long-run average costs at price *TL* before union, and are now making excess profits in *H*. This will cause the supply curve in *L* to shift bodily to the left until the combined *H* + *L* supply curves wipe out the price difference between L and H, representing the end of the opportunity for producers in L to make excess profits in H. Unlike Shibata, I therefore conclude that price differences cannot persist in a FTA for goods of area origin (for an alternative explanation of this, see El-Agraa in El-Agraa and Jones, 1981, Chapter 3) and that the price level of the most efficient area producer will prevail – under the conventional assumptions, of course.

It follows from this conclusion that a FTA is more trade-creating and less trade diverting than a tariff-averaging customs union – see Chapter 2. It also tends to be less detrimental to non-member interests, since exports to L need not diminish and may well expand in the short run, allowing world producers to gain a foothold from which it may be difficult to dislodge them at a later date once producers in L have expanded capacity. Finally, returning to Figure 5.1, if a horizontal line is drawn mid-way between TL and TH, representing the CET of a tariff-averaging customs union, it is clear that the FTA avoids an oft-neglected cost to customs union, namely, the increased level of protection in L. This is fine for producers, of course, since marginal capacity can be brought into use and efficient plants will make excess profits, but the economy as a whole suffers from misallocation and consumers suffer a direct consumption loss. This does not occur in the case of FTAs, and is one reason why low tariff countries tend to prefer them to customs unions.

TOO GOOD TO BE TRUE?

Against all these (static) advantages two drawbacks must be pointed out.

(1) DISTORTION IN RESOURCE ALLOCATION

It is commonly objected that because the FTA offers different levels of EP, allocation distortions will occur. Two comments need to be made in this connection. First, if we maintain our initial assumptions (especially with regard to our 'perfect' origin system) it can be shown that intra-area free trade sets a natural limit to distortions arising from this source. Secondly, the amount of misallocation will depend on whether the origin rules are strict or generous.

Let us consider the following example (Figure 5.2): Sweden[6] imports man-made fibres (cost = 25), spins them (adding another 25 to the value

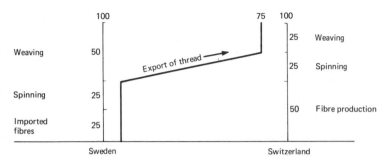

FIGURE 5.2

of the fibres) and weaves them into cloth (adding another 50), giving a total cost for cloth in Sweden of 100. The Swedish tariffs on fibres, thread and cloth are designed to ensure that the inefficient weaving function is given a high level of EP.

In Switzerland, on the other hand, a different tariff structure obtains, designed to ensure that fibres are produced locally. Spinning and weaving enjoy low or possibly negative levels of EP, and are therefore highly efficient.

If trade is freed for goods of area origin, without tariff harmonisation taking place, the Swedish spinning industry will displace the Swiss (Swedish thread costing 50 instead of 75), but Swiss weavers will displace the Swedes (their costs being 25 instead of 50). The total cost of making cloth will be 75:25 (fibre imported into Sweden) + 25 (spinning in Sweden) + 25 (weaving in Switzerland). People will simply stop making fibres in Switzerland, and weaving in Sweden. Neither the high level of EP in Sweden for weaving nor the high level of explicit protection in Switzerland for fibres will attract investment. Both have become redundant because of free trade with a more efficient partner. In terms of efficiency of resource allocation, the efficient segments have been encouraged to expand and the inefficient ones to contract.

From this example, it can be seen that the danger of misallocation arises not from *high* levels of EP, but from *low or even negative* rates of protection. The latter is a rare but by no means unheard of phenomenon. Returning to our numerical example, it is illustrated by the hypothetical Swiss spinning industry which is indeed discriminated against: it is as efficient as the Swedish, but burdened by negative EP. If negative as well as positive EP is embedded in the tariff structure we shall be in a familiar second-best situation, where a move towards improved efficiency co-exists with conditions favouring inefficiency. If positive EP exceeds negative EP (the more common situation) then movements towards improved efficiency will outweigh those towards inefficiency.

Many authors have suggested that FTAs would generate spontaneous pressure towards a harmonisation of EP rates, in order to prevent efficient activities from being penalised by negative EP. Indeed, there is some merit in the argument. Returning to our hypothetical example, we see that Swiss fibre producers will be unable to sell their goods, even to their own efficient down-stream local spinners (since the FTA price for thread is 50). They will either strive to become more competitive or go out of business. In the first case, Swiss spinners may be able to survive; in the second, they will go the same way as the fibre producers – out – unless the Swiss government notices in time that it is unnecessarily throwing away a perfectly healthy industry along with the inevitable loss of a dud one, and that a reduction of the redundant tariff would save it.[7]

This discussion raises the question why governments would discriminate against the activity in the first place. In fact, most tariff structures are progressive, namely, levying nil or negligible rates of duty on imported raw materials and semi-processed manufactures, intermediate rates of duty on competent and industrial inputs, and high rates of duty on finished goods. Both governments and industry are well aware that raising the cost of intermediate goods penalises all down-stream sectors, and tariff structures are on the whole designed to favour the higher value-added down-stream segments. However, if EP rates are positive, no distortions arise in a FTA from the lack of harmonisation, as noted above. Perhaps it is for this reason that there is little evidence of conscious tariff alignment in EFTA or the AFTs, although the low (and generally declining) absolute levels of protection anyway limit the scope for large negative EP rates.

(2) RULES OF ORIGIN

Returning to our hypothetical numerical example, it can be seen that the ability of the Swiss to displace Swedish weavers depends on free intra-area trade in thread, half of whose value consists of non-area fibres. Were origin rules to specify that, say, 60 per cent of the value had to be produced in Sweden, then Swiss weavers would not have access to cheap thread and would not be able to displace the Swedes.

However, if the area preference were worthwhile and the differences in efficiency were large enough, entrepreneurs would soon find a way of adding the required extra amount of area content and shipping thread to Switzerland at a slightly higher cost.

From these remarks it should be clear that rules of origin may fulfil more than one purpose. The obvious one is to stop non-member goods from enjoying the area preference: this can be accomplished by specifying some 'reasonable' uniform level of area content [50 per cent being the benchmark actually used in EFTA-(I)]. A less apparent function is to use the origin system to concentrate the demand for intermediate goods on area producers. The reason for the assumption concerning a 'perfect' non-distorting origin system above should now be clear. Indeed, the origin system is the key to the nature of the FTA: if it is generous, it will encourage trade creation; if it is restrictive, it will foster trade diversion.

This holds true irrespective of the height of the individual country tariffs. Thus a group of high-tariff countries forming a FTA with generous origin rules would still tend to be more trade-creating than a tariff-averaging customs union (since the highest tariffs would become redundant, and prices within the area would be governed by the lowest of the high tariffs): conversely, a group of low-tariff countries forming a FTA with strict origin rules might well turn out to be more trade-diverting than a tariff-averaging customs union. Of course, this does not alter one of the basic conclusions of customs union theory, namely, that a high level of protection *vis-à-vis* third countries will tend to cause an excess of trade diversion over trade creation.

In practice, this means that the analysis of a FTA's origin rules, though not perhaps the most fascinating of tasks, is most revealing. The rules of origin of EFTA-(I), though generally considered to be a model of liberalism, contained a couple of darker areas (textiles and chemicals) – see Price, 1974, pp. 158–60 and 162–7 – while the rules of origin imposed by the EC in the AFTs are visibly less generous (Curzon 1974, pp. 234–5). Very briefly, whereas EFTA-(I) rules of origin offered two alternative methods of acquiring origin status (50 per cent value-added within the area of fulfilment of a 'process' criterion), EC–AFT rules specify only one method (a *combination* of a value *and* a process criterion); also, whereas the EFTA 50 per cent criterion was softened by a 'basic materials list' (some 200 imported basic materials which, if transformed or incorporated in the area, counted towards the area content, irrespective of where they came from) the EC rules of origin contain no such list; also, by using the fob export price as the denominator, EFTA producers could add to the area content the cost of handling from the factory to the port of exit, whereas the EC value-added criteria are based on the ex-factory price; also most of the EC's value-added criteria require more than 50 per cent local value-added whereas in practice EFTA's implied considerably less; finally, whereas EFTA created a group of seven countries within which origin status could be accumulated multilaterally, the AFTs, being bilateral treaties between the EC and each individual EFTA country, do not permit multilateral cumulation across EFTA for the purposes of EFTA-EC trade.

This last point is important, if read in conjunction with the generally stricter origin requirements outlined earlier. It implies that there is an incentive to concentrate EFTA industrialists' demands for intermediate goods and components on EC suppliers, to the detriment of both other EFTA and non-European suppliers.

The EFTA countries fought this provision from the outset, and obtained a minimal concession from the EC during the AFT negotiations: the right to so-called 'diagonal' cumulation. This arcane term allows goods *which have acquired* origin status under *one* AFT to be incorporated or transformed into new products in a parallel AFT without losing their origin status under the *first* AFT. However, this is not considered to be a substantial concession, and EFTA countries continue to strive for what is known as 'simplification' and 'full cumulation'.[8]

There is some evidence that the AFTs have indeed caused an unusual concentration of trade flows in the EC to the detriment of EFTA and third-country suppliers in certain sectors, and especially in semi-manufactures – as expected (see Table 5.6). Thus, the EC has raised its share of EFTA's imports of semi-manufactured goods from 55.7 per cent in 1973 to 63.4 per cent in 1978, at the expense partly of EFTA (down from 26.7 per cent to 22 per cent) and partly of developing countries (down from 7 per cent to 5 per cent). Textiles display a similar trend. A corollary to this development is the growing trade deficit that

TABLE 5.6   *Impact of rules of origin on the structure of EFTA trade (% share of designated trading partner in EFTA imports)*

	Raw materials		Chemicals		Other semi-manu-factures		Textiles	
	1973	1978	1973	1978	1973	1978	1973	1978
EC	34	36	69	69.5	55.7	63.4	56.8	63
EFTA	17.6	17.6	13	12	26.7	22	27.5	20
LDCs	21	17	3.4	2.5	7	5	4.3	5.5

SOURCE   GATT, *International Trade*, 1978/1979.

TABLE 5.7 *Evolution of EFTA: balance of trade, 1973–1979 in m. US $*

	1973	1979
USA	− 900	− 1 650
Japan	− 710	− 1 370
EC	−6 500	−11 160
OPEC	− 360	− 1 700
LDCs	+ 340	+ 1 960
Communist countries	+ 110	− 1 300
Total deficit	**−5 710**	**− 12 380**

SOURCE EFTA Secretariat, *EFTA – Past and Future* (Geneva).

EFTA countries run with the EC, as firms concentrate their demand for intermediate goods on EC suppliers (see Table 5.7). In fact, the EC ran a trade surplus with EFTA of 11.1 billion US dollars in 1979, which more than offset the 7.6 billion US dollars trade deficit with Japan of which it complained so bitterly. The silver lining to this large and growing trade deficit is that it puts the small EFTA countries into a stronger negotiating position than would otherwise have been the case.

Finally, it should perhaps be recorded that the EFTA countries relinquished their own liberal origin system, and adopted the EC-AFTs, for the purpose of intra-EFTA trade, on the grounds that it was too complicated to administer two different sets of rules. This may also help to account for the sharp drop in the share of intra-EFTA trade.

In summary, a FTA will tend to be more trade-creating, in the sense of replacing a high-cost source of production by a lower-cost source, and less distorting of long-term resource allocation:

(a) the more generous its origin rules;
(b) the rarer the cases of negative EP;
(c) the lower the general level of protection *vis-à-vis* the rest of the world, since, if this condition is fulfilled, the scope for large allocative distortions due to non-harmonised tariffs is reduced.

These conditions do not supersede, but are complementary to, the conclusions reached concerning the welfare implications of customs unions discussed in Chapter 2.

THE COST FOR THE NEUTRALS OF REMAINING OUTSIDE THE EC

The most interesting practical question raised by the present complex structure of European economic integration as far as the neutrals are concerned, is whether the AFTs are a good or bad substitute for full membership of the EC.

They do offer free trade in industrial products – by far the most important category of goods exchanged between EFTA and the EC. But as we have seen, this free trade contains distorting elements. However, the trade-diverting impact of the EC origin system should, in practice, not be exaggerated, because the EC's level of protection is mostly fairly low, and many of its industries remain competitive in world-market terms (see Table 5.8). For instance, although the rules of origin for chemicals are strict and potentially trade-diverting, the loss for EFTA is probably minimal because industrialists are likely to have bought from EC suppliers anyway since they are among the world's most efficient producers. The story is of course different in textiles, but here the old EFTA rules of origin were also restrictive, and the intention is and was clearly to keep trade creation to a minimum.[9]

There remains the vexed question of steel, where current EC policies may be imposing negative EP on down-stream industries and where heavy subsidisation is clearly distorting competition. EFTA steel producers (in Austria and Scandinavia) are being asked to respect the EC's minimum prices in their exports to the EC. This is already bad enough, but what of the steel contained in automobiles, machinery and appliances made in EFTA? These at present enjoy an artificial advantage due to the fact that EFTA manufacturers can purchase steel at low world prices plus the (low) EFTA tariff. Furthermore, it would be a mistake to think that this is necessarily to the long-term benefit of the EFTA countries as a whole. Resources may be pulled into down-stream steel-using industries which will have to be shed again once the artificial stimulus is removed (as it is almost bound to be). Even if it were not, the neutrals' comparative advantage might lie in quite another direction, yet their pattern of industry would in part be determined by policies adopted in the EC over which they had no direct say. This is an example of a distortion that can occur in EC–EFTA trade when a whole sector is taken out of the domain of the market-place and placed in the tender care of the government, while still being subject (nominally) to free trade rules.

In short, if the EC's steel policy is a foretaste of more to come in other

TABLE 5.8 Weighted averages of tariffs on manufactured goods (% of import value)

	Integration		Kennedy	Enlargement	Tokyo MFN	MFN
	1960 →	1967	→ 1972	1977	→ 1980	→ 1985
Austria	18.0	13.6	8.3	1.1	11.2	7.8
Finland	6.9	3.5	2.0	0.5	4.4	3.2
Norway	4.1	1.9	1.2	0.3	2.6	1.7
Sweden	6.6	3.9	2.4	0.7	4.2	2.8
Switzerland	4.5	3.7	2.2	0.6	2.8	1.9
Denmark	5.4	2.9	1.9	0.7	7.4	5.0
UK	14.8	11.4	7.0	3.1	7.4	5.0
W. Germany	6.1	4.5	2.6	1.3	7.4	5.0
France	12.6	4.9	1.9	1.0	7.4	5.0
Italy	13.8	5.6	2.2	1.2	7.4	5.0
Benelux	7.4	4.0	2.0	1.1	7.4	5.0

SOURCE *EFTA Bulletin*, June 1980, p. 10.

'embattled' (see Grey 1981) or declining sectors of industry, then EFTA countries will suffer growing distortions in terms of efficient resource allocation in their own economies, whether they like it or not.

Besides this potential cloud on the horizon, the main source of loss for EFTA citizens and entrepreneurs in the present AFT system is in the absence of preference in EC markets for services and trade in factors. Banking, insurance, transport, communications, data storage, processing and exchange, engineering blueprints, design, technical consultancy and so on, are not included in the AFTs, but are very much part of the neutrals' economic landscape, and are among the 'second generation' of integration issues being discussed in the EC.

One of the concessions which the EC made in the 1972 negotiations, on which the EFTA countries pin much hope for the future, is the so-called 'evolutionary clause'. This permits either party in a bilateral AFT to raise a question in any field not covered by the arrangement, which it thinks would be in the interests of their respective economies to develop.[10]

Is this clause merely a symbolic concession, devoid of practical meaning, or will it allow the neutrals to participate in the EC-wide market for services as and when it develops? The answer seems to be that the spirit represented by the evolutionary clause offers an opportunity of which some EFTA countries make more than others. The EC is in principle willing to cooperate, and indeed sometimes initiates the discussion. But EFTA countries will find that the EC is ill-equipped to respond to initiatives on their part because it cannot tie itself in an agreement with a non-member until a 'common' policy has been worked out. Once it is there non-members may join, or not, according to whether there is a mutual will to reach agreement. But there is very little scope for *negotiation* as one normally understands it, since the give and take of bargaining implies a flexibility on the part of the EC which it simply does not have. EFTA countries have to keep within the confines of the EC Commission's mandate, or run the risk of seeing it sent back to the Council of Ministers for modification. This not only takes time, but may in fact jeopardise the whole negotiation by allowing the Council to have second thoughts. The EC is therefore in an incomparably stronger position in any negotiation initiated by an EFTA country.

The record for agreements extracted from the EC is held by Switzerland, which has achieved the astonishing score of 80.[11] Most of these, however, are on trade-related subjects, such as the definition of a 'Swiss' watch (i.e. how much Hong Kong content it may contain) or trade on cheese. Actual 'second generation' agreements have been few in number. Switzerland, along with some other EFTA countries, participates in the Euronet, COST and JET projects. It is in the process of negotiating an agreement covering the right of establishment of non-life insurance companies on a reciprocal basis; it participates unilaterally in the European Monetary System (by pegging the Swiss franc to the German mark) but the link is tenuous and the Swiss National Bank is not under any external obligation to maintain a fixed relationship; and (after a revealing two-year resistance backed by popular referendum) has finally decided unilaterally to adopt summer daylight saving time in line with its EC neighbours.

One really cannot resist philosophising on the psychology of integration at this point. The Swiss people have accepted the conclusion of the most far-reaching economic treaty of recent Swiss history, and the subsequent conclusion of scores of subsidiary agreements regulating details affecting many aspects of Swiss economic life; they have agreed to origin rules which are not wholly to their advantage. But when it came to adopting European Summer Time, they said no: the cows, it was said, would refuse to let down their milk an hour earlier. But behind the farcical aspects of this display of Swiss sovereignty lay a real issue. The Swiss, no different from anyone else, dislike having to accept the EC *diktat*. As long as it expresses itself in obscure technicalities, no popular resistance occurs; but the minute it affects people's daily lives, no matter how trivially, feelings will run high. Yet, as the story of summer time in Switzerland shows, the cost of refusing the EC *diktat* is likely to be greater than the cost of accepting it. The inconvenience of living with an elephant, no matter how benign, is simply a fact of life which our mouse, no matter how nimble, has to put up with.

Indeed, returning to our initial question, there are definite economic costs to remaining outside the EC for the small EFTA countries. Inside, they would be able to influence 'second generation' policies in their formative stages, exercising veto rights over elements they might particularly dislike; they would even be able to initiate and promote policies of their choice and bargain them off against other policies of interest to their larger partners. All this is at present denied to the EFTA neutrals.[12] On the other hand, they enjoy the considerable economic benefit of not having to participate in the CAP, and the smaller advantage of not having to adopt the CET, which is on the whole higher than theirs. These advantages are probably at a peak, in the sense that sooner or later something will be done to reduce the cost of the CAP, while the costs of non-participation in 'second generation' policies are still more potential than real. I therefore reach the following conclusion:

at present, and for some time to come, the neutrals probably bear no net cost, and may even derive a net economic benefit from non-participation in the EC. However, this situation is likely to reverse itself with time, if and when the EC outgrows the farm problem and concentrates its energies on creating a true common market embracing services and trade in factors.

NOTES

1. EFTA MFN tariffs on manufactured goods being on the whole rather low (with the exception of Austria and Portugal) there was not much scope for sizeable trade diversion in net welfare terms (see Table 5.8).
2. Sowell (1980) provides a modern re-statement of this important insight.
3. It should be emphasised that shifts in the ratio of imports to apparent consumption are indicative of the existence of net trade creation (if the ratio increases) or of net trade diversion (if the ratio declines) but that they do not measure it precisely in welfare terms. For that one would need to know not only the volume of trade created or diverted, which the shift factor provides, but also the difference in costs between the old and the new source of supply. Thus a large volume of trade might be diverted, but this would be of little importance in welfare terms if the difference in cost between the world's lowest-cost supplier and the partner source were minimal. Such precision will not be attempted here (see Chapter 2), although it may be kept in mind that as EFTA MFN tariffs tend to be low, rather small coefficients would probably need to be applied to gross volume figures to extract the true welfare gain or loss.
4. In this measure, the EFTA Secretariat has related imports of manufactured goods to apparent consumption on a *value-added basis*, that is, strictly speaking, comparing apples and pears, since trade figures are collected on a gross turnover basis, while domestic production figures (as extracted from the national accounts statistics) are collected on a value-added basis. However, *gross* output per sector (also estimated by the EFTA Secretariat) tends to over-estimate apparent consumption and is considerably less accurate than the value-added concept.
5. Applying a known figure, namely imports of manufactured goods into (Little) EFTA in 1972 and 1976, to these ratios, it is possible to derive apparent consumption in US dollar terms, and hence the gross volume of trade created (in US dollars):

	Apparent consumption	*Import of manufactures*
1976	73 bn	50 bn
1972	51 bn	31 bn
Difference	**22 bn**	**19 bn**

The proportion of the growth in apparent consumption supplied by imports thus seems to be 86 per cent (19 bn US dollars out of 22 bn). However, this ratio is exaggerated because of the value-added/gross turnover problem mentioned in Note 4.

We can also apply these ratios to known absolute amounts, namely the increase in manufactured imports from EC to EFTA in 1972–76, in order to determine how much of the trade creation noted earlier can be attributed to the AFTs:

EFTA imports of manufactures from EC (in US dollars)

1972	19 bn
1976	30 bn
Difference	**11 bn**

= 58 % of the gross volume of trade creation
(11 bn US dollars out of 19 bn)

6. Any resemblance to a real country is purely accidental and unintentional.
7. Note that 'drawback' (namely, the restitution of import duties paid on intermediate goods which are transformed or incorporated in another product and subsequently exported) is not permitted on intra-EFTA or intra-AFT trade. This constitutes an added incentive to members to ensure that viable activities are not penalised by redundant tariffs.
8. After almost ten years of constant pressure it is thought that the EC was ready to concede the point. However, the arrest in Zurich in the summer of 1980 of the two French customs officers, allegedly conducting an investigation on Swiss soil has, it appears, cast a pall on proceedings.
9. The US Commerce Department, which has sponsored an effort to expand US textile exports to Europe (under the 'Textile and Apparel Export Expansion Programme') has complained that the EC–EFTA rules of origin 'are designed not only to prevent trade deflection (selling goods in a low tariff market for trans-shipment to countries with a high tariff) but also to act as a specific trade barrier to our textile imports' (*Financial Times*, 16 February 1981, p. 3).
10. See Binswanger and Mayrzedt (1972, pp. 84–7) for a discussion on what the evolutionary clause seemed to imply in 1972. It has come up to expectations as far as scientific cooperation is concerned, but not in respect of monetary cooperation or industrial policy.
11. Commission des Communautés Européennes, *La Suisse et la Communauté*, 1980.
12. See, Blankart (1979) on a possible solution to the problem. Blankart (chief Swiss negotiator in Switzerland's relations with the EC) proposes that the EC should consult its EFTA partners during the formative stage of 'second generation' policies. The question is whether the EC member states would be prepared to add yet one more consultative step to an already heavily burdened decision-making process.

6 The Council for Mutual Economic Assistance[1]

Paul Marer and John Michael Montias

INSTITUTIONAL ARRANGEMENTS IN THE CMEA

MEMBERSHIP AND AFFILIATION

Four types of affiliation with the CMEA are possible: full membership, associate membership, non-socialist 'cooperant' status, and 'observer country' status. In addition, several countries have been identified as 'interested' in some form of affiliation.

Ten countries had *full membership* at the end of 1979: the six nations which formed the CMEA in January 1949, namely the USSR, Bulgaria, Czechoslovakia, Hungary, Poland, and Romania (Albania had joined about a month later but has taken no part in CMEA's activities since 1961); the GDR (1950), Mongolia (1962), Cuba (1972), and Vietnam (1978). Members can decide whether to participate or not in CMEA programmes according to the 'interested party' provision of the CMEA charter.

Since 1964 *associate membership* status has governed the affiliation of Yugoslavia which participates in 21 of 32 key CMEA institutions as if it were a full member.

Non-socialist cooperant status has been granted to three countries: Finland in 1973 and Iraq and Mexico in 1976. Since these countries have no foreign trade plans and their governments cannot conclude agreements on behalf of firms, cooperant countries do not participate in the work of CMEA organisations. Each country has mixed commissions, composed of government and business representatives, which sign various kinds of 'framework' agreements with CMEA's Joint Commission on Cooperation, especially established for this purpose. The agreements are subsequently 'accepted' by the relevant permanent commission of the CMEA but the implementation is up to the interested CMEA country(ies) and cooperant country firms.

Observer status appears to be a designation applied to a mixed group of communist or communist-leaning governments. The group's composition changes from time to time, depending mainly on political developments. At one time, for example, the People's Republic of China and North Korea were 'observers'. At the end of 1978, Afghanistan, Angola, Cambodia, Ethiopia, Mozambique, and South Yemen had negotiations under way with the CMEA to explore the possibility of a Yugoslav-type associate membership. Occasionally, some countries in this group are invited to attend CMEA Council sessions as observers.

Interested country appears to be a designation for a group of less developed countries whose composition has also changed over time. For example, Egypt, Chile under Allende, and Bangladesh were interested countries at an earlier period. At the end of 1978, seven less developed countries were reported to have an interest in the possibility of a Finland-type cooperant status: Guyana and Jamaica, with which official talks were said to have been under way, and Angola, Colombia, Costa Rica, India, and Venezuela, which were said to have been considering the matter.

MAIN ORGANISATIONS

CMEA's main policy and administrative organisations and the linkages among them are shown in Figure 6.1.

The CMEA Council is the organisation's supreme policy-making body; each full member has one vote. The Council is convened about once a year; sessions deciding important matters are usually attended by the party first secretaries. The Council's recommendations must be approved by each country, after which bilateral or multilateral agreements or treaties must be signed as a basis for implementation.

The Executive Committee is the executive body of the Council. It proposes statements and recommendations to be considered by the Council, supervises the work of all other CMEA bodies, and monitors the implementation of CMEA agreements and treaties. It meets at least once every two months.

The Secretariat, located in Moscow, carries out the day-to-day operations of the CMEA. It has a large, multinational staff headed by a citizen of the USSR. Many of its departments correspond in name and function to those of the various special-purpose Council committees and permanent commissions (see below); other departments are responsible

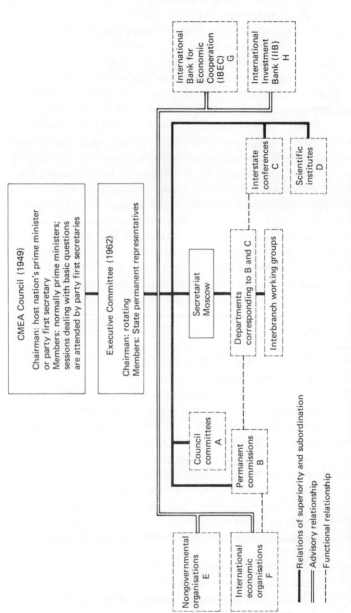

Source   H. Trend, 'Economic Integration and Plan Coordination under COMECON' in K. Robert and J.F. Brown (eds), *Eastern Europe's Uncertain Future* (New York: Praeger, 1977)   Figure 6.1; miscellaneous CMEA documents.

FIGURE 6.1   *CMEA Organisation*

for interbranch coordination, arranging interstate conferences, and other functions.

The key line functions of the CMEA are performed by three *Council* committees, set up in 1971, and a large number of *permanent commissions*, most of them established during the 1950s and 1960s. The *Committee on Cooperation in Planning*, comprised of the chairmen of the central planning bodies of the member countries, comes close to being a supranational planning agency for dealing with specific economic problems. This committee is the main CMEA body responsible for the coordination of the five-year and long-term plans of the member countries. It has a special permanent working group on energy. The other two *Council* committees are the *Committee on Scientific Technological Cooperation* and the *Committee on Cooperation in Material and Technical Supply*, each dealing with problems suggested by its name.

The *permanent commissions* are generally organised along branch lines, but some are responsible for functional areas, such as health, statistics, currency, standardisation, and so on.

In addition to these organisations, the CMEA also has two regional banks (see below); a large number of scientific institutes; interstate conferences on *ad hoc* problems; intergovernmental commissions dealing with specific issues; and many conferences of non-governmental organisations which maintain loose ties to CMEA organs. It has been estimated that more than 100 000 persons are involved directly in carrying out various CMEA functions and sponsored activities.

Of special interest in connection with CMEA integration are the few production enterprises jointly owned by firms in member countries. We have been able to identify from CMEA sources nine such enterprises (see Marer and Montias, 1980 and 1981 for a listing). The fact that only a few, relatively small-scale, jointly owned enterprises have been established during the past two decades reflects the financial and other institutional obstacles that hamper cost-accounting and profit-sharing. Many of the existing arrangements are little more than repayment in kind for the other side's deliveries of capital assets (usually on credit) and current inputs. These joint enterprises may thus be regarded as domestic enterprises of the country in which they are located, with several special provisions regarding credit obligations and direct foreign trade rights (Brus 1979, p. 168).

After the adoption of the *Comprehensive Programme* in 1971 (see below), and in accordance with the trend toward enhancing the role of large industrial units (associations) in individual countries, a new type of organisation was created, the so-called International Economic

Association (IEA). Their purpose was the concrete coordination of joint economic activities in research and development, production, service, and foreign trade. IEAs have a looser organisational structure than the joint enterprises. We have been able to identify from various CMEA sources nine IEAs (see Marer and Montias 1980 and 1981 for a listing).

The IEAs are legal entities of the country in which their headquarters are located; hence they are not organs of the CMEA, although they do have a close working relationship with CMEA bodies, especially the permanent commissions.

To begin operations, certain assets are put at the disposal of the IEAs and they are expected eventually to become self-financing by the revenues and profits generated in their operations. According to a comprehensive Western study of IEAs, none of them has yet attained full solvency (Ginsburgs forthcoming,).

The significance of the joint enterprises and the IEAs lies in the possibility that they may provide the legal and experimental basis for creating socialist multinational corporations, which potentially could play an important role in CMEA integration. To be sure, the consensus of Western opinion is that the difficulties of determining accurately costs, prices, and meaningful exchange rates, as well as other problems, such as differences in applicable legal norms and tax statutes among the countries, greatly limit the scope and operation of the IEAs, which *cannot* be considered socialist multinational enterprises (Lavigne 1975). Concluded another Western observer:

> Due to their small number, their mostly very limited functions and their special financial and currency arrangements, the [joint enter-prises and the IEAs] are not to be considered as a new qualitative element of international cooperation within CMEA. . . . It is un-likely that, in the foreseeable future, an autonomous initiative could be taken by [them] for developing new mechanisms of integration which would involve a limitation on the member countries' sovereignty. On the contrary, an improvement of methods and forms of CMEA integration will have to create the conditions for a better functioning of the IEAs (Machowski 1977, pp. 194–5).

While legally not a part of the formal CMEA structure, the two regional banks must be discussed in conjunction with other CMEA institutions.

The *International Bank for Economic Cooperation* (IBEC) was established in 1964 by the full members of the CMEA to perform bookkeeping operations arising from commercial transactions among the members, to issue trade credits and thereby promote multilateralism within the region, and to carry out financial operations with banking institutions outside the region. IBEC's statutory capital was set at 300 million transferable rubles (TR) – an artificial unit of account described in the following section. Each country's quota was determined in proportion to its share in intra-CMEA trade. But since loanable TRs can be 'created' only through an export surplus in intra-CMEA trade, and since all members cannot be net exporters simultaneously, it is not clear how, or whether, the paid-up capital in TRs has actually been transferred to the Bank, as prescribed, by all members.

IBEC performs as planned its intra-CMEA bookkeeping function and has been expanding considerably the volume of transactions with Western banks in convertible currencies, but it has not been able to promote multilateralism within the bloc in any significant way.

The *International Investment Bank* (IIB) was established in 1971 by the full members of the CMEA to help finance investments in the member countries, including the joint CMEA projects. Statutory capital was set at 1 billion TR, 30 per cent payable in convertible currency, the rest in TR. Each country's quota is proportional to its share in intra-CMEA trade. As in the case of IBEC, how the IIB 'creates' loanable TR funds is not clear. The fundamental issue is: when the Bank issues paper credits in TRs, what freedom does the recipient country have in choosing the investment goods it needs from the other CMEA countries to build a project? This point has not been clarified in the CMEA literature. One possibility is that a member's TR quota subscription takes the form of a hypothetical (or tentative) list of pledged investment goods; the other is that a granting of IIB credits must be preceded by successfully concluded negotiations between the prospective debtor and creditor countries, specifying the investment and repayment commodities that will be shipped, including all terms and conditions. In either case, the mobilisation of TR credits must be exceedingly difficult.

In recent years, the IBEC and the IIB have both borrowed substantial convertible currency sums from Western financial institutions. It has been shown that the convertible-currency operations of these two CMEA banks have tended to facilitate regional integration, while the intended original main purpose of these institutions, promoting CMEA integration through the introduction and increased use of the TR, has not been achieved (Brainard, 1980).

The basic statistics for the main members of the CMEA are given in Table 6.1. These are self-explanatory.

THE PRICE MECHANISM IN INTRA-CMEA TRADE

CMEA countries employ a different pricing mechanism in East–West trade and in intra-CMEA trade. With partners outside the bloc, they trade at current world market prices, while prices in intra-bloc trade are linked to Western world market prices of an earlier period, according to various formulas periodically agreed upon since shortly after World War II. There is bargaining in the CMEA not only about the kinds of goods as well as the quantities to be traded but also about prices, because it is difficult to find 'the' world market price. Different capitalist markets can be taken; price quotations may vary from actual prices because of rebates, quantity discounts, and so on, or may differ as between particular buyers and sellers due to quality factors, the effects of tariffs and other trade barriers, conditions of payment, and transport and insurance costs, all difficult to isolate. And since intra-CMEA prices are based on average world prices for a commodity over a period of years, the process of averaging multiplies the large choice.

The essence of price-determination in CMEA trade was pinpointed by a leading Soviet specialist on the CMEA:

> The exporter will naturally propose prices that are advantageous to him or that at any rate cover his production costs. In the price selection process, the importer is also guided primarily by the level of his production costs. Thus, in negotiations, both sides cite prices that satisfy their notions of effectiveness of exchange and subsequently arrive at some variant as a result of 'bargaining' (Mitrofanova 1979, p. 9).

Formally, the basis for setting prices in intra-CMEA trade has taken the following course: during 1945–50, prices were based on current capitalist world market prices; the period 1951–3 was the era of 'stop prices', when negotiators relied on the latest prices in effect before 1950, to avoid the distorting effect of inflation due to the Korean War; during 1954–7, a situation existed in which 'stop prices', their adjusted version, and current world market prices existed side by side, creating much friction.

TABLE 6.1 *CMEA basic statistics*

	Population* § (millions)	Area (km²)	Density (km²)	GNP† (billion US $)	Per capita GNP (US $)	GNP growth rate 1970–7 (%)
Albania	2.6	28 748	87	2	740	6.3
Bulgaria	8.9	110 912	79	24–28	2 720–3 200	6.8
Cuba	9.7	114 524	84	7.9	810	–1.2‡
Czechoslovakia	15.1	127 869	117	70–71	4 610–4 720	4.6
GDR	16.8	108 278	155	80–96	4 770–5 660	5.3
Hungary	10.7	93 030	113	33–37	3 040–3 450	5.6
Mongolia	1.6	1 565 000	1	1.5	940	1.6
Poland	35.1	312 617	112	110–128	3 130–3 660	7.7
Romania	21.9	237 500	90	69	1 750–3 180	9.8
USSR	261.0	22 402 000	11	966	3 701	4.4
Vietnam	52.0	329 556	151	8.9	170	n.a.
Yugoslavia	21.9	255 804	86	52	2 390	5.4

* Mid-1978
† 1978. There are two estimates for some countries. These come from the World Bank (underestimate) and Project on National Income – see Marer, 1981.
‡ Per capita growth rate.
§ The percentage of workers without jobs is uniformly low, hovering near zero in Albania, Bulgaria, Czechoslavakia, GDR, Hungary, Poland and Romania. In Yugoslavia it is comparable to Western levels.

SOURCE World Bank Atlas 1980; P. Marer and J. M. Montias, *East European Integration and East–West Trade* (Bloomington: Indiana University Press, 1980).

The 1958 ninth session of CMEA in Bucharest adopted the following new rules of price determination: (1) average 1957–58 world market prices would be introduced in 1959; (2) prices would remain fixed for several years, except for new or improved products; (3) the so-called 'half-freight principle' was adopted, under which the importer pays the equivalent of 50 per cent of the hypothetical transport cost from the recognised world market centre for that commodity to its own border; and (4) clarification was made of what constitutes acceptable documentation of the world market price in bilateral negotiations (Marer, 1972).

Average 1957–58 world market prices remained in effect until about 1965. For 1965–70, average world prices of 1960–64 were used; for the 1971–75 period, the agreement was to base intra-CMEA prices on average world prices of 1965–69. However, in early 1975, prices were revised, at Soviet insistence, one year ahead of schedule. For the year 1975 only, prices were based on average world prices of the preceding five years for most goods and for the preceding three years for a few commodities, notably oil. The world market price explosion of the mid-1970s also prompted the CMEA countries to change their method of price formation, replacing the principle of keeping prices fixed for five years with a moving average formula: intra-CMEA trade prices are now revised annually on the basis of world prices of the immediately preceding five-year period.

IMPACT OF THE ECONOMIC SYSTEM, POLICY AND THE ENVIRONMENT ON CMEA INTEGRATION

ECONOMIC SYSTEM AND INTEGRATION

The foreign trade activities of a traditional centrally planned economy (CPE) are determined or influenced by the following institutional arrangements:

(a) In each country, production and trade levels are set by highly placed officials in the party or in the government and carried out by the ministerial hierarchies concerned. Plans – sets of *ex ante* production and trade decisions slated to be carried out in a given period by producers and foreign trade enterprises (FTEs) – are geared to a system of interlocking material balances. Decisions are implemented via orders that come down through hierarchic lines. Information about the environment of producers is transmitted chiefly from subordinates to superiors in the hierarchies.

(b) FTEs, subordinated to the Ministry of Foreign Trade, buy output from producers for export and sell imports to producers and wholesalers. The monobank in each country, on behalf of the FTEs, pays producers for goods exported and charges consumers for goods imported in local currency. The producer of export and the user of import deals with the FTEs only, so he is isolated from the foreign buyer of his export or foreign supplier of his import. Managers of producing enterprises and FTEs are subject to material incentives for fulfilling physical output or foreign trade plans, for cutting down on production costs, and in certain instances for carrying out other assigned tasks. Given this system, quality and orientation toward the needs of the user often leave much to be desired. Observes a Hungarian author:

> It occurs that the technical parameters of Soviet machines and equipment and their cost norms, (i.e., cost of operating the machines) are less favourable than those of the most up-to-date Western ones. This is known already before the purchase and necessitates compromises on the part of consumers (Schweitzer, 1977, p. 326).

(c) Export and import transactions entered into by the FTEs with non-CMEA countries are valued according to current world market prices, and settled in a convertible currency; with CMEA countries transactions are valued according to an agreed upon set of past ('historical') world market prices and settled in TRs. The TR is an artificial accounting unit which takes a world market price expressed in a convertible currency and translates it into rubles at the prevailing official exchange rate for the ruble.

(d) The official exchange rates of the individual CMEA countries in terms of convertible currencies or *vis-à-vis* the transferable ruble are set arbitrarily and may not reflect or even approximate the equilibrium exchange rates based on the purchasing power of the currencies or some other equilibrium concept. FTEs, therefore, must keep two sets of books in domestic currency: one expressing the value of transactions with foreign buyers and sellers translated into domestic currency via the official exchange rate, and the other expressing the value of transactions with domestic sellers of exports and users of imports according to the domestic prices fixed (to some degree arbitrarily) by the domestic authorities in the country. The 'gain' or 'loss' on foreign transactions reflected by the difference in the two sets of books is settled automatically with the state budget, a procedure known as 'automatic price equalisation'.

(e) Within the CMEA, representatives of each country negotiate the pattern of specialisation in production with other CMEA members either bilaterally or multilaterally. The exchange of goods among countries is almost always agreed upon bilaterally. Prompted by the domestic planning system in the CMEA countries, which is based on 'material balances', trade negotiations in the CMEA focus mainly on the type and quantity of goods each country wishes to import. When negotiating the quotas to be included in the five-year agreements, it is necessary to forecast domestic demand for all kinds of machinery as far ahead as eight years because plan coordination in the CMEA begins three years before the current plan period ends. Practically speaking, this is a difficult situation, not designed to facilitate the ready matching of product specifications in the exporting and importing countries.

(f) Bilateralism discourages economic integration in several ways. One reason is that barter deals tend to be struck to keep bilateral accounts in approximate balance. Any surplus demand beyond an exporter country's planned supply must be purchased outside the CMEA. It is for this reason that the value of a given surplus or deficit with one CMEA partner, expressed in transferable rubles, is indeterminate and cannot be used automatically to offset deficits or surpluses with other CMEA partners. Lack of convertible currency sometimes leads to egregiously inefficient decisions. Hungary, for example, has a chemical complex whose operation requires a large quantity of salt. About 35 miles from the complex, across the border in Romania, is one of Europe's largest salt mines. But Romania ships the salt to the USA and other countries where it gets paid in convertible currency while Hungary imports salt from Algeria because that source does not require a direct outlay of scarce hard currency. Sometimes such problems are solved by agreeing to settle certain intra-CMEA trade transactions in convertible currency, a growing tendency which may be favourable to bloc-wide integration insofar as it mitigates the integration-reducing effects of bilateral clearing accounts.

(g) There is no mechanism in the CMEA for joint risk taking. Risks inevitably arise when a country undertakes an investment to build export capacity for the CMEA (or for the world) market. Demand in the CMEA (as in the world market) may fluctuate due to technological or other factors or because central planners in partner countries change their minds regarding imports. The risks of specialisation for the CMEA market fall relatively more heavily on the smaller East European countries than on the USSR because the former can specialise in only a relatively few products so their risks are concentrated, while the USSR produces and specialises in many products, so its risks are spread more widely.

Since the early 1950s, when the above described 'pure' foreign trade system was in force throughout the bloc, partial reforms have been implemented at various times and in varying degrees by all CMEA countries and comprehensive reforms were introduced in Hungary in 1968 (Marer, 1981). Have economic reforms changed the basic mechanism of foreign trade within the CMEA?

Three types of partial reform measures may be identified: reforms in the planning mechanism, in the foreign trade monopoly, and in the domestic price and exchange rate systems.

The essence of planning reforms is a reduction in the number of quantitative plan targets set by the central planner, leaving some flexibility to the ministries and producing enterprises to determine the composition of output. Decisions to incorporate a line of production, an investment project, an export or an import commitment into the plan may be based on, or justified by, calculations of costs and returns made with the aid of domestic or foreign-currency prices. Yet, the essential features of traditional material balancing and central supply allocation have remained unchanged in all countries except Hungary.

Reforms in the monopoly of foreign trade were prompted by a recognition that the functional separation of foreign trade from domestic production is inefficient. Various schemes have been introduced, therefore, to make FTEs and producing enterprises more equal partners, including the granting of foreign trade rights to selected industrial firms. Still, the fundamental lack of interest of producing enterprises in earning more foreign exchange by improving the quality of products or by finding new export items has not changed.

Reforms in the domestic price system were undertaken so that prices would reflect more accurately production costs, including the cost of imports. But because there is no consensus in these countries on how to set prices to reflect both costs and relative scarcities, or on how long prices should remain fixed, and because strong vested interests oppose any major price change, prices tend to be arbitrary and still play only a small allocative role. Various reforms were also undertaken to forge a more meaningful link between domestic and foreign prices. Exchange-rate-type coefficients are permitted to influence, to a greater or lesser degree, some export and import choices. But given the shortcomings of the domestic price systems and the mechanisms under which taxes mop up the greater part of enterprise profits and wipe out the bulk of its losses (bankruptcies are not permitted), these modifications in the price mechanism do not have a substantially different effect on enterprise decisions than automatic price equalisation did under the traditional system.

Hungary's comprehensive economic reform in 1968 abolished detailed plan instructions to enterprises, based prices on factor costs while allowing some prices to be flexible to reflect demand also, and established more realistic exchange rates to link foreign and domestic markets operationally. But the influence of the market is still circumscribed by the monopoly power of many enterprises, which remain protected from foreign competition, and by the pervasive use of direct and indirect instruments of state invervention.

We conclude that, notwithstanding the introduction of partial reforms in all CMEA countries since the late 1950s and the nurturing of the comprehensive reform that has been evolving in Hungary since 1968, the 'traditional' foreign trade mechanism is still essentially intact, at least as far as trade within the bloc is concerned. What forces are generated by the 'system' for and against CMEA integration?

First, the system places on producers constraints that are not conducive to integration with foreign markets. Since producing for the foreign market is more difficult as a rule than supplying the domestic market, most firms are fundamentally disinterested in exports. The enterprise is ordered to export to fulfil the plan rather than to make a profit; the firm's existence in most cases is not threatened in any fundamental way by its inability to export or to compete efficiently with imports. Since most exporting firms also produce for the domestic market, even when managerial bonuses are tied to foreign exchange earnings, the maximum bonus can usually be achieved more easily by skilful bargaining with the planning authorities or by fulfilling the domestic plan than by gearing up for exports. Even when nominal bonuses for exports expansion are substantial, the marginal rate of taxation of personal income is so high in some countries that the *de facto* export incentive is insignificant. These generalisations seem to be valid even for the majority of Hungarian industrial producers. There are exceptions, to be sure, in all CMEA countries: enterprises that have a long tradition of producing for foreign markets (e.g., pharmaceuticals in Hungary, optical equipment in the GDR, ships in Poland) or enterprises whose top management is entrepreneurial and has strong lobbying power to obtain the resources necessary to produce for export. (This does not mean, of course, that these firms earn their foreign exchange efficiently.)

The information system in the CMEA countries is much too coarse to enable the policymaking hierarchy to make fine-tuned specialisation and trade decisions based on any small differences in relative scarcities between their country and the economies of the other CMEA members. To illustrate: in the late 1960s, when Poland and Czechoslovakia agreed to produce tractor parts and components for each other's markets, there was so much uncertainty and debate about what each part or component was worth that they finally entered into a barter agreement in which 10 kg. of exports was exchanged for 10 kg. of 'similar type' imports; the uncertainty about whether this kind of specialisation yielded gains or losses was a factor in the decision to abandon this specialisation agreement.

Decisionmakers in the CMEA countries probably do not perceive the necessity of evening out differences in relative scarcities among countries. They are moved to action by perceived shortages and deficits in the availability of goods or by calculations of costs and returns showing a conspicuous advantage in engaging in certain lines of exports or in replacing expensive domestic production by imports. Neither the material balances (which at least ensure a modicum of consistency between input and output decisions) nor the calculations comparing foreign-exchange prices with domestic costs (based ultimately on administered prices) can supply accurate guidelines for specialisation and trade policies.

Investment to expand export capacity may occur because exports are necessary to pay for imports or, in the case of the less developed members of CMEA, because exports in certain 'modern' branches of manufacturing are prestigious. There is no *a priori* reason to believe that the resulting investments will be efficient in volume or in composition. For example, about ten years ago Bulgaria decided to specialise in electronic pocket calculators. It started to export calculators to Hungary (probably also to other CMEA countries) for 100 TR each. Finding the price too high, Hungary attempted import substitution and started to produce calculators. But since it found that the value of components it had to import from the West was $15 and that it could import the finished product for about the same price, Hungary stopped production and began to import calculators from Hong Kong (Pécsi, 1977 p. 318).

For many decisionmakers in CPEs, every imported good is a 'deficit item', and any branch of domestic production that can be expanded to replace it is a worthy candidate for investments. While there may be no policy of 'import-substitution across the board' handed down from the highest levels of the government, such an attitude is fostered for balance-of-payments reasons, by a misperception of scarcity, and by a fear that dependence on inputs imported from socialist partners may jeopardise fulfilment of the plans in case of supply breakdowns. Diversification of production to hedge against the vicissitudes of supply may be just as rational a response to this source of uncertainty at the national level as it is at the enterprise level. This pattern of enterprise behaviour in CPEs is conventional wisdom in the East European and Western literature on the topic. Unless the import supply of a product can be nailed down through a CMEA-sponsored specialisation agreement supplemented by an enforceable long-term contract with the exporting country, it is likely that the one-time 'shortage' will sooner or later disappear as a result of a capacity-expanding investment in the importing country. But, paradoxically, attempted import substitution cannot reduce the imports of the relatively small countries of Eastern Europe, but only transform their composition. If previously the country was importing commodities that have been replaced with new domestic capacity, then the new import requirements will consist of goods made necessary by the process of import substitution itself.

This discussion of systemic considerations leads us to the conclusion that decisions by branch ministries, industrial associations, or enterprises are unlikely to move the system in the direction of intra-bloc comparative advantage and may well move it in the opposite direction. An active integration policy must be conducted at the top to combat tendencies toward isolationism at the lower levels.

ECONOMIC POLICY AND INTEGRATION

Given the economic system in the CMEA countries and the system-determined mechanism of foreign trade in the bloc, what *integration policies* are pursued by members of the CMEA? First we will discuss the evolution of key policy recommendations for integration, especially those by the USSR, and the concrete measures taken up to now to implement them. Next, we will call attention to certain *domestic policies* of the CMEA countries which affect regional integration outcomes directly or indirectly.

The economic system previously described perpetuates the fundamental lack of interest of producers in becoming integrated with customers and suppliers in other countries. For this reason, the integration policies of member countries must focus on the mechanism of state-to-state relations rather than on domestic economic policies which would make CMEA integration more attractive to producers and consumers. That is, integration must be planned by the state at the highest level and imposed on the ministries, trusts, and enterprises. This is recognised by a Hungarian observer who writes:

> In general, the special requirements of consumers are enforced only in those particular cases when the central organs themselves exercise pressure on producers to take them into account (Schweitzer, 1977, p. 327).

Tracing the efforts during the three decades of CMEA's existence to find policies acceptable to all members reveals how difficult it is first to reach agreement about specialisation, then to find a workable CMEA mechanism, and finally to implement agreed policies effectively in each country. Linked closely with alternative policies on specialisation, suggestions for reforming the CMEA mechanism have ranged from proposals for a supranational authority which would create the traditional institutions of central planning at the regional level, to those favouring greater reliance on market mechanisms.

The best known proposed integration policy was that advocated by the USSR during 1962–64 for CMEA to become a supranational organ. The Soviets proposed that CMEA should make decisions and allocate resources *ex ante* rather than to try to coordinate *ex post* the decisions taken by the national planning authorities. This proposal brought to the surface the fear of the comparatively small East European countries that bloc integration under a supranational authority would mean more and more domination by the USSR. The most uncompromising stand against this type of integration was taken by Romania, whose ruling party issued its famous 1964 statement, which brought the conflict to world attention:

> . . . forms and measures have been proposed such as a joint plan and a single planning body for all member countries. . . . The idea of a single planning body for all CMEA countries has the most serious economic and political implications. The planned management of the national economy is one of the fundamental, essential, and inalienable attributes of sovereignty of the socialist state . . . transmitting such levers to the competence of superstate or

extrastate bodies would turn sovereignty into a meaningless notion. (cited in Montias, 1967, p. 217).

In the face of Romania's firm stand (and perhaps remembering that intensified pressure on Albania just a few years earlier had led to that country's defection from the bloc) the USSR decided not to press its proposals.

The 1964–70 period was one of much discussion, debate, and experimentation in each CMEA country about needed reforms in the traditional centrally planned economic system. In addition, the proposals usually contained suggestions to reform the CMEA mechanism also. One such proposal, most clearly articulated by Hungarian economists, favoured a greater reliance on market mechanisms for socialist integration. The advocates of this approach predicted better prospects for the realisation of gains from regional specialisation and for the maintenance of greater national autonomy. Other proposals, including those by Soviet economists, favour planned integration relying on the traditional concepts and institutions of central planning (McMillan, 1978).

After the Czechoslovak events of 1967–68, it became more urgent for the USSR to promote the cohesiveness of the CMEA network through which it could maintain its dominion without resorting to coercion. The USSR probably also wanted a system of regional integration that would place external limits on the economic reforms undertaken by any East European country. At the same time, this system would better compensate it than the then current CMEA price and trading system for becoming an increasingly large net supplier of energy and raw materials to Eastern Europe (see the next section.) Accordingly, Soviet economists began to float new proposals in the late 1960s. Realising that supranational planning was not politically feasible, they thought that it could be approximated, nevertheless, through joint planning of the regional economy's key sectors.

The outcome of this debate was the 1971 *Comprehensive Programme* for socialist integration. Although the document appears to be a compromise between those advocating market mechanisms and those favouring a joint planning approach, the emphasis since 1971 has been clearly on joint planning and the initiation of joint investment projects in priority sectors. Aspects of the *Comprehensive Programme* which stress the market approach to socialist integration, such as its timetable to introduce a degree of convertibility into CMEA currency relations or to establish direct, autonomous trade links among enterprises in the different countries, appear to have been more lip service, or perhaps a recognition of need rather than a statement of resolution (McMillan, 1978).

With respect to the latter point, a reform proposal that was codified in the *Comprehensive Programme* is the classification of traded goods into three categories: 'important commodities' with fixed quantities in physical terms; fixed value quotas with physical contents to be negotiated subsequently between buyer and seller; and 'non-quota goods'. It was envisioned by the reformers that trade at least in the third category would encourage direct export–import links between autonomous producer and user enterprises. But due to the many institutional obstacles, the trade flows in this third category have remained small (about 2 per cent, some say between 2 and 5 per cent of intra-bloc trade) so that the reformists' hopes were not realised:

> It [is] clear that any extension of enterprise autonomy would remain meaningless as long as the functions of COMECON money continued to be passive, subordinated to barter-type exchange. In turn, the activation of money [would] require major changes in the system of exchange rates, . . . in domestic prices and [in the economic management system] (Brus, 1979, p. 167).

To reduce the fears of the East European countries about compulsory supranationalism, one important compromise recognised by the *Comprehensive Programme*, which appears to have become a permanent feature of the CMEA, is the 'interested party principle'. This permits member countries to participate only in those CMEA projects or programmes in which they have a material 'interest'.

Three types of activities contained in the *Comprehensive Programme* have been stressed: improved plan coordination, cooperation in long-term 'target' programmes, and joint CMEA investment projects. With respect to the first two, it is difficult to learn from the CMEA literature how much has been agreed upon in principle only, whether comprehensive and detailed blueprints for implementation have yet been accepted, or the extent to which implementation of these programmes is under way. Our understanding about the status of these activities at the end of 1979 is the following.

Improved plan coordination

The old way was that 'coordination' began when for all practical purposes the national plans had been completed and the pattern of investment (formally not subject to coordination) already decided. Coordination used to mean little more than exchanging background information preparatory for bilateral trade negotiations. Improved plan coordination today means that the procedure begins earlier (three years before the end of the current quinquennium) so that there is at least the possibility that, as a result of discussions, a member country's investment plans would be altered (Brus, 1979). Moreover, a 1973 agreement specified that each country must include a special section in its national plan document for 1976–80, elaborating the specific economic details of its integration measures.

Plan coordination appears to involve a standardisation of economic information concerning projects that involve a long-term linking of two or more CMEA economies. This should facilitate a better assessment of what is really going on in the CMEA and checking the bilateral and multilateral consistency of national plans, but it does not appear to affect the substance of CMEA integration.

Cooperation in long-term target programmes

This involves selected sectors and key projects of major importance, where coordination takes a more binding and all-embracing form. The blueprint for this type of cooperation reportedly consists of (Trend, 1977): (1) joint forecasting for 15 to 20 years of production, consumption and trade trends to identify prospective shortages and surpluses; (2) coordination of medium- and long-term plans for the sector's main branches of production and key commodities; (3) joint planning of the production of selected key commodities, and joint research and development programmes; (4) continuous exchange of information on planning experiences. It has been agreed that cooperation in long-term target programmes should encompass five sectors: fuels, energy, and raw materials; machine building; industrial consumer goods; agriculture, especially feedstuffs; and transportation. Joint planning of production has been agreed on in principle for selected commodities.

Implementing these programmes would involve substantial investments by the East European countries in the USSR beyond those detailed in the next section. But in June 1980 the CMEA adopted a policy that once again places the emphasis on 'cooperation and specialisation' in manufacturing in preference to so-called 'joint investment projects' (Pécsi, 1981). But the systemic obstacles to specialisation in manufacturing remain formidable.

Joint CMEA investment projects

These represent the major new form of CMEA activity. About a dozen such projects were being implemented during the 1976–80 five year plan, most of them located in the USSR. The biggest by far is the Orenburg gas pipeline; other large ones include asbestos mining facilities at Kiembayev, a cellulose plant at Ust Ilim, and an electric power transmission line between the USSR and Hungary. The planned value of joint CMEA projects in 1976–80 was 9 billion TRs (approximately $14.5 billion), about half financed by the USSR, the other half by the East European countries.

Our understanding, briefly, of the role of the joint projects is as follows: Since the *Comprehensive Plan* was accepted, and contrary to the reported policy change in 1980, the USSR has been pressing the other countries to participate in such projects, pointing out that its territory has the natural resources which most of these joint projects are designed to exploit or transport, and that these investments represent partial compensation for supplying its CMEA partners with energy and raw materials – hard goods which today the Soviets can readily sell to Western countries for convertible currency.

The East European countries argue, on the other hand, that investing in the so-called CMEA joint projects – which take the form of the delivery of labour, capital and consumer goods, and the provision of technical know-how for projects located on Soviet soil – is not necessarily economic from their point of view. They cite the high manpower and hard-currency costs of these projects, the low interest rates received, and the disadvantageous terms of repayment, made in kind yet valued in continually depreciating TRs as intra-CMEA prices follow the rise of prices on the world market. The East European countries recognise, however, that these liabilities must be juxtaposed with assurances that the promised supplies will be available in the future.

While the system determines or narrowly confines the channels through which policies can be implemented, and the environment imposes restrictions on each country's set of possible actions, there are still many options for policymakers to give effect to their preferences on matters of integration. First, the preferences of the highest authorities in the various CMEA countries and the policies that they inform differ a good deal with respect to the nature and the extent of specialisation that they are willing to accept. Bulgaria, has specialised in exports of agricultural products, both raw and processed, as far as was compatible with her goal of rapid industrialisation. In contrast, Romania has neglected her agriculture until quite recently to press all available resources into industrial expansion. Within the industrial sector, Romania and Bulgaria also differed in that the former insisted on 'balanced, complex, multisided development', meaning that no branch of industry was to be sacrificed for the sake of reaping the advantages of specialisation, whereas the latter was distinctly more willing to go along with CMEA-wide specialisation.

Not all members of CMEA have the same preference, relative to the other goals they may pursue, for promoting the economic interests of CMEA as a whole. In more recent years, the USSR at times appears to have forsaken its short-term economic advantage, for example by its willingness to become an increasingly large net supplier to Eastern Europe of oil and other 'hard goods' at a time when those commodities could have been sold more advantageously on the world market. To be sure, policies on such matters involve difficult-to-quantify trade-offs between a country's economic and political objectives and may well involve economic or political *quid pro quos* between the USSR and the countries in Eastern Europe. For example, there could well be a link between the GDR's economic and military assistance to countries in sub-Saharan Africa and the level, the composition, and the prices of goods it trades with the USSR. To establish this point more firmly, however, would require more information and study.

The attitudes of individual CMEA members towards trade and industrial cooperation with Western countries, and their reliance on Western credits, differ considerably. The share of the industrial West in the total trade of the European CMEA countries ranges from about 20 per cent for Bulgaria to almost 50 per cent in the case of Romania and Poland. Only Romania and Hungary permit equity joint ventures within their borders with Western corporations; Poland allows only small-scale joint ventures in certain sectors. The acceptance of Western credits, or the active search for them since the early 1970s, range from avid in the case of Poland and Bulgaria, to eager in the case of Hungary, the GDR and Romania, to cautious in the case of Czechoslovakia. Western credits facilitate the expansion of trade with the West, both through an immediate rise in imports by the credited nation and an eventual rise in exports to repay the loans.

In spite of these differences within the CMEA, there was a substantial expansion of all CMEA countries' trade with the West during the 1970s. Increasing reliance on imports from the West – whether energy, raw materials, semimanufactures, grain, technology, or consumer products – reflects the growing unavailability (in adequate quantities or quality) of products most in demand from CMEA suppliers, which is a consequence of the economic system, as well as the easy availability of Western credits, and new policies by the CMEA countries.

The relationship between East–West trade and CMEA integration can be both complementary and competitive. Complementarity obtains, for example, insofar as the enlarged scale of production for the East European countries, prompted by export-specialisation for the CMEA market, may facilitate production for the Western market also. At the same time, the inflow of Western goods, technology, and managerial know-how can give an impetus to product specialisation in the CMEA. Some imports from the West and a few of the industrial cooperation agreements with Western firms are motivated in part by the desire of the smaller East European countries to be designated the sole (or at least principal) supplier of machinery or other products under CMEA specialisation agreements (Marer, 1980). For Western corporations, the possibility of penetrating the entire CMEA, especially the Soviet market, through industrial cooperation with an East European partner can be an important commercial motive. These kinds of complementarities are illustrated by the 1972 agreement between the US firm International Harvester and the Polish firm BUMAR to jointly manufacture crawler tractors in Poland (Garland and Marer, 1981).

Examples of complementarity between East–West commerce and CMEA integration should not suggest that the two are typically complementary and mutually reinforcing. Many examples can illustrate just the opposite. The CMEA countries have no common agreed strategy regarding the purchase of Western technology or regarding industrial cooperation with Western firms. This causes unnecessary duplication of effort among them. For example, during the first half of the 1970s, every European CMEA country bought polyvinyl chloride (PVC) technology from the West and planned to export a large part of the output to pay for the import. Lack of coordination in the CMEA, inadequate CMEA-wide planning for domestic utilisation of the output, and long delays in installing the plants (during which worldwide overproduction had cut the world price of PVC by nearly half) have resulted in excess production capacity and cut-throat competition to sell PVC for convertible currency.

East–West trade and CMEA integration can be competitive in other respects also. The substantial expansion of the CMEA countries' trade with the West during the 1970s has created economic links that cannot easily be severed. The large indebtedness of the CMEA countries to the

West mortgages a significant share of East Europe's future exports to the West, with self-evident consequences for CMEA integration.

ENVIRONMENTAL VARIABLES AND INTEGRATION

The most remarkable aspect of the environment of CMEA, in contrast to that of the EC is the disparity in size, resource endowment and political power among its members. The USSR accounts for roughly two-thirds of the population and aggregate GNP of the bloc and it is endowed with over nine-tenths of its crude oil, gas and iron ore resources.

As well endowed as the USSR is, there is a deficit supply in the communist bloc in natural resources, minerals, foodstuffs and other primary commodities. This is in part a consequence of forced industrialisation, which required a growing quantity of these resources for domestic industries and for exports, and the wasteful use of materials in production. The deficit is caused in part also by the fact that primary commodities can be traded more easily outside the bloc for convertible currencies, and in part because in the CMEA they are underpriced relative to manufactured products (as compared to world market prices). This relative underpricing (much less pronounced since 1975 than before) is the outcome of the bargains struck by the individual CMEA members in bilateral and multilateral negotiations, and hence of the policies underlying the negotiating stance of each member. But once prices have been decided on, the relative scarcity of 'hard goods' and abundance of 'soft goods' become exogenous (i.e. part of the environment) for each CMEA member. Countries relatively well supplied with natural resources, or which are net exporters, are pressed by those that cannot provide them. The former, chiefly the USSR but also to a lesser extent Poland and Romania, hold the trump cards. They exert bargaining power by tying their deliveries of primary products to sales of soft goods, chiefly manufactured commodities that for one reason or another the purchasers would not otherwise have wished to buy.

The disparities in the levels of industrial development of CMEA members is another factor inhibiting integration. One might expect that the faster growth of the least advanced members (Bulgaria, Romania) and the gradual evening out of levels of development in the bloc (a matter on which CMEA's ideologists are given to boasting) would tend in the long run to reduce the importance of this impediment to integration. This, however, is by no means certain, in view of the 'brute-force' nature of the development of the latecomers to industrialisation. As long as the technological gap between the more and the less advanced members of the bloc persists, the former will not, in general, abandon lines of production to the latter and become dependent on suppliers that may not be capable of meeting their requirements. The technological gap, in general, is not likely to narrow as rapidly as disparities in GNP per capita.

The enlargement of the CMEA by the incorporation of Mongolia in the early 1960s, Cuba in the early 1970s, and Vietnam in 1978 (Laos, Afghanistan, and Cambodia during the 1980s?) makes integration more difficult, for political and institutional reasons, even if these countries play only a marginal role in CMEA specialisation agreements. Given their locations, their membership would appear to serve principally Soviet foreign policy interests, according to which the East European countries are called upon to subsidise these less developed allies of the USSR.

A critical environmental factor for CMEA is the low mobility of factors of production between the socialist countries, especially within Eastern Europe proper. The initial decision not to open Eastern Europe to the free movement of labour and capital may be traced to Soviet policies imposed on East European clients in the early postwar period. These actively discouraged the formation of deep commercial ties among the East European countries. But those policies eventually became a part of the CMEA economic environment. With few exceptions there have been no significant transfers of labour within the bloc. In addition, these economies do not take advantage of low-cost foreign labour from countries outside the bloc, such as the EC imports from Portugal, Spain, Greece, Turkey and Yugoslavia.

Until recently, capital exports from one CMEA nation to another have also been small and were often determined *ex post*, when credits were granted to finance an unplanned imbalance in (visible and invisible) trade flows, or on the basis of political considerations. An example of the latter is the flow of Soviet credits granted to several East European countries to finance their deteriorating terms of trade with the USSR after 1975, when energy prices were raised. Such Soviet credits, agreed upon by leaders at the highest levels, often cannot be utilised fully by the East European countries because the goods they need the most, energy and raw materials, are not available and what is readily available (e.g. standard machinery, watches, cameras, and so on) is not wanted. In recent years, large credit transactions have been initiated under the so-called joint CMEA investment projects discussed earlier.

According to the neo-classical theory of international trade, given differences in factor endowment in a group of countries, low factor mobility should be conducive to even greater intensity of trade than if factors were free to move. But under conditions where intra-industry trade, which is not particularly related to specific factor endowments, predominates, lack of mobility is likely to impede trade rather than promote it. CMEA integration, no matter how defined, would move to higher levels if energetic measures were taken to transfer labour and capital across frontiers to those uses where they might be expected to be most productive on the margin. But such transfers are impeded by the inability to calculate reliably the benefits and costs of such integration measures.

Let us now turn to the impact of events external to the region on CMEA integration. The rapid growth of trade with the West during the 1970s has made the East European countries, and to a lesser extent the USSR, increasingly sensitive to international economic disturbances, such as the OPEC-triggered energy crisis, rapid world inflation, and Western recession. OPEC's action in 1973–74 increased the opportunity cost to the USSR of supplying energy and raw materials to Eastern Europe, thus intensifying pressure for the USSR to reorient its export supplies to the West. Although the actual reorientation was modest because of political considerations, it has forced the East European countries to rely more and more on alternative sources for energy and raw materials, which is clearly dis-integrative. However, to the extent that the world market price explosion increased the cost of Soviet energy and raw materials to Eastern Europe (although with some time lag), the East European countries have had to export more to the USSR to finance their deteriorating terms of trade. They also had to become more willing to invest in the large energy and raw material projects located in the USSR. Both of these outcomes may be viewed as integrative, even though the cost-benefit calculations on the joint projects are unclear and the terms of investment participation are in dispute.

Perhaps the most important effect of world events since 1973 on CMEA integration was the impact of developments on the international financial markets. Large OPEC surplus funds had to be recycled just when the deep Western recession reduced corporate demand for loanable funds, creating large excess liquidity on the world financial markets. The recession also induced Western governments to subsidise the financing of their country's exports. These developments, combined with the new political environment created by detente, brought about a situation in which exceedingly large private and official credits were made available by the West to the CMEA countries. At the end of 1979, the gross indebtedness of the six East European countries and the USSR to the West was about $70 billion, the net indebtedness (subtracting the assets of the CMEA countries held in Western banks) was in excess of $60 billion. Because of the availability of these credits, the extraordinarily rapid expansion of imports from the West was not, in our view, at the expense of CMEA integration (induced as the expansion was though in part by the shortcomings of CMEA). Intra-bloc trade continued to expand during this same period, although at a slower rate.

The impact of CMEA's large indebtedness on the future of CMEA integration is exceedingly difficult to assess. Much will depend on the productivity of the borrowed resources in terms of generating hard-currency exports. Although the debt may continue to rise (some experts foresee the possibility that it may well double during the 1980s), the need to service it makes claims on resources. As the ability of the CMEA countries to import from the West is impaired, now or eventually, by the requirements of debt service, this may give an impetus to an improved intra-bloc division of labour.

There is another environmental consideration: successive international crises (political, like those relating to events in Afghanistan, or economic, relating to the growing difficulties that CMEA countries are encountering on Western markets due, among other reasons, to protectionism) are supporting those in Eastern Europe who argue that the CMEA, but especially the USSR, offers a more stable and more easily accessible market and source of supply than does the West.

No simple generalisations can be made about the impact of the external economic environment on CMEA integration. The expansion of East–West commerce has set in motion both centrifugal and centripetal forces in the CMEA; their strength and impact differ from time to time and from country to country.

FUTURE PROSPECTS

Where does the CMEA stand today, as it begins the fourth decade of its existence, and what are its prospects for the 1980s?

It is our impression that, once again, the CMEA has reached an impasse. No significant initiatives appear to have been taken in recent years to conduct intra-CMEA economic relations more efficiently. Coordination of national plans and joint planning focus on the last stage of production for key commodities, without much attention to the interconnectedness of production with other branches. While there are a number of highly visible CMEA mining and transport projects, these undertakings can be justified for the most part on the basis of resource endowment or engineering capacities. Even on these projects there is much dispute between the host and the investing countries about who is contributing how much and how equitable are the repayment arrangements. Joint projects in manufacturing, which must be based on commercial considerations and supported by cost calculations and financial arrangements acceptable to all parties, have not yet materialised on any significant scale. Successful CMEA integration, i.e. increased specialisation in manufactures, requires uniform valuation criteria among the countries. This in turn will become possible if and when in every CMEA country, domestic price relatives of tradeables approximate prices on the world market and national currencies become convertible. As a minimum, the prices and exchange rates used to make decisions on CMEA specialisation must simulate world market prices and equilibrium exchange rates.

There are two key determinants of the future of CMEA integration: First, the course of domestic economic reforms in the individual CMEA countries is important because the fundamental systemic constraints limiting CMEA integration are rooted in the domestic institutions of CPEs, whether traditional or partially reformed. Second, the attitude of the USSR is important because the policies of the East European members of the CMEA are to some extent constrained by the policies adopted by the organisation's most powerful member. The more developed East European countries are fundamentally much less conservative about comprehensive economic reforms than the USSR. This is so not only for political reasons but also because the role of foreign trade is relatively small in the Soviet economy. A further reason is that in the USSR the best-trained individuals, particularly in fields involving contacts abroad, can be found near the top of the party and government hierarchies, whereas in Eastern Europe the disparity in the quality of technical–managerial personnel is not so pronounced. This reduces in Eastern Europe the risk (from the point of view of the system's directors) of allowing middle-management to engage in foreign operations (Ginsburgs, forthcoming, p. 35). These considerations help explain why Soviet leaders are less willing to tamper with the country's domestic economic mechanisms or move toward currency convertibility, which would necessitate changing domestic prices. For East European countries, on the other hand, improved efficiency of foreign trade, including a more effective CMEA integration, is very important, although the constellation of economic and political forces supporting and opposing comprehensive reforms differs from country to country. Paradoxically, one of the reasons why the issue of improved regional integration is pressing on all members is the rising cost of energy and their large indebtedness to the industrial West, which make it imperative for all countries to use their resources and to trade more efficiently.

Given all the obstacles that must be overcome to achieve integration in today's environment and in the framework of a central planning system that is not conducive to this end, in the long run there appear to be only two ways of cutting the Gordian knot. One option is the imposition of supranational authority over the members whereby policies working for integration would be ordered by the 'centre'. Although Moscow probably prefers this solution, Kremlin leaders know that the USSR incurs significant political costs when it uses force overtly to gain its ends. This gives the East European states some room for manoeuvre. The second option is comprehensive economic reforms, a key component of which must be economic (as opposed to administrative) decentralisation, a reform in the price mechanism, and the introduction of currency convertibility. At the very least, the evaluation of proposed CMEA projects and specialisation agreements must be based on generally accepted cost-benefit calculations, even if the CMEA trade and financial mechanism remains unchanged for the time being. An intermediate solution might lie in an initiative by an East European subgroup of CMEA to undertake comprehensive domestic economic reforms and simultaneously to move toward subregional integration. In any event, the key to the choice lies in the politico–economic preferences of the leaders in the USSR. They will choose among these options to achieve more rapid and far-reaching integration if and only if the gains they expect from this 'common good' outweigh the expected political losses they are likely to suffer under any alternative course.

THEORIES AND MEASUREMENT OF CMEA INTEGRATION

Economic integration has traditionally been equated with the division of labour in a geographical region, although it is usually not made clear what minimum level of trade would justify speaking of integration. More recently, economic integration is said to consist not only of the internationalisation of the markets for goods and services but also for those of capital and labour, technology and entrepreneurship, money and credit, as well as of the supporting economic institutions – see Chapter 1.

The institutional aspects of integration cannot be measured with statistical indicators, but their effects will presumably be reflected in the level and composition of trade and other kinds of measurable economic links among members of a regional group. In discussing CMEA integration East European economists tend to focus on institutions that foster or hinder integration; Western economists, by contrast, seek statistical measures of commercial ties among countries belonging to any regional group.

At this juncture it is appropriate to ask: can the EC and the CMEA be compared? It should be noted that characterising the EC countries as 'capitalist' and the CMEA countries as 'socialist' is an over-simplification. There is significant state ownership and control over the means of production in the EC as well as a degree of supranational planning. Conversely, market-type relations can be found both in the domestic economies of individual CMEA countries and also in their relations with each other. However, the basic features of the two integration groups justify characterising them as essentially market-oriented or centrally planned.

The fundamental difference between market-oriented and centrally planned types of economic integration can be found in the institutions facilitating or hindering integration. In Western economies, in spite of the expansion of the public sector and other deviations from 'perfect competition', the bulk of international commerce is conducted by private enterprise, seeking profit opportunities wherever it can find them. Hence, a reduction or elimination of barriers to the movement of goods, factors of production and money across national boundaries goes a long way towards integration. By contrast, once the market is replaced by central planning, all movement of goods and factors within the region (as well as transactions with outsiders) requires an explicit action by the governments involved. The integration of CPEs demands, therefore, more overt management and thus a more elaborate bureau-cratic structure.

The fundamental similarity between the two types is that the purposes behind efforts to integrate tend to be similar: better division of labour (i.e. improved specialisation) desired as a source of economic growth; economic discrimination in favour of members; and enhanced political power for the integration group. The stronger countries (the USA in the OECD, the USSR in CMEA) usually hope that closer economic ties will lead to closer political ties and eventually to political unification; weaker countries seek the benefits of being associated with a strong group but resist any significant loss of national independence and freedom of action in the international arena.

Focusing on market-type economies, sophisticated statistical indicators have been developed by Western economists and political scientists to measure aspects of integration from the point of view of a single member of a group or for a group of countries *vis-à-vis* other groups or the rest of the world (see Chapter 3). Statistical measures of integration tend to give meaningful insights when applied to the same country or a group of countries over time. Less meaningful are attempts to compare integration among countries or groups of countries at any given moment. The reason is that it is so difficult to hold 'all other things constant' – see Chapter 3 and El-Agraa (1980, Chapter 5). Among the important variables that will influence comparative outcomes are the economic size of the countries (regions) and the size disparities within the groups, level of development, resource endowment, distance from main suppliers and key markets, the economic policies pursued (such as import substitution vs. export expansion), the political objectives and relations of the countries within an integration group, and the group's economic and political relations with the rest of the world. It is not possible to isolate simultaneously the effects of these and other variables on integration outcomes because the statistical sample of integration groups is limited. No union of countries can therefore be compared meaningfully with the EC, which itself is undergoing continuous transformation as new members are added and political conditions in the member countries change – see Chapter 4.

Finally, comparisons of the integration outcomes of market and planned economies, i.e. the EC v. the CMEA, encounter special difficulties. One is the problem of calculating identical statistical measures for both groups. Note that, if the CMEA is viewed as a Western-type customs union because its members discriminate against outsiders, this would be reflected in the CMEA countries' preference for higher-priced or lower-quality domestic or bloc suppliers. That is, the CMEA aggregates its preferential trading area by implicit quotas rather than by preferential tariffs or explicit quotas. Moreover, even when it is possible to calculate nominally identical measures for the EC and CMEA, institutional differences can undermine the validity of parallel statistical interpretation. Rather than indicating successful integration, a relatively large volume of intra-bloc trade, such as during the 1950s, may only reflect underlying systemic or externally imposed commercial and financial barriers to extra-regional trade. Our efforts in the next section will therefore be limited to the conceptualisation and measurement of economic integration in the CMEA.

The economic integration of socialist countries may be viewed from the vantage point of the authorities in these nations, as they perceive the problem, or as Western economists would envisage it, in theory or in practice. In this section, we present both points of view, along with some appropriate methods of measuring progress towards integration.

The perception of CMEA policymakers as to what might represent progress towards integration is undoubtedly more subtle and complex today than it was two or three decades ago. At that time it was generally believed that any decision tending to increase trade among CMEA members at the expense of trade with non-members promoted bloc integration, which was deemed to be a good thing. An indicator of such progress widely used at the time was the percentage of each member's total trade carried on with other members of the bloc. Viewed thus, the integration of the communist bloc reached its highest point in the 1950s, when every member of the CMEA, including the USSR, conducted a larger part of its trade with other members than it does today, even though the organisation itself was dormant. Lack of opportunities to trade outside the bloc, largely due to the Western strategic embargo, contributed significantly to this apparent integration.

Today, CMEA policymakers concerned with the pace of integration would place considerable weight on the 'deepening' of the intra-CMEA division of labour, that is, on increased specialisation within branches and on 'vertical' specialisation by two or more countries contributing inputs, components, or final assembling capacity to manufacture a product. 'Deepening', of course, does not necessarily increase the share of intra-CMEA trade in the total trade of the bloc. Two CMEA members, each agreeing to specialise in a particular line of production, may find that as their output and exports of the specialised products expand, their imports from the West needed to sustain the increased output have to be stepped up *pari passu*. Gains in real income due to specialisation may also lead to larger imports from non-member countries.

Numerous books and articles published in the CMEA countries on specialisation approach the statistical measurement of integration by citing increases in the absolute volume of trade, the share of trade turnover accounted for by CMEA partners, the number of signed bilateral and multilateral trade and specialisation agreements, or the share of trade accounted for by various (usually poorly defined) specialisation or industrial cooperation agreements. That is, the statistical indicators most often relied upon to show integration tend to be based on supply data. No reference is made, as a rule, to conditions that must be met or states that must be reached to have achieved some acceptable or desired level of (static or dynamic) integration among the CMEA countries. A representative review article presenting the kinds of evidence CMEA economists often rely on to measure CMEA integration is one by a GDR economist which has appeared in a leading Soviet journal, also available in English (Morgenstern, 1978).

A more sophisticated measure of integration sometimes used by CMEA economists, as well as by the United Nations' Economic Commission for Europe, is the 'delta coefficient', which is the ratio of a region's actual share of intra-bloc trade to its hypothetical share. The ratio is calculated on the assumption that intra-bloc trade is proportional to the region's share in total world exports and imports (UN 1971). To illustrate with hypothetical figures: if the EC were to account for 35 per cent of total world exports and 30 per cent of total world imports, then the hypothetical share of intra-EC trade would be 10.5 per cent of world trade (35 per cent × 30 per cent). If the actual share were, say, 15.75 per cent, the 'delta coefficient' would be 1.5 ($= 0.1575 \div 0.105$) – for a variant of this measure see Fink (1977). But, in our view, these measures of integration are only very approximate indicators of the extent to which a bloc of countries trading in a protected common market has achieved specialisation according to its members' comparative advantage. One reason is that a bloc's share in world trade may be depressed by a policy of systematic 'trade aversion' on the part of its member countries, or by discrimination against the bloc by outsiders. Yet, net 'trade creation' in intra-bloc exchanges may not be large enough to compensate for the drop in trade with the rest of the world. In such a case, the delta coefficient would rise without any increase in intra-bloc specialisation taking place. Stating the problem differently: if the EC's higher foreign trade intensity than that of the CMEA, measured by trade/GNP ratios, is not properly considered, the delta coefficients will underestimate the trade integration of the EC and overstate that of the CMEA.

There is a more fundamental problem, however, with any type of indicator that relies on changes in trade shares among members of a preferential group. A decrease in the share in the face of an increase in the absolute volume of intra-bloc trade surely does not indicate a decline in regional integration, just as an increase in the share in the face of a stagnating or declining volume of intra-bloc trade does not signal an increase in integration. Thus, the decline in the CMEA's delta

134   *International Economic Integration*

coefficients between 1971 and 1976 was almost certainly due to increased Soviet and East European trade with the West rather than disintegration of CMEA. Moreover, the requirement of bilateral balancing within the CMEA encourages tied trade and re-exports, so that even changes in the absolute volume of intra-bloc trade may not necessarily indicate a corresponding change in the degree of integration (for a comprehensive review see Marer and Montias 1980, 1981 and van Brabant, 1980).

Our preference is to measure integration in the framework of the neo-classical paradigm, under which a necessary and sufficient condition for complete integration would be that the relative prices of any pair of goods in every member country should be the same (adjusted for transportation costs). A *process of integration* would then consist in moving from an initial state, where relative prices differed significantly in each country, through a series of states, each marked by a convergence of relative prices compared to the last.

Among CPEs (or, for that matter, among market economies where the state plays an active role in production and investment decisions), convergence towards equal price relatives is a necessary but not a sufficient condition for integration because government planners may order, or induce, levels of output or investment projects that are inconsistent with comparative advantage. In fact, there is considerable evidence that in the CMEA countries investment decisions are often systematically made with an eye to equating relative scarcities within each country.

Let us examine the problem of measuring progress towards integration along neo-classical lines. In the light of our definition of an integration process, price and quantity indicators should be used to measure changes in the degree of integration. But in CPEs, prices and costs generally diverge from marginal rates of transformation in production (due, among other factors, to low capital charges and to large differences in the extent of indirect taxes and profits levied on various goods). Moreover, wholesale accounting and retail prices have not had much influence on the planners' choice of tradeable goods, nor have the prices of exports and imports been reflected systematically in wholesale and retail prices. In this situation, it would be difficult to use changes in the relative prices of goods to give even an impression of the extent to which relative scarcities within CMEA have tended to converge or to diverge over time.

On the quantity side, the question is how to measure the convergence or divergence of relative outputs among countries over time. The method we suggest is analogous to the measurement of changes in the distribution of incomes or wealth using the Lorenz curve approach. Take as an example the statistics of production of metal-cutting lathes, which we assume to be available for all countries in CMEA in comparable measurement units. What is the percentage of the total CMEA output of these goods in a given year represented by the smallest producer (say, Bulgaria) or of the two smallest producers, and so forth, until the entire output is accounted for? The results may be plotted on a Lorenz curve, with the number of states shown on the abscissa and the cumulative shares of total output they represent on the ordinate. Of interest then would be the changes in the position of the curve observed through time. Clearly, progress towards integration will be marked by greater 'inequality' or a larger coefficient of variation, that is, by each curve lying farther from the 45° line than the last.

To see what the results of a systematic study with this measure might yield, we selected a sample of 14 products from the CMEA statistical yearbooks. Data availability limited the samples to relatively highly aggregated products, such as lathes, tractors, and so on. According to our definition, a movement toward specialisation would show a more unequal distribution of production, i.e. the smallest three or four producers accounting for a declining share of total CMEA output over time. As could have been predicted, this indicator of integration during 1950–76 shows dis-integration among CMEA members for most products, largely because the countries that produced the smallest relative outputs during the 1950s (Bulgaria and Romania) have increased their shares of total bloc output over time. During 1950–60, a trend towards specialisation is found only for 3 out of 13, during 1960–70 for 4 out of 14, and during 1970–76 for 5 out of 14 products.

This particular application of the proposed measure is far from ideal, if only because we cannot rest a generalisation about CMEA integration or dis-integration on 14 arbitrarily chosen and quite aggregated products. There is also the following conceptual problem. One usually thinks of increased specialisation as one country *expanding* output at the expense of other countries; but if one country *reduces* output to let several other countries expand production a little, might that not also be construed as a move towards increased specialisation? This is in fact what we found in the case of tractors: during 1960–76, Hungary and the GDR were both giving up the production of this item (their absolute production figures were declining), yet during the same period, the combined shares of the four smallest CMEA producers were rising, so that the statistical results cannot give an unambiguous answer.

We computed the coefficient of variation of the percentages of output of the 14 commodities represented by the different members of CMEA. (The greater the coefficient, the greater in principle the degree of integration.) To refine this measure, which is strongly influenced by the large share of the USSR in the total CMEA output of most of these commodities (close to two-thirds), and to detect whether subregional integration might be taking place among the six East European countries, the coefficient of variation was computed both including and excluding the USSR. The results did not contradict the findings reached earlier. Our tentative conclusion is that 'dis-integration' appears to have been taking place in the CMEA between 1950 and 1970 as the less developed countries installed capacity to produce many products that were previously the monopoly of the more industrialised members, but after 1970 this trend appears to have been halted and some specialisation decisions implemented (for details of calculations and further approaches see Marer and Montias 1980, 1981).

These statistical results illustrate the problem of quantifying the proposed measure of integration. One may argue, for example, that working with more disaggregated products, which would distinguish, say, lathes of various dimensions and degrees of automatic control, might show more positive results on specialisation, since individual members of CMEA are more willing to agree to specialise in narrowly defined than in broadly defined product groups.

The neo-classical framework for analysing specialisation and integration has lately come under attack among Western economists. One of its chief drawbacks is that it has little to say about the extraordinarily rapid growth of intra-industry exchanges and about the related phenomenon of balanced trade within sectors and even within subsectors in trade among developed market economies.

In many developed countries the share of foreign trade in GNP has increased only moderately. Yet the intensity of trade *within* practically all *industrial* sectors has increased drastically, in some cases by some 50 to 100 per cent during the last decade. The reason for this apparent paradox is that the composition of GNP of many industrial countries has shifted from high-trade to low-trade sectors, mainly from manufacturing to services, public services in particular.

What explains the success of increasing intra-industry and the failure to deepen inter-sectoral specialisation after the elimination of tariffs? Balassa's explanation for the EC focuses on product differentiation and strong promises to protect existing industries. He finds that the elimination of tariffs has led to increased exchanges of consumer goods and specialisation in narrower ranges of machinery and intermediate products. 'The increased exchange of consumer goods is compatible with unchanged production in the consumer goods industries of each of the participating countries while changes in product composition can be accomplished in the framework of existing machinery and intermediate products industries' (Balassa, 1974).

Focusing on the effect of successive tariff reductions among GATT countries, Hufbauer and Chilas (1974) explain the failure to deepen intersectoral specialisation in terms of the process of bargaining for the mutual concessions that paved the way for the expansion of trade among these developed nations. They argue that the negotiators, in the framework of GATT, swapped tariff concessions, which had to be more or less balanced to receive domestic support from the industries that were likely to be affected. Often the consent of a powerful firm could be obtained for an import that might threaten its sales only if a countervailing concession could be secured for one of its exports.

With regard to the protection of domestic industries, the situation within CMEA seems to be analogous, particularly as regards the mutual trade of its East European members. CMEA negotiations on reciprocal deliveries take place within specialised commissions, one for each industrial sector like machine-building, chemicals, textiles, and so forth. In this framework, concessions are likely to be 'balanced'. There is little chance that one country will concede an export surplus to one or more other members in the goods under the jurisdiction of one commission in counterpart for the opportunity of running a surplus in the goods subject to negotiation in another commission.

To illustrate the point let us look at trade in machinery which has grown much faster than in other products, especially among the six East European countries, where in just ten years the share of machinery in their mutual trade increased from about 40 per cent to 54 per cent. The main reason for this was the rapid increase in the machinery exports of the less developed countries, especially those of Bulgaria and Romania, and also of Poland, principally to the more developed markets of the GDR and Czechoslovakia. Thus, the large export and import surpluses of the 1950s and 1960s in intra-bloc trade in machinery, and in the corresponding offset categories of raw materials and foodstuffs, diminished over time as 'tied' reciprocal deliveries became the framework for trade within the CMEA.

Intra-industry trade among developed nations cannot be explained satisfactorily by specialised factor endowment or by any of the standard theories of the neo-classical paradigm. Neither can its advantages be measured in terms of the familiar gains-from-trade arguments. The explanations now being looked into by theorists run in terms of economies of scale and product differentiation in imperfectly competitive markets, while the advantages of trade without specialisation may be attributed to the broadening of consumer choice, the limitation of the power of oligopolies, and the enlarged possibilities for the transmission of technology. It can hardly be claimed that expansion of balanced intra-industry trade, so characteristic of exchanges among both Eastern and Western nations, promotes the type of integration that reduces or eliminates differences in relative scarcities among trading partners, at least to the same extent as inter-sectoral trade might be expected to. In our view, despite the advantages that we have listed, its potential for facilitating growth or increasing consumers' welfare is definitely inferior to what we would associate with a freer type of trade.

NOTE

1. Earlier versions of this chapter appeared in Marer and Montias (1980, 1981).

7 The East African Community[1]

Arthur Hazlewood

INTRODUCTION

The East African Community (EAC) was established in 1967 by the Treaty for East African Cooperation between Kenya, Tanzania and Uganda. The Community of the three partner states formally came into existence on 1st December of that year. No such precise date can be set for the Community's demise, but the middle of 1977, when the partner states failed to approve the 1977–78 budget for the Community, comes closest to it, and may be taken as the date of its demise in the legal sense. Effectively the Community came to an end earlier that year, soon after the completion by an outside authority (the Caribbean economist, William Demas) of a review of the Treaty and the submission of recommendations, when Kenya set up her own airline and Tanzania closed her border with Kenya. The Community died, therefore, well before its tenth birthday could be celebrated, and just as its new headquarters building was completed.

Since the Community ceased to exist, relations between its former partner states have fluctuated in cordiality, if that is the word for them. A dominating influence has been the state of affairs in Uganda since the Tanzanian army drove out the dictator, Amin. Suspicion of Tanzania's plans for Uganda coloured Kenya's view, and in its turn Tanzania was no less suspicious of Kenya. Some easing of attitudes seemed in prospect following a meeting of Presidents Moi and Nyerere in May, 1979, but no substantial progress was made.

The presidents met again in January, 1980, together with the then-President of Uganda, in what was hailed in the press as the first meeting of the heads of state of the three countries in a decade. 'The achievements of today's meeting are tremendous', President Nyerere declared (*Weekly Review* 4 January, 1980). But that was optimism. The heads of state met next in April that year, in the company of the President of Sudan. On the instructions of that meeting, ministers of the former partner states assembled in April to receive the report of the mediator (a Swiss diplomat, Dr Umbricht) who had been commissioned to recommend on the division between the three countries of respons- ibility for the assets and liabilities of the Community. Tanzania's attitude was that there could be no agreement on other matters until the affairs of the Community had been properly wound up. Press reports (*Weekly Review* 16 May, 1980) have it that the winding-up would involve Kenya's paying Shs. 678 m. and shouldering a long-term debt of Shs. 1664 m., which may be explanation enough of why at the end of 1980 mediation was still proceeding, though at an imperceptible pace.[2]

This chapter begins by explaining the background of the Treaty for East African Cooperation. It then outlines some main features of the Treaty and analyses the issues which arose between the partner states during the life time of the Community. (A study of economic integration in East Africa up to the early months of 1973 is contained in Hazlewood, 1975.) It concludes by posing questions which, it is suggested, must be answered to the satisfaction of participants if an integration scheme is to succeed. Table 7.1 gives basic statistics for the EAC.

When the Treaty was signed, after negotiations between the three countries in the Commission for East African Cooperation, known as the Philip Commission (after its Chairman Professor Kjeld Philip of Denmark), it was widely regarded as an instrument for achieving economic development and progress through cooperation. The Com- munity soon attracted applications for membership or association from neighbouring countries, though not all were serious, and the partner states carried on rather desultory negotiations with the applicants for several years. It seemed at one time possible that a zone of cooperation in Eastern Africa could come into existence around the nucleus of the Community States, achieving something like the economic community of Eastern Africa which the United Nations had earlier been trying to bring into existence.

Indeed, the United Nations, particularly through its various regional commissions, has for many years been prominent in propagating the view that regional integration and cooperation is an important device for fostering development, especially industrial development, in the countries of the Third World. There have been many attempts at economic integration in different parts of the Third World, but nowhere has there been even a proposal for a scheme covering so wide a range of

TABLE 7.1(a) *EAC basic statistics*

	Area (km²)	Population (millions) 1961	Population (millions) 1978	Density (per km²) 1978	GDP m. EA£ at current prices 1961–3 (average)	GDP 1971	GDP 1976	GDP 1977	Per capita GNP 1978 (US$)	Per capita GNP average annual growth 1960–78 (%)	Agriculture 1960	Agriculture 1978	Industry 1960	Industry 1978	Services 1960	Services 1978
Kenya	582 646	8.4	14.9	26	243	576	1 296	1 681	330	2.2	86	79	5	8	9	13
Tanzania	945 087	9.4	16.6	18	212	442	1 018	1 252	230	2.7	89	83	4	6	7	11
Uganda	236 036	6.8	12.8	54	163	469	n.a.	n.a.	280	0.7	89	83	4	6	7	11

(The last six columns fall under the heading: *Distribution of labour force (% of labour force)*.)

TABLE 7.1(b) *Wage employment (thousands)*

	All sectors 1967	All sectors 1973	All sectors 1977	Manufacturing 1967	Manufacturing 1973	Manufacturing 1977
Kenya	601	762	903	74	94	118
Tanzania	347	473	474	31	59	81
Uganda	257	348	n.a.	44	40	n.a.

TABLE 7.1(c) External and inter-territorial trade (EA £ m.)

	Kenya				Tanzania				Uganda			
	1967	1974	1976	1977	1967	1974	1976	1977	1967	1974	1976	1977
Exports: external	59	170	279	440	85	139	193	225	65	113	n.a.	n.a.
inter-state	26	48	67	62	4	11	13	2	13	4	n.a.	n.a.
Total	**85**	**218**	**346**	**502**	**89**	**149**	**205**	**227**	**78**	**117**	n.a.	n.a.
Imports: external	107	353	394	529	67	272	238	301	41	47	n.a.	n.a.
inter-state	13	13	13	2	14	19	33	9	16	31	n.a.	n.a.
Total	**120**	**366**	**407**	**531**	**81**	**291**	**271**	**310**	**57**	**78**	n.a.	n.a.
Balance: external	−47	−183	−115	−89	+18	−133	−45	−76	+24	+66	n.a.	n.a.
inter-state	+13	+35	+54	+60	−10	−8	−20	−7	−3	−27	n.a.	n.a.
Total	**−34**	**−148**	**−61**	**−30**	**+8**	**−141**	**−66**	**−83**	**+21**	**+39**	n.a.	n.a.

NOTES AND SOURCES
Exchange rates: US $1 = approx. KShs. 7.1, TShs. 8.1 EA £1 = Shs. 20. Until recently the Shillings of the three countries were at par.
Population
1961 Source: East African Statistical Dept., *Economic and Statistical Report.*
1978 Source: World Bank, *World Development Report,* 1980
Gross domestic product
Sources: *Economic and Statistical Report;* Kenya, *Statistical Abstract 1979;*
Tanzania, *Economic Survey 1977–78*
Gross national product
Source: *World Development Report,* 1980
Rate of inflation
Source: *World Development Report,* 1980
Trade
Note: Inter-state trade is that between Kenya, Tanzania, and Uganda. Figures may not add to totals because of rounding.
Sources: *Economic and Statistical Report;* Kenya, *Statistical Abstract;* Tanzania, *Economic Survey.*
Labour force
Note: Labour Force consists of wage employment plus self-employment, which is by far the larger component
Source: *World Development Report,* 1980.
Wage employment
Sources: *Economic and Statistical Report;* Kenya, *Statistical Abstract;* Tanzania, *Economic Survey.*

activities within so highly organised a system, as that of the East African Community. Yet within a decade the scheme had collapsed leaving the wreckage of the arrangements in such an atmosphere of hostility and recrimination that three and a half years later the borders between Kenya and Tanzania remained effectively closed.

INTEGRATION BEFORE THE TREATY

It is, in fact, possible to interpret the establishment of the Community not as a stride forward in cooperation but as a stage in a process of disintegration. Although it would be difficult to understand this view from a simple reading of the Treaty, it is comprehensible when the Treaty is seen in its historical context. There had, indeed, been even closer integration of the economies of the three countries before any of them achieved independence. In barest outline, the integration arrangements had comprised a customs union with a common external tariff and free trade between the countries, common customs and income tax administrations, common transport and communications services (railways, harbours, posts, telecommunications, airways), a common university, common research services, and a common currency. By the time the Treaty was signed, however, the common currency had been abandoned, after the failure to find an acceptable system of East Africa-wide central banking, and the operation of the customs union was being seriously inhibited by quantitative restrictions.

The integration arrangements, which had their origins in the early years of the century, were in the past of course 'colonial' and could not have been expected to continue unchanged into the era of independence. Most dissatisfaction was with the distribution of the benefits of integration. Change was essential once integration became voluntary and not enforced by the colonial power, because it was firmly believed in Tanzania and Uganda that the arrangements worked overwhelmingly to the benefit of Kenya. The customs union, it was believed, worked to the benefit of Kenya as the most industrially developed country of the three, and as the headquarters of the various common services were established in Kenya, the employment and income creating benefits of the services were believed also to accrue mainly there. The extent to which these beliefs were justified is not entirely uncontroversial, but it was the strength of the beliefs that counted.

The independence settlement, which established an East African Common Services Organisation to replace the High Commission of colonial days, provided for a redistribution of revenue in favour of Tanzania and Uganda, but this proved an inadequate measure, and restrictions began to be imposed on trade between the countries. Discussions about the establishment of an East African Federation came to nothing, and an *ad hoc* agreement on industrial location, known as the Kampala Agreement, was not implemented. Relations between the countries were rapidly deteriorating when the Commission which negotiated the Treaty (composed of ministers and an outside chairman) was appointed.

THE TREATY

The Treaty was intended to put cooperation between the partner states on a firm footing of mutual advantage, and not simply to paper over the cracks in the old structure of colonial relationships. It set up a formal structure for administering the Community institutions and provided measures to achieve an acceptable distribution of the benefits of cooperation between the states. The main features were: the introduction of a device known as the transfer tax to give limited protection for industries in the less developed states against competition from those in the more developed; the establishment of an East African Development Bank (EADB) which was to allocate its investments disproportionately in favour of Tanzania and Uganda; the relocation of the headquarters of some of the common services, including the Community Secretariat, so that they were not concentrated in Kenya. The Treaty made no more than formal reference to agriculture.

During the life of the Treaty separate universities were established in the three partner states and the assessment and collection of income tax ceased to be a common service, but a new institution, the East African Management Training Centre, was added, and survives, with additional countries participating. An Eastern Africa National Shipping Line was also established, but outside the community and including Zambia as an owner along with the three Community countries. It survived the collapse of the Community, but closed down with massive debts in March, 1980, two of its ships having earlier been seized by creditors in Europe. Formally the main structure, including the common external tariff (CET), stood until the final collapse, but the 'common market' became increasingly a dead letter and some of the common services became effectively disintegrated. The EADB survived the final collapse but in a largely moribund condition.

ISSUES BETWEEN THE PARTNER STATES

It would be convenient if the failure of the Treaty to achieve its intentions could be attributed to some single cause. In reality there were so many interacting influences and issues, some deriving from the Treaty and some not, that no simple lesson can be easily drawn from the experience of the EAC. Nor is it sensible to allocate the 'blame' for the break-up. One way to classify the issues that arose between the Partner States, and which affected the course of cooperation, is into those which were (a) dealt with in the Treaty, even if inadequately; (b) not dealt with in the Treaty, but which could have been by amendment or extension of the Treaty; (c) of a kind not amenable to settlement by Treaty. This is not an entirely satisfactory classification of the issues, and some can be seen to fall under either (a) or (b), but it is a helpful way to approach an examination of them.

COMMUNITY GOVERNMENT

The Treaty established a complicated institutional structure to administer and control the Community. In addition to a secretariat there were a number of councils, at which discussions took place between representatives of the partner states, and an East African minister and assistant minister for each partner state. Ultimate control rested with the authority composed of the three presidents. Although in the end the structure proved powerless to ensure the survival of the Community, its effectiveness should not be judged by the experience of the period following the coup which took place in Uganda in January, 1971. It can be objected that the system relied too much on harmonious relations between the presidents, and that control of the Community collapsed when relations became bad, and the source of initiative for the continuation and development of cooperation died. It is also true that even during the first few years the existence of the Authority seemed to deprive lower levels in the administration of the Community of initiative and of willingness to seek solutions to issues between the partner states by compromise. The structure of control encouraged the pursuit of national interests and discouraged compromise, because there was always the Authority to reach an agreement in the end. And in the first three years of the Community's existence it did reach agreement, for although the history of the Community even before the Uganda coup can be read as a lurch from crisis to crisis, the Authority was adept at resolving crises.

There is something to be said for the view that a system which encouraged compromise at a lower level – ministerial rather than presidential, and among officials – would have made the relations between the partner states less crisis-prone and the Community machinery of cooperation smoother running. There is also something to be said for the view that the secretary-general and the secretariat had too limited powers, as all decisions required the specific agreement of the partner states. However, it is certain that at the time the Treaty was signed, the partner states would have been unwilling to allow any delegation of powers to the secretariat of the Community. The importance of sovereignty in the first flush of independence would have prevented any delegation of powers, and gives credence to the view that arrangements which require a surrender of sovereignty if they are to work efficiently – even if they go no further than a commitment to consultation before decisions are taken – are exceptionally difficult for new nations.

Unanimous or majority rule is a related issue. The partner states did not agree, and certainly would not have agreed, to action by majority decision. In a community of three members majority rule is in any case difficult because of the risk that one country may find itself repeatedly in a minority of one. But even in a larger community it is almost inconceivable that majority rule would have been acceptable, and unanimity would have been even more difficult to achieve in a larger grouping.

The issue of the enlargement of the Community is, in fact, one which the Treaty could have dealt with in principle, but did not. The Treaty allowed negotiations for the accession of new members, but it did not provide for it. The Treaty could certainly have been adapted for a larger Community, but it is probably true that only Zambia was ever a serious applicant, so a solution to the issue of unanimity or majority rule could hardly have been found in that direction.

TRANSFER TAX

The most important matter with which the Treaty attempted to deal was the distribution of the benefits of cooperation. The integration of states which are at different levels of development tends to concentrate further development in those already most-developed, and to result in an unequal distribution of the benefits of cooperation. For an integration scheme to be born and to survive, every member must be satisfied and must remain satisfied with the distribution of the benefits. Measures to achieve an acceptable distribution, which would not be achieved in an unregulated common market, are therefore an essential feature of an integration scheme. The treaty dealt with this matter partly in a chapter entitled 'Measures to Promote Balanced Industrial Development', which provided for the transfer tax and the EADB. It is evident that the mechanisms of the Treaty were inadequate, given the context within which they operated, to persuade the partner states that continued cooperation was worthwhile. But it is not self-evident that the mechanisms of the Treaty were inherently inadequate, let alone inappropriate, for their purpose.

The transfer tax is sometimes seen as a device for encouraging the duplication of industries within East Africa, whereas the rationale of the common market was to avoid such duplication and to enable industries to enjoy economies of scale resulting from access to the whole East African market. But this criticism seems to derive from a misunderstanding even though in practice it may be true that uneconomic duplication took place – steel-mills and tyre factories have been given as examples (though in reality they may not have been of uneconomic size). The rationale of the transfer tax system was that it would allow Tanzania and Uganda temporarily to protect from Kenyan competition industries which could operate efficiently on a scale provided by their national markets. For these industries, the encouragement of duplication was the whole purpose of the transfer tax, not an unwelcome and unintended side-effect. There were other, large scale, industries the location of which would not, according to this rationalisation of the system, be affected by transfer taxes, because only a single plant would be economic for the whole of East Africa. Herein, however, lies the weakness of the rationalisation: the distinction between the two types of industry is nothing like so clear cut as the rationalisation presumes, and if sufficient incentives are provided, industries with important economies of scale could be duplicated to serve national markets at high cost. Such inefficient duplication cannot be blamed on the transfer tax. As formal fiscal incentives differed little between the partner states it is probable that practices incompatible with the Treaty, including discriminatory purchasing by state trading corporations (see below) and quantitative restrictions on imports, were the major cause of inefficient duplication of industries, and that the transfer tax was never really given a fair trial.

EAST AFRICAN DEVELOPMENT BANK

The effectiveness of the EADB as an equalising device may be questioned because of the limited scale of its activities. By the end of

1975 its investments in total were little more than twice the original contributions of the partner states. On average the annual commitment of funds by the Bank accounted for no more than 4 per cent of industrial investment in the partner states. It may be that a much larger scale of operations was expected by the less-developed partner states when they agreed to the constitution of the Bank. But the EADB did rapidly achieve the prescribed distribution of its investments between the partner states (until its activities in Uganda were disrupted by political developments) and it is possible that if the Community as a whole had proved a success, outside finance would have become available to enable the scale of the EADB operations to increase substantially. However, the most important role of the Bank could be seen as to act as a catalyst for complementary industrial development rather than to undertake a major part of industrial investment itself. And in that respect there is certainly reason to question its effectiveness. The projects in which the EADB invested (textiles, sugar, paper, tyres, cement, for example) do not appear particularly relevant to the aim of making the economies of the partner states more complementary. It would have been difficult for the Bank alone to pursue this aim. It could have done so if agreements had existed between the partner states on a pattern of industrial specialisation into which the EADB's investments would fit. But regional planning, which is discussed later, did not get very far during the life of the Community.

COMMON SERVICES

A further mechanism in the Treaty for distributing the gains from cooperation more equally was the relocation of the headquarters of the common services, which was combined with some decentralisation of their operations. Perhaps too much was expected from these changes, because the greater part of the local expenditures made by the services, and of the employment provided by them, continued to benefit Kenya. Perhaps rather more than half of all the activities of the common services were in Kenya, and a third in Tanzania, by the early 1970s. Uganda with probably less than a fifth of the total received least from the arrangements. A high proportion of the activities of the services continued to be in Kenya in consequence of her higher level of development, as well as of geographical factors, and a fundamental change in the distribution could only occur in the longer run with relatively greater economic growth in Tanzania and Uganda. Whatever the redistributive benefits through the common services, the increased costs imposed by the relocations and decentralisations were a serious problem.

In the event, the common services, far from being a mechanism for regulating the distribution of the benefits of cooperation and reinforcing the desire for integration, became a disruptive influence. In particular, the crisis in the railways was an immediate cause of the breakdown of cooperation. Without the inefficiency and financial inadequacy of the Railways Corporation, the Community might have survived until Amin was ousted and have had a second chance of effective life.

TRANSPORT ISSUES

In fact, several issues concerning transport, and the related issue of tourism, caused tensions between the partner states. The Kenya tourist industry benefited from access to the game parks of northern Tanzania. They were generally included in a circuit for Nairobi-based tourists, using Kenya vehicles. Although payments were obviously made for the use of Tanzania's hotels and game parks, and for other goods and services, nonetheless it was strongly contended by Tanzania that she received only minor benefits from the traffic. Geographical convenience made northern Tanzania a natural part of a Nairobi-based tour, and at the time it would have been implausible to expect a cross-border tour to be based anywhere else. Arusha could have been an alternative base, but not until there had been a very substantial expansion in the infrastructure for tourism and a change in Tanzania's somewhat ambivalent attitude towards the industry. Tourism is an industry where a redistribution of the benefits rather than a relocation of activities was the way to maximise total benefits and improve their distribution. A greater share for Tanzania would have required an agreement permitting discriminatory charges and other measures, and such arrangements could have been brought under the Treaty. The closure of the border and the disappearance of cross-border tourism with the collapse of the Community must have reduced the total benefits of tourism. Although it has stimulated Tanzania's interest in tourism, and she may be gaining more from tourism than in the past, the gains could have been greater still from cross-border tourism with an equitable distribution of the benefits.

A substantial road traffic developed between Kenya and Zambia, crossing Tanzania. The benefits of the trade accrued to Kenya where it imposed costs on Tanzania from the use of Tanzanian roads by heavy vehicles. Tension arose between Kenya and Tanzania over this issue.

Tanzania eventually closed the border to Kenya's heavy vehicles, even before the general border closure.

Competition between road and rail was also a cause of tension. The growth of road transport in Kenya was seen as a benefit to private business at the expense of the jointly-owned public railway. In fact, the issue was a good deal more complicated than that, competition between road and rail being a. matter of long standing in East Africa – see Hazlewood, 1964. Although it is probable that the railway was the lower-cost carrier of petroleum products, they were a high-rated traffic in the railway's tariff. This high charge by the railway made the carriage of petroleum products by road profitable, and large investments in road tankers had been made by private interests in Kenya. It was at this traffic in petroleum products that the argument just reported was mainly directed. As it happens, however, the investment in road tankers in Kenya took place at a time when large investments in railway rolling stock would also have been needed if the railway were to be able to handle the traffic. In any case, the opening of a publicly-owned pipe line from the coast to Nairobi to carry petroleum products, displacing both road and rail, suggests that a juxtaposition of private and public transport interests was too simple an interpretation of the issue. Nevertheless, the simple interpretation had some effect in souring relations between Kenya and Tanzania, and certainly the gain from both road and pipe-line operations accrued to Kenya.

The omission from the Treaty of detailed provisions for road transport followed naturally from the fact that it did not exist as a common service. The issues arising could nevertheless have been dealt with under the Treaty. The costs imposed by the use of Tanzanian roads by heavy vehicles from Kenya could have been dealt with by the levying of appropriately heavy charges, so long as the charges did not formally discriminate in favour of Tanzanian vehicles, and so long as funds were available and time allowed to reconstruct roads to the standard needed to carry the very heavy Kenyan vehicles. The issues of road – rail competition were discussed in the Communications Council, one of the Community institutions established by the Treaty, but much more needed to be done to produce and implement a plan for the coordinated development of surface transport throughout East Africa. Without it, transport issues were a disruptive influence on the Community.

STATE TRADING

Transport coordination was an old issue left unsettled by the Treaty in which the absence of a settlement led to strains between the partner states. A new issue of the same kind was that of state trading, which came into prominence soon after the Treaty was signed. The Treaty was implicitly written for a common market of market economies, in which marketing decisions were based on prices. The transfer taxes were designed to protect national industries while preserving a preference for the goods of other partner states over goods from outside East Africa. The whole system was based on the assumption that the transfer tax and the external tariff would establish certain price relationships, and that purchasing decisions would be based on those prices. This assumption became rapidly out of date with the growth of state trading in the partner states. State trading corporations, with a monopoly of purchasing for distribution, could be directed, and might be expected even without direction, to discriminate in favour of domestic suppliers, and there was a belief that this was happening, whatever the truth of the matter. Rules were drawn up for the regulation of state trading, though they would have been difficult but not impossible to enforce. It must be said, however, that state trading could have been turned into an integrating rather than a disintegrating device if it had been able to operate within a system of, and as an instrument for the implementation of, inter-state planning.

PLANNING

It might be argued that the relevance of inter-state planning in an integration scheme of developing countries is enhanced by the extent to which industrial development is undertaken with foreign capital, and in particular by trans-national corporations. In a largely *laissez-faire* scheme, including a scheme where the market is rigged by a device such as the transfer tax, even if fiscal incentives are harmonised, the members will be competing for the favour of foreign firms, and consequently their bargaining power will be drastically reduced. There will be duplication of investments which will dissipate the gains, and the gains in any case will go mainly to the foreign enterprise. This possibility provides a further argument for inter-state planning to reinforce cooperation, but its relevance to East Africa is a good deal diminished by the apparently unwelcoming face at times presented by Tanzania to foreign enterprise. Be that as it may, the development of manufacturing in Kenya by transnationals led some to the view that by importing from Kenya, Tanzania was allowing herself to be exploited by these concerns.

It would be too easy, in fact, to blame the absence of planning for the failure to solve these problems and, indeed, the whole issue of the distribution of the benefits of cooperation. If planning, particularly of the development of industry, is a *sine qua non* of successful regional integration, as some authorities believe, the failure to undertake such planning was obviously a major cause of the collapse of the Community. Planning is one of the matters which fall partly under (a) and partly under (b) in the classification proposed earlier. It had a place in the Treaty where provision was made for an economic consultative and planning council, and a committee of officials, the East African Committee of Planners, was set up. Planning was not simply something the framers of the Treaty forgot. Of course, the Treaty could have given a central role to planning, and established a planning instead of a pricing mechanism to deal with the distribution of industry. But it is certain, particularly as it was so soon after the failure of the Kampala Agreement on the allocation of industries, that a planning system would not have been accepted. There would have been no treaty signed if that had been its central feature. After the Treaty was signed and the Community came into being, there was certainly much activity within its planning Secretariat: reports were compiled and discussions held with the partner states. Although some progress was being made, planning proposals never came anywhere near to implementation.

It may be that successful regional planning would have required a much greater degree of harmony between the member states than existed in East Africa. No time was allowed for this proposition to be tested, however, as the advent of Amin to power in Uganda brought the planning process to an end.

BALANCE OF PAYMENTS PROBLEMS

Another issue which falls partly under (a) and partly under (b) of the classification, in that it was neither ignored in the Treaty nor given sufficient importance, concerns the balance of payments and foreign exchange problems of the partner states. The issue was to become more serious and express itself in ways which it may be guessed were not fully foreseen at the time the Treaty was drawn up.

The settlement of net indebtedness arising from inter-state transactions had in effect to be in foreign exchange. There was a provision for the extension of credit by a state in surplus in inter-state trade to one in deficit, but the maximum credit was relatively small, and the scheme was in fact never brought into use, though there may have been informal inter-state lending. The provisions of the Treaty were to the advantage of Kenya, which relied on a surplus in inter-state trade to balance a significant part of her deficit in external trade. It is unlikely that Kenya would have accepted a scheme which provided for balances to be inconvertible and which did not allow her to earn foreign exchange from inter-state trade, given that she had accepted discrimination against herself in the form of the transfer tax and the investment allocations of the EADB, and given the lower free market rates of Tanzania and Uganda Shillings. But the resulting large foreign exchange costs of inter-state settlements had very serious consequences.

Foreign exchange scarcity, though it was already a problem, suddenly became of major importance with the rise in oil prices, and to save foreign exchange became a major preoccupation of governments. It would have been consistent with a commitment to East African cooperation if inter-state transactions had been immune from restrictions. But that was not to be, and in the application of restrictions to imports there was no discrimination in favour of imports from other partner states.

A perhaps unforeseen effect of foreign exchange scarcity, which played an important part in the collapse of the Community institutions and in souring the atmosphere in the last years of their existence, was the imposition of restrictions on the transfer of funds from the regions to the headquarters of the common services. It is unnecessary to rehearse the sorry tale of squabbles and recriminations, and the charges and counter-charges of responsibility for the failure to transfer funds. The blame cannot be entirely attributed to the desire to save foreign exchange, for, if the affairs of the common services had been in better order it would have been more difficult for payments to be stopped on exchange control grounds. And in any case, the railway losses became so large that the regions could not have transferred enough to headquarters, independently of any concern for foreign exchange. But the fact is that the common services, already in a state of disarray, were fundamentally disrupted by the drying-up of the flow of funds to headquarters, where lay the responsibility for large expenditures, including the purchase of equipment and loan charges. This disruption in the financial operation of the services led directly to their effective dissolution as common institutions and to the collapse of a major part of the structure of the Community.

AMIN

The founders of the Community could not have been expected to legislate against the appearance of General Amin, and his seizure of power is one of the matters which was not amenable to settlement in advance by Treaty. Nevertheless, the crucial position of the Authority, to which reference has already been made, raises again the question of whether a different structure of control would have been less sensitive to such events. The Authority did not meet after Amin came to power in Uganda, although after initial disruption the essential business was conducted by obtaining the agreement of the members individually. Even if it had met, the Authority would have been unable to operate in the old way. The political atmosphere was not conducive to the smooth operation of the Community, let alone to that progressive extension of cooperation which some have seen as necessary for success. Uganda ceased to be an effective participant in Community discussions and the balance of the Community's tripartite structure disappeared.

IDEOLOGY

Nor is it easy to see that the Treaty could have done anything about the growing ideological division between 'capitalist' Kenya and 'socialist' Tanzania, if these shorthand terms may be allowed to represent the positioris of the two governments. When there were all the other disruptive influences at work, the different ideologies of the governments of Kenya and Tanzania certainly made cooperation increasingly difficult, particularly as they were used from time to time as pegs on which to hang mutual political abuse. However, too much can perhaps be made of this cause of dissension as the reason for the inevitable collapse of the Community. After all, procedures for dealing with the problems created by the establishment of state monopoly trading corporations had been devised by the Community secretariat, though they had not been implemented. Certainly, determined proseletisation of one side by the other could make cooperation impossible. But it would be a conclusion of despair that mutually beneficial economic cooperation requires a close similarity of social and political outlook. And it must be emphasised that the fundamental assumption on which the Treaty was based was that integration was a 'positive sum game' from which all could benefit, particularly in the longer run when the volume of mutually beneficial intra-Community trade had expanded. In the words of the Treaty

It shall be the aim of the Community to strengthen and regulate the industrial, commercial and other relations of the Partner States to the end that there shall be accelerated, harmonious and balanced development and sustained expansion of economic activities the benefits whereof shall be equitably shared.

And here, perhaps, we come to the heart of the matter. As time went on the partner states increasingly behaved as if they believed it was in fact a 'zero sum game', or even a 'negative sum game'.

CHANGING PERCEPTIONS

There was, it must be admitted, some justification for such a belief, to an extent indeed because of the way the partner states had behaved. The benefits from the common market began to disappear with the duplication of industries. The benefits of the common services were dissipated in inefficiencies and financial difficulties. With increased road competition on the Mombasa–Nairobi rail route, and with extra rail traffic in Tanzania arising from the construction of the Tanzania–Zambia railway (itself established as a separate entity from East African Railways), the pattern of cross-subsidisation within the railway system shifted, and Tanzania appeared to be benefiting less than before from the joint system. TAZARA was established outside the Community, and the increase in imports from China under the agreement for financing the local costs of the railway, Tanzania having failed to obtain support from Western donors or international institutions, had an adverse effect on inter-state trade.

But even more important than the objective situation was the perception of the partner states about the costs and benefits of the system. If the perception of the partners is that there are gains for all, then the bargaining is about how much each shall benefit, and only if one partner is pushed to the limit will it be worth its while to withdraw. Even where it is such a positive-sum game, however, the perceptions of the partners may be inconsistent. One partner may think it is not receiving enough of the benefit, at a time when another partner thinks it has itself been pushed to near the limit. There is reason to think that the perceptions of Tanzania and Kenya, respectively, were something like this when the Treaty was signed. It is doubtful if Kenya would have accepted a more unfavourable bargain. It would be a mistake to think that at the signing of the Treaty the Kenya ministers and officials were chortling at the thought that they had made a very advantageous deal. Yet Tanzania may have felt that the Treaty gave her little more than the minimum she was prepared to accept, and developments in the succeeding years may have made her even less satisfied.

Although the definition and the measurement of the 'gap' between the levels of development in Kenya and Tanzania are fraught with difficulties, which are enhanced by the different ends of 'capitalist' and 'socialist' societies, the gap evidently did not narrow and may have increased in the perceptions of both Tanzania and Kenya, despite the growth of industry in Tanzania. Given that the growth of the Kenya economy was to a significant extent the consequence of the welcome it gave to foreign investors, a route to development of which Tanzania to say the least was wary, at least in rhetoric, the equalising mechanisms of the Treaty were attempting to swim against a strongly flowing stream. That inequality was perceived to remain or increase led to a loss of interest in cooperation, because of hubris in Kenya, where the ill effects of a loss of exports to Tanzania and Zambia may have been greatly under-estimated, being concealed by the boom in the price of coffee, and because of despair in Tanzania at cooperation with Kenya as a route to development. All in all, there was a change in the perceived benefits of continued cooperation and in the perceived costs of dissolution. Perceived as a zero- or negative-sum game the Community had no future, even though the perceptions may have been erroneous.

Perceptions, or rather misperceptions, entered also into the final break-up. It is possible that both Kenya and Tanzania misperceived the 'sticking-point' of the other, and so took a position from which withdrawal was impossible, and which made break-up inevitable, even though neither wanted it and both saw benefits in continued cooperation. On this view, the final collapse of the Community was the result of a poker game in which everybody lost.

OTHER INFLUENCES

Interest in East African cooperation was crumbling also for other reasons. Reference has already been made to the coup in Uganda as disrupting her relations with Tanzania. It did more than that. It removed Uganda as a serious member of the common institutions, and had an eroding effect throughout the structure of the Community which can hardly be exaggerated.

In addition, the focus of political interest in Tanzania moved towards the south. The future of Zimbabwe, and Tanzania's position as a front line state, attracted political attention at the highest levels and, it may be suspected, diminished the concern with the strengthening of East

African relations. If this is so, it would be one reason why the crisis-solving function of the Authority ceased to be effective.

This discussion has been in terms of the interests and benefits of the partner states, but the states are not monolithic and within them there are different interests which would be affected differently by the success as by the failure of cooperation between the states. A full understanding of the brief history of the Community is impossible without an understanding of how that history was both affected by and affected these various interests. It is a matter very difficult to research, and largely unresearched, but it is of importance. And much the same must be said about external interests – foreign governments, international institutions, transnational corporations. So far as the transnational corporations are concerned, there is a simple-minded view that cooperation in East Africa fell victim to their hostility; there is the equally simple-minded view that it was only these corporations which benefited from the integration arrangements. Both views can hardly be correct, and it is probable that they are both wrong. Nevertheless, the role of transnationals in the integration and disintegration processes, as well as that of other external interests, might reward study.

QUESTIONS

It has already been remarked that there was no single cause of the death of the East African Community, no single inadequacy in the regulating instruments, but rather a multiplicity of ailments, each of which by itself could have been survived, but which together were too much for the weakened body to bear. Nor can it be said that the Community was killed: rather it faded and died from a lack of interest in keeping it alive, though not without a nudge or two along the road to the grave, and not without some squabbles between the heirs to the estate. In short, the political will was lacking in the partner states to keep the Community in being.

Spilt milk is, proverbially, not worth crying over. However, it may be worthwhile to examine the reasons for the spillage, particularly if to do so will help to prevent a similar waste in the future. It is perhaps surprising that the death of the Community has not killed the apparent interest in regional integration schemes of varying degrees among developing countries, in Africa and elsewhere. There are still schemes in various stages of development in different parts of the world. Certainly the members of new schemes elsewhere would not have the history of disagreement which in East Africa began with the unregulated common market of colonial times. A well-designed new scheme which fully met each member's perception of the costs and benefits, if such a scheme could be designed, would not have the tensions created by years of controversy. On the other hand, most groupings lack what might be expected to be the valuable lubricants for smoothly working cooperation of common languages, as with English and Swahili in East Africa, and the common educational background provided by Makerere for some politicians and for many of the generation of civil servants who took over the administration of all three East African countries at independence. ECOWAS (the Economic Community of West African States) and the proposed preferential trading area for which 16 Eastern and Southern African countries signed a treaty of intent in March, 1978, and which was seen as a first step in a process of regional integration, are two schemes that might benefit from the lessons of the East African Community.

It is not easy to summarise the lessons for the planners of other schemes, so that they can be learned by rote. Perhaps the best approach is to list some of the questions about the requirements for successful regional integration that are suggested by a study of the Community's history:

1. Is it necessary only that all members of the scheme should benefit, or must they benefit equally, or must the poorer or less developed members gain most, or must even the gap between the members in their wealth and level of development actually narrow over time? The last is a very strong requirement, because it is perfectly possible for the gap to widen, even though the integration arrangements themselves have a strong equalising element.
2. Is there a limit to the difference in levels of development and 'economic size' of members of a grouping beyond which integration cannot work? Are giants and pygmies incompatible cohabitants?
3. Are members willing to take a longer-term view, and to see the benefits from cooperation grow with the growth of trade between them, or do their assessments inevitably have a short horizon within which transactions between them, and hence the benefits of cooperation, are likely to be small?
4. If there are gains from the scheme for the members as a whole and for every member individually, can it be ensured that they all

perceive the benefit, and do not have incompatible perceptions of the distribution of the benefits?

5. Are the members prepared to agree on a common system of fiscal incentives to encourage an acceptable distribution of investment between them and to prevent the competitive offering of concessions to investors?

6. Is it possible for the operation of the scheme to be insulated from the effects of foreign exchange scarcity in the member countries?

7. Is a substantial degree of regional planning over such matters as the location of new industries and the pattern of industrial specialisation essential to achieve an acceptable distribution of the benefits of integration?

8. If so, are the member countries prepared to accept the constraints imposed on them by such planning?

9. How does such planning cope with strong preferences by potential investors about the location of production?

10. Is a complex or 'package' scheme, embracing different fields of cooperation, as in East Africa, where some parts of the scheme may be of particular benefit to some member(s) and other parts to others, most likely to lead to all members perceiving that there are benefits from membership?

11. Would a less comprehensive scheme, in which areas of cooperation with the greatest potential for conflict were excluded, be more viable?

12. Would 'functionally specific' arrangements of limited scope be the best bet?

13. What should be done if a major element of an integration scheme works so badly as to threaten the future of the whole scheme?

14. Would provisions in the Treaty for a common agricultural policy have been a cohesive influence in the Community? Is it important to include agriculture in integration arrangements for countries where it is the major economic activity?

15. Is the view correct that integration must 'go forward' or decline?

16. Is a broadly similar ideology in the member countries essential for success?

17. Is it in fact in ideology or in their approach to practical negotiations in which governments need to be relatively similar?

18. Is continuing political harmony between the states essential and must it go beyond the minimum of good will without which cooperation would be impossible?

19. Must the members be willing to surrender sovereignty to the extent of allowing decisions to be reached by majority vote?
20. Must the members be prepared to delegate substantial powers to the bureaucracy of the scheme?
21. Can a scheme be protected from the effect of a wavering commitment to integration at the highest levels in one or more of the partner states?
22. Is the absence of political rewards at the regional level likely to reduce the political will and interest in integration below the minimum necessary for success?
23. What is the balance of influence within each country and what interests will be harmed or benefited by the progress of integration?
24. What external influences are at work and which favour and which oppose integration?
25. Are the expected gains from industrialisation to serve a protected regional market great enough to make it worthwhile surmounting the difficulties, given the possibilities for manufacturing for extra-regional export, including export to developed countries through the medium of multinational corporations? The expectation will differ from country to country according to the size of its domestic market and its competitive ability in international markets. Is a firmly affirmative answer from every member necessary if a grouping is to have strong prospects of success?

The answers to at least some of these questions might seem obvious, but the implications of such answers have not always been taken into account in regional integration proposals. And unless the founders of regional integration schemes in developing countries are satisfied with their answers to all these questions their efforts may be described, in Dr Johnson's words on the second marriage of a man whose first had been unhappy, as the triumph of hope over experience.

NOTES

1. This chapter is a revised version of 'The End of the East African Community: What are the Lessons for Regional Integration Schemes?', *Journal of Common Market Studies* September 1979. I am grateful to the editor of the journal for permission to use the article. In revising it I have been greatly assisted by written comments on the original article by Professor R. H. Green, though it should not be assumed that he agrees with everything in the chapter.

2. A cordial meeting was reported to have taken place on 27 December, 1980, between President Moi and the new, post-election, Prime Minister of Uganda 'for discussions on trade, communications and border security', *The Times* 29 December 1980, and President Moi and Obote met in Western Kenya on 5 January 1981. The three presidents met on 17 January – together with the president of Zambia – and agreed to meet frequently 'to establish political will as a basis for promotion of trade and other forms of cooperation', but the Kenya–Tanzania border remained closed.

8 The West African Economic Community

Peter Robson

INTRODUCTION

The West African Economic Community (*Communauté Economique de l'Afrique de l'Ouest*, or CEAO), not to be confused with the Economic Community of West African States (ECOWAS), represents·the third attempt of the majority of the states[1] created out of the former federation of *Afrique Orientale Française* (AOF) to maintain and improve their previous economic links. The two earlier attempts, resulting in the establishment of UDAO in 1959 and of UDEAO in 1966, both failed. The reasons for their failure are numerous and complex and some are now mainly of historical interest. Technical, administrative, political and economic factors all played a part, including a natural desire on the part of newly independent countries to utilise their principal instrument of fiscal policy, namely the tariff, in the interests of development. But an overriding reason for the failure of the two previous initiatives was the inherent defectiveness of an orthodox customs union as an instrument of regional cooperation in the conditions of Africa in the 1960s. Some much needed improvements were made in UDEAO, notably in its acceptance of the necessity of intraregional tariff protection in a bloc which lacked a regional policy, and in the establishment of a permanent machinery of administration, previously lacking. In its almost exclusive concern with trade liberalisation, however, UDEAO remained an expression of an approach that Tinbergen (1965) had designated as 'negative integration' – see Chapter 1. Its convention was hardly at all concerned with measures of 'positive integration' of a kind designed to make the market area function effectively or to promote other broader policy objectives in the union. These omissions were to play a large part in the failure, in its turn, of UDEAO, which had become apparent to all parties by 1969. Its members determined nevertheless to make another effort to resolve the problems which had arisen. They chose to do so by embarking on more ambitious arrangements for regional integration going well beyond the removal of trade barriers and the formation of a customs union and involving other measures to promote regional economic cooperation on an equitable basis. In doing so, their choice echoed approaches that were being attempted at that time in other African groupings to deal with essentially similar difficulties. The outcome was the Treaty of Abidjan which came into effect in 1973 on its ratification by Ivory Coast, Senegal, Mali, Mauretania, Niger and Upper Volta. This chapter discusses the progress of the Community in the eight years which have elapsed since its establishment and the principal problems and issues which confront it today.

THE ECONOMIES OF THE MEMBER STATES

Since any well-grounded appreciation of the operations of the Community must hinge on an understanding of its constituent economies, it is appropriate to commence with an outline of the economic conditions and recent development of the member states. Perhaps the most striking characteristics of the Community are its immense land area, small populations and generally low incomes. In 1978 (see Table 8.1), the Community's total population amounted to some 31 million which occupied an area larger than the whole of Western Europe and roughly half the size of the USA. Population distribution is very uneven, for much of this vast territory is predominantly Sahelian in character and of low or negligible agricultural productivity, and in these areas crop production must at present be confined largely to riverain flood plains such as those of the Niger and Senegal rivers.

The aggregate GNP of the Community in 1978 amounted to some $11600 million (IBRD 1980), of which the Ivory Coast accounted for more than half. Average income per capita amounted to $366. All the member states fall into the low-income category, except for Ivory Coast, which with a per capita income of $840–higher than in any other African country south of the Sahara except South Africa – falls squarely into the middle income group.

The pattern of economic growth experienced by the Community's members during the past two decades is rather mixed. Although exceptionally high rates of growth of real GDP were recorded by Ivory

TABLE 8.1(a)   West African Economic Community Population, Income and Growth

	Population (millions) 1978	Area (km² thousands)	Population density (inhabitants per km²)	Rate of population growth (1970–78)	GNP Aggregate ($m)	GNP Per cent of total Community	GNP Per capita ($1978)	GNP per capita (average annual growth per cent) 1960–78	Real GDP growth (average annual growth per cent) 1960–70	Real GDP growth (average annual growth per cent) 1970–78
Ivory Coast	7.8	322	24.2	5.6	6 580	56.8	840	2.5	8.0	6.8
Upper Volta	5.6	274	20.4	1.6	870	7.5	160	1.3	3.0	−0.2
Mali	6.3	1 240	5.0	2.5	760	6.6	120	1.0	3.3	4.6
Mauretania	1.5	1 031	1.5	2.7	420	3.6	270	3.6	8.1	2.3
Niger	5.0	1 267	3.9	2.8	1 110	9.6	220	−1.4	2.9	2.4
Senegal	5.4	196	27.6	2.6	1 836	15.9	340	−0.4	2.5	2.2
Community	31.6	4 330			11 576		366			

SOURCE   The World Bank, *World Development Report 1980*, Annex, World Development Indicators.

TABLE 8.1(b) *West African Economic Community distribution of GDP (per cent) and growth rates (Annual averages)*

	Agriculture				Industry				Manufacturing				Services			
	1960–70		1970–78		1960–70		1970–78		1960–70		1970–78		1960–70		1970–78	
	% share	Rate of growth	% share	Rate of growth	% share	Rate of growth	% share	Rate of growth	% share	Rate of growth	% share	Rate of growth	% share	Rate of growth	% share	Rate of growth
Ivory Coast	43	4.2	21	3.9	14	11.5	23	10.0	7	11.6	13	7.5	43	9.7	56	7.2
Upper Volta	62	–	38	–3.6	14	–	20	1.4	6	–	13	1.6	24	–	42	2.7
Mali	55	–	37	2.0	10	–	18	9.2	5	–	12	–	35	–	45	5.2
Mauretania	59	2.4	26	–2.3	24	12.8	37	2.1	3	18.0	11	2.9	17	17.0	37	7.6
Niger	69	3.3	43	–0.2	9	13.9	27	8.6	4	–	10	–	22	–	30	4.2
Senegal	24	2.9	26	3.3	17	4.4	25	3.9	12	6.2	19	4.1	59	1.7	49	1.0

SOURCE The World Bank, World Development Report 1980, Annex, World Development Indicators.

TABLE 8.1(c) West African Economic Community trade growth and export structure

| | Merchandise trade ($m) | | Average annual growth rate (per cent) | | | | Terms of trade (1970 = 100) | | Per cent share of merchandise exports | | | | | | | | | | Value of manufactured exports $m | |
| | Exports | Imports | Exports | | Imports | | | | Fuels, minerals, metals | | Other Primary commodities | | Textiles and clothing | | Machinery and transport equipment | | Other manufactures | | | |
	1978	1978	1960–70	1970–78	1960–70	1970–78	1960	1978	1960	1977	1960	1977	1960	1977	1960	1977	1960	1977	1963	1977
Ivory Coast	2 322	2 325	8.8	8.5	9.7	10.6	89	94	1	4	98	89	0	2	–	2	1	3	7	161
Upper Volta	57	210	14.4	8.5	7.8	9.4	75	89	0	–	100	95	0	–	0	1	–	4	1	3
Mali	107	219	3.1	7.7	–0.4	5.0	91	93	0	–	96	98	1	–	1	1	2	1	–	2
Mauretania	119	181	55.2	–0.8	4.6	6.3	112	68	4	87	69	9	1	–	20	–	6	4	3	6
Niger	158	346	6.0	13.2	11.9	5.5	90	78	–	31	100	35	0	1	0	0	0	33	1	56
Senegal	391	788	1.2	4.4	2.7	4.7	91	100	3	13	94	80	1	1	1	–	1	6	9	36

SOURCE   The World Bank, *World Development Report 1980*, Annex, World Development Indicators.

Coast for the whole of the period 1960–78, those of the other members were very much lower. Rates of growth of per capita real GNP, reflecting the impact of both population growth and profit and interest remittances abroad, were naturally much lower and, at best, hardly more than modest, exceeding $2\frac{1}{2}$ percent only in Ivory Coast and Mauretania. Actually negative real per capita growth rates are recorded for Niger and Senegal.

At the beginning of the 1960s all six countries were fairly typical in their economic structures of low-income primary producing economies in that the principal domestic determinant of economic activity was the production of primary products for export. This is reflected in the generally high share of agriculture in the GNP for all countries except Senegal, where industrial and service activities had been developed in Dakar on a scale quite disproportionate to Senegal's own domestic requirements to serve the needs of the AOF as a whole.

Agricultural production in the Community is undertaken mainly by traditional agriculturists, partly for subsistence but partly for the market. Modernised plantation and estate agriculture is also found, in particular in Ivory Coast (where its operation has underpinned the substantial growth and diversification of agricultural production in recent years), to a limited extent in Mali (in rice and groundnuts), and in Upper Volta (sugar). Cash crops are mainly produced for export, but some, e.g. cotton and to a limited extent rubber and certain food crops, are important ingredients of local consumption and manufacture. The most important cash crops include cotton, coffee, cocoa, groundnuts, sugar cane, rice, rubber and pineapples. Most members are highly specialised on one or two of these: Senegal (groundnuts), Mali (cotton and groundnuts), Upper Volta (cotton), Niger (groundnuts and cotton). At the beginning of the period, Ivory Coast's agricultural production was also highly specialised, and three-quarters of its export earnings were produced by coffee and cocoa. By 1975, although these two crops continued to be important (accounting in that year for nearly a half of export earnings), others such as cotton, rice, sugar, pineapples and rubber had become quite significant. Livestock rearing, often with a nomadic base, is of major importance in several countries, including Mali, Upper Volta, Mauretania and Niger. Other important natural products include timber in Ivory Coast and fish in Mauretania.

It is still the case today that the domestic economic performance of the CEAO countries is heavily dependent on agriculture and livestock production, and the unsatisfactory growth record of some of the Sahelian member states is attributable largely to the severe impact of the droughts of the early seventies upon this sector. Nevertheless, during the past two decades important structural changes have occurred in two of the Sahelian member states and in Ivory Coast so that it is no longer only Senegal whose economic performance is significantly influenced by activity in other productive sectors. In the Sahelian countries of Niger and Mauretania mineral development is the source of the changes, and this has largely mitigated the disastrous impact which drought would otherwise have had on their incomes. Throughout the period 1960–78, Mauretania enjoyed a substantial income from the production and export of iron ore. In 1978 income from this source, which accounted for more than 25 per cent of GNP and 75 per cent of export earnings, exceeded that generated by agriculture and animal husbandry. Niger's mining sector –of mere recent origin – has similarly constituted the major dynamic element. Although income generated in mining has not yet overtaken agriculture's contribution to GNP, growing incomes from uranium production have enabled Niger to recover fairly quickly from the effects of drought and have supported growth in other sectors. The other member state whose economic performance has become significantly dependent on developments outside agriculture is Ivory Coast – in its case, as a result of its success in creating a varied modern manufacturing sector. In 1978 income generated in Ivory Coast's manufacturing sector surpassed that of agriculture in its contribution to GNP, despite the considerable absolute expansion in agricultural production that had also been achieved simultaneously. The rapid development of Ivory Coast's manufacturing industry during the past two decades was based initially on the managed substitution of domestic products in its large and growing home market for goods previously imported from Dakar. This was reinforced by bilateral trade deals with Senegal and by the development of exports to other countries of the Community, notably Upper Volta and Mali. Outlets were also successfully created outside CEAO in the West African region. In this wider though admittedly still limited intraregional trade, Ivory Coast has even succeeded in becoming West Africa's leading exporter, far outstripping Nigeria and Ghana. Ivory Coast's remarkable industrial growth is based not only on its natural advantages in the shape of a substantial domestic market, access to a labour force, and relatively low energy costs, but also on the provision of generous industrial incentives. It has enabled Ivory Coast to overtake Senegal's initially dominant position in several major industrial sectors and to establish very strong positions in others. An inevitable consequence of Ivory Coast's industrial growth has been that industrial development in Senegal has displayed a less dynamic picture for much of the period, reflecting the adjustments forced on it by increased competition from Ivory Coast in that country's domestic market, in Senegal itself and in other countries of the group. Senegal's industrial sector nevertheless continues to generate a relatively large share of GNP (comparable to that of agriculture) and during the past decade its manufacturing sector generated a larger share of its GNP than that of any other member of the group. In the land-locked states of the Community and in Mauretania, there has been some expansion of the industrial sector from modest beginnings, but their relative importance, mining apart, is very much smaller than in Ivory Coast and Senegal.

In its character, the industrial structure which has grown up in the Community is not untypical of countries at these levels of development. In terms of a broad product classification the most important industrial group, measured in plant numbers (this is not a very satisfactory indicator of relative importance, but regular censuses of manufacturing are not available for comparable dates for all member states – these statistics of plant numbers are derived from a Community enumeration for 1975), is the food, drink and tobacco industry which in 1975 numbered 88 plants. The chemical industry – a heterogeneous group which includes both traditional products such as paints and matches and others such as plastics which are based on newer technologies – was in second place with 52 units. In third place came the textile industry which numbered 32 units. Industries linked to construction and building, which are effectively protected by the high costs of transporting the finished products, are also important (25 units). The same consideration partly accounts for the importance of industries assembling transport goods such as coaches, autocycles and bicycles. Mechanical and electrical industries on the other hand were relatively little developed, and most of the plants in this category are small units of an artisanal character, typically involved in repair work.

The industries that have been established fall into four distinct categories: (i) industries processing agricultural products for export (such as cotton ginning and groundnut processing); (ii) industries subjecting certain imported products to a limited degree of additional processing; (iii) industries producing, with mainly local ingredients, relatively simple import substitutes such as cement, bricks, textiles and beverages by means of simple technologies; (iv) industries, of a processing or assembly kind, involving more sophisticated products and techniques. Both Ivory Coast and Senegal possess all four types, but the industrial sectors of the land-locked countries and Mauretania are largely confined to the processing of primary products and minerals for export and to the production of simple import substitutes.

Of the 336 enterprises recorded in the 1975 enumeration, 139 were located in the Ivory Coast (most having been established after 1960) and 102 were located in Senegal. In terms of shares of output value, Ivory Coast may account for some three fifths, and Senegal for a quarter, with Upper Volta, Niger and Mali accounting for some 5 per cent. Within each country, industrial development is highly concentrated in one or two development poles which can offer infrastructure, a suitable labour force and markets.

From the standpoint of integration, a noteworthy aspect of the industrial development of the CEAO countries is its heavy dependence upon investment by transnational enterprises based in Europe and America. In the industrial sectors of all countries except Mali, where the public sector is more important, and to a lesser extent in Upper Volta, the larger enterprises are generally affiliated with foreign companies which own the bulk of the capital. In the case of textiles, for example, except in Mali, most of the large and medium enterprises in CEAO are affiliates of foreign enterprises which own between 60 and 100 per cent of the capital. Some transnational enterprises operate in only one member state, where they may compete with other similar enterprises, but many do business in more than one member state, as does the important locally-based Blohorn group. Distribution is also undertaken by enterprises such as CFAO and SCOA which operate in more than one country.

THE PROVISIONS OF THE TREATY OF ABIDJAN

The Community's objectives as expressed in Title 1 of the Treaty clearly reflect the more positive approach to economic cooperation which has been espoused in this latest measure. The expressed aim of the Community is to promote a harmonised and balanced economic development of the member states. Active policies of cooperation and integration are to be pursued in a variety of fields to bring this about and steps are to be taken to develop trade in agricultural and industrial production on an organised basis.

The basis of the Community is to be the creation of a unified regional market in which products of local origin circulate freely without quantitative restrictions. This is to be brought about by (i) the establishment of a common external tariff (CET) within 12 years; (ii) the introduction of free trade in products of local origin (such as livestock, agricultural products, fish and mineral products) which have not undergone industrial processing (*produits de cru*); and (iii) the institution in approved cases of a special preferential import duty regime termed the Regional Cooperation Tax (*Taxe de Coopération Régionale* or TCR) for traded manufactured products which originate in member states. Where applied, this involves the substitution of a single duty (the TCR) at an effectively lower rate in place of all import duties that would otherwise be levied at importation. The level of the TCR is fixed on a product by product basis by the Council of Ministers. Internal indirect taxes imposed without discrimination on both imports and domestic products may be levied additionally. Conventional customs union arrangements for the circulation of transferred imports, and the reimbursement of corresponding duties, are specified in Protocol 1 and in a subsequent ministerial decision (12/77/CM).

A novel feature of the Treaty is that it makes provision for the payment of compensation to offset the revenue-loss (*moins-value budgétaire*) arising from the importation of products subject to the TCR to the extent of two-thirds of the assessed loss. Compensation is effected through the Community Development Fund (*Fonds Communautaire de Développement*–FCD). FCD derives its resources from contributions from member states which in total are equivalent to the aggregate assessed revenue loss. Each member's contribution to FCD is determined by its relative share of the global value of intra-CEAO exports of manufactures for the year in question. The difference (equivalent to one-third of the assessed revenue losses) between the receipts of FCD and its compensatory payments is made available to support projects of Community interest.

Apart from its concern with trade and customs, the Treaty also contains potentially important provisions relating to the development of common Community policies in other fields. These include the requirements for the preparation of a draft programme of industrialisation at the zonal level, to be submitted to the Council within three years of the coming into force of the Treaty; the preparation of a draft statute for multinational corporations; and the preparation within two years of proposals for harmonising the fiscal conditions for investment. Joint policies and measures are also envisaged in various other sectors of economic activity, such as scientific and technological research, energy production and distribution, development of industry and mining, development of tourism, meat production, coordination and development of transport and communications, although no time-table is specified for their implementation and the content of the policies is undefined. To implement common policies, the Treaty established community offices for agricultural development, industrial development, trade promotion, livestock and meat, and fisheries. Other important provisions of the Treaty (Title 5) relate to the free circulation of persons and capital and the right of establishment.

Unlike the situation in some other arrangements for regional integration, it was unnecessary for CEAO to give much attention to monetary and payments problems since all of its members except Mali and Mauretania participate (together with Benin and Togo), in a common central bank (BCEAO) and share a common currency–the CFA franc, which is tied to the French franc. Effectively, the Malian franc has also been freely interchangeable with the CFA franc at a fixed parity in recent years.

To operate the Community, provision is made for the establishment of four main Community institutions in addition to the FCD, namely, the Conference of Heads of State, the Council of Ministers, the Secretariat-General, and the Court of Arbitration. With the exception of the latter, all of these institutions are in operation.

The provisions of the Treaty are potentially quite far-reaching and their full implementation would imply a high degree of economic integration among the member states. Coupled with fiscal compensation, a properly elaborated programme of incentive harmonisation, regional industrial development and transport improvements could go far to ensure that, in certain key spheres at any rate, the interests of each member state would be broadly served by integration – which the previous arrangements were unable to do. Whether the arrangements envisaged would suffice to make a significant contribution to the basic aim of balanced economic development of the member states, if by that it is meant to imply a reduction in the existing wide disparities of income and growth, is more doubtful. In the light of the physical conditions of the least developed members of the group, it is arguable that any prospect of a substantial reduction in disparities is more likely to be dependent on the impact of mineral discovery and exploitation and substantial inflows of foreign aid aimed at agricultural improvement, than on the contribution of the integration arrangements themselves, useful as they may be in promoting industrialisation and more balanced economic structures.

TRADE LIBERALISATION AND THE TCR

Although the Community clearly sets out to be much more than a trade bloc, a major objective of the CEAO is nevertheless to promote intra-

Community trade, and in this respect the TCR is clearly a pivotal feature of the arrangements. It is not an entirely novel kind of integration preference, being similar to the *taxe unique* of UDEAC (Robson, 1968), but the precise form it has taken, and in particular its automatic link with fiscal compensation, makes it unique. Eligibility for its benefits is not automatic. The level of the tax is determined for each enterprise, product and country by the Council of Ministers, which considers only applications that are put forward by the Government of the country in which the enterprise seeking TCR status is domiciled.

Progress with the introduction of the TCR was initially slow, but by 1977 it was well advanced, and by June 1979 a total of 361 approvals had been granted to 188 enterprises for 472 products or groups of products. Of these enterprises, 101 were located in Ivory Coast, 11 in Upper Volta, 12 in Mali, 1 in Mauretania, 5 in Niger and 58 in Senegal (*CEAO, 1979, Fonds Communautaire de Développement, Prévisions de Recettes 1980, 2è version*). The approvals determined up to 1979 covered most of the industrial products satisfying the rules of origin, which alone could be considered for TCR treatment. The principal exception – and it is a large one – concerned trade between Ivory Coast and Senegal, much of which, until 1979, remained outside these arrangements as a result of a bilateral trade agreement inherited from UDEAO, which was allowed to continue for the initial five-year period of the life of CEAO.

Although the Treaty lays down no principles for determining the levels of the TCR, certain guidelines have been adopted by the Secretariat in formulating its own recommendations to the Council and these are often reflected in the rates established. Firstly, in order to reduce the competitive disadvantages of the least developed member states, TCR rates on their products are often fixed at lower levels than those imposed on the similar products of Ivory Coast and Senegal. Likewise, the landlocked countries and Mauretania often accord lower rates for products traded amongst themselves as compared with rates charged on similar products coming from Ivory Coast and Senegal. Secondly, in the interests of promoting the use of local raw materials and of developing inter-industry linkages, products using local raw materials or locally manufactured intermediate inputs are treated more favourably than products utilising foreign-produced inputs. A third relevant consideration is the existence or absence of a product in the importing country similar to that for which another country requests a TCR regime.

The rate differentiation produced by the adoption of these guide-lines constitutes the principal practical manifestation so far of CEAO's expressed concern with balanced and co-ordinated development. Necessarily, the absolute levels established for the TCR also reflect the varying levels of import duty that are imposed in member countries as well as their levels of internal indirect taxation which remain applicable to CEAO imports, since these two tax charges jointly determine the effective preference against third countries which any given rate of TCR provides. In this connection it may be noted that Senegal, Upper Volta and Mauretania impose relatively high tariffs whilst those of Ivory Coast and Mali are more moderate and that of Niger is low.

The degrees of preferences *vis-à-vis* third countries that have been established in CEAO under the TCR by the application of these considerations are naturally very variable, but they are commonly substantial, producing a TCR rate of some 40–60 per cent of the corresponding effective import duty charge. In a smaller number of cases, the preferences are much higher, producing in one or two instances abatements of the order of 90 per cent, while in yet other cases only very modest preferences, of some 10 per cent or thereabouts, have been conceded to originating products.

INTRA-CEAO TRADE

What then, is the pattern of trade amongst the CEAO countries, which for *produits de cru* and manufactures of local origin is underpinned by the arrangements which have been described? Although aggregate data on recorded trade among CEAO countries are unreliable, partly because of the inconsistent treatment of transit items, it is not open to doubt that the two more advanced coastal members, Ivory Coast and Senegal, typically enjoy substantial favourable balances whilst the other countries are all substantially in deficit.

Dependable statistics are available for intra-Community exchanges of manufactured products. Table 8.2 relates to such exchanges, whether or not the products concerned are subject to TCR. It can be seen that total trade in manufactured products amounted to some 20000 million. fr. CFA. Of this total, Ivory Coast and Senegal together accounted for about 98 per cent of total intra-group exports and trade between those two countries amounted to about a quarter of this component of total intra-Community trade. Both Ivory Coast and Senegal enjoyed substantial favourable trade balances on their intra-Community trade in manufactures, while the other countries incurred varying but substantial

TABLE 8.2 *Intra-Community trade balances in manufactured products 1976 (m. fr. CFA)*

	Exports	Imports	Balance
Ivory Coast	10 316	3 038	+ 7 278
Upper Volta	194	2 394	− 2 200
Mali	182	7 158	− 6 976
Mauretania	3	4 153	− 4 149
Niger	58	1 405	− 1 347
Senegal	10 030	2 636	+ 7 394
	20 784	**20 784**	−

SOURCE Adapted from *Rapport d'Activité*, CEAO; 1977/78.

deficits. Between Ivory Coast and Senegal, trade in manufactures was roughly in balance.

In the context of CEAO, particular interest attaches to that part of intra-Community trade in manufactures which is subject to TCR. For 1978 the total value of imports subject to the TCR amounted to 7886 m. fr. The principal importer was Niger, which accounted for about 31 per cent of the total, followed by Mali, which accounted for 27 per cent, and Upper Volta whose share was about a quarter. The two more advanced members, namely Ivory Coast and Senegal, accounted for relatively modest shares of these imports, namely 6.9 and 4.6 per cent respectively, but this results from the exclusion from the TCR regime until 1st January 1979 of bilateral trade between those two countries under an agreement which antedates the establishment of the CEAO. This trade represented a very high proportion of total intra-group trade in manufactures and a still higher proportion of trade potentially eligible for TCR treatment. From 1979 this trade has been incorporated into the TCR system.

The commodity composition of intra-Community trade in products subject to the TCR is also of interest. In 1978 cotton thread and cloth accounted for about a quarter of the trade, while coffee extract and lubricating oil, of roughly equal importance, jointly accounted for between a fifth and a quarter of the total. The remaining products traded were diverse. Among the more important categories are plastic products, vehicle parts, household enamel ware, footwear, cigarettes, bicycle tyres and tubes, biscuits, beer and plywood. The product groups enumerated accounted in 1978 for three-quarters of intra-group trade in TCR products. In almost every case the principal sources of supply were Ivory Coast and Senegal.

FISCAL COMPENSATION AND THE DISTRIBUTION OF COSTS AND BENEFITS

One of the most important respects in which the CEAO differs from its two predecessors – UDAO and UDEAO – is that provision is made for the payment of fiscal compensation for revenue losses. These provisions represent an attempt to alleviate important economic problems which typically arise in customs unions and economic groupings – see Chapter 2.

The need for some such measures – though not necessarily of this form – stems from the fact that economic integration among developing countries typically gives rise to distributional problems, which, if not dealt with, may ultimately disrupt the bloc – as indeed resulted with the predecessors of CEAO. Firstly, the static costs of trade diversion often fall disproportionately on the least developed members. Secondly, the least developed members may also be exposed to net adjustment costs and, indeed, enduring costs from trade creation, if, unlike the case assumed in the neoclassical theory of integration, resources are immobile and unemployment exists. Thirdly, disproportionate costs may arise for the least developed members in particular, in the shape of a reduction in their freedom to protect new industries because of the constraints imposed on their use of tariff and other policy instruments by their membership obligations.

It is unlikely that these problems of balance and equity can be wholly satisfactorily resolved without an effective regional policy, perhaps embodying administrative control over industrial development and its location, or at least the adoption of market instruments having a similar effect. No regional group has yet developed wholly adequate policies in these areas, but several, including CEAO, have tried to alleviate the problem of the imbalance in the costs of trade liberalisation by resort to fiscal compensation.

In CEAO fiscal compensation is payable by reference to revenue losses arising in the process of trade liberalisation. Its rationale is nevertheless not to offset revenue losses *per se*, but to offset the impact or static costs of trade diversion, which themselves represent losses of national income. These costs arise whenever, as a result of preferences, imports from a member country replace imports from a lower-cost source outside the group. If then, because of a polarisation of economic development and wide disparities in the levels of economic development of the participants, intra-group trade is markedly unbalanced, as it is in CEAO, a convincing case for compensation can be made out and there is justification for basing it on revenue losses (Robson, 1980, pp. 179–80).

Under the Treaty, fiscal compensation is payable to member states in respect of the revenue losses deemed to be incurred as a result of the provision of intra-Community preferences under the TCR. These losses are defined as the difference between the duties which would be imposed on a product imported from a third country not subject to '*droit de douane*' and the duties imposed under the TCR regime. The *droit de douane* is a relatively small component of the fiscal import duties charged by the members of CEAO – now 5 per cent – and was in effect the means by which a two-column tariff was operated.

Required inter-budgetary transfers are effected through the FCD. The Treaty provides for compensation as of right to be paid to each member state to the extent of two-thirds of its assessed losses. A further amount equal to one-third of the aggregate assessed losses is distributed on a discretionary basis among member states to support national development projects of Community interest. The distribution of this discretionary part of FCD is determined by the Conference of heads of state. For the initial five-year period, it was decided to distribute it solely amongst the least industrialised members, that is, Niger, Upper Volta, Mauretania and Mali, according to a key which reflected their relative GNPs per capita (1976 Acte No. 12/76, CEAO *Journal Officiel*, no. 3, 1976).

Table 8.3 illustrates the forecasted operation of FCD for the year 1976, based on the Secretariat's initial estimates of trade and of revenue losses. On this basis it can be seen that the operations of FCD in 1976 would have resulted in a net redistribution of fiscal resources towards the least-developed member states of some 1.5 billion fr. CFA. Two-thirds of the transfer would have been in the form of an untied budgetary transfer, whilst the remaining one-third would have taken the form of earmarked payments to support specified national development projects. For 1976, supported projects included equipment for customs services, urban water supply, animal health projects and industrial promotion centres.

With transactions at this level, FCD's operations would hardly be of major budgetary importance for the member states, and the contribution to balance and integration which could have been made by the FCD at these levels would be modest. For the two net contributory countries, namely Ivory Coast and Senegal, the calculated contributions are equivalent to some 0.7 per cent and 0.9 per cent of their respective ordinary budgets. For the recipients, the calculated amounts receivable are rather more significant, being equivalent in total to 3.3 per cent of

TABLE 8.3   *CEAO Community Development Fund (FCD) 1976 (M. Fr. CFA)*

| | Estimated intra-CEAO industrial exports | | Contribution to moins-value | Estimated receipts | | | | | | Estimated net contribution (+) or receipts (−) | |
| | Value | % of total | | Fiscal compensation | | Support for development projects | | Total amount receivable | | Amount | As % of budget revenue |
				Amount	% of total	Amount	% of total	Amount	% of total		
Ivory Coast	15 700.1	60.8	1 385.7	403.8	26.6	–	–	403.8	18.6	+981.9	0.7
Upper Volta	341.5	1.3	30.1	421.2	27.7	206.6	31.8	627.8	28.9	−597.7	3.3
Mali	403.0	1.6	35.6	122.4	8.1	206.6	31.8	329.0	15.2	−293.4	1.3
Mauretania	1.6	(0.008)	0.2	299.2	19.7	76.1	11.7	375.3	17.3	−375.1	(1.6)
Niger	110.3	(0.4)	9.7	146.7	9.6	160.7	24.7	307.4	14.2	−297.7	1.4
Senegal	9 282.9	35.9	819.3	126.7	8.3	–	–	126.9	5.8	+692.4	0.9
	25 839.4	100.0	2 280.6	1 520.4	100.0	650.0	100.0	2 170.2	100.0	Net +110.4	

SOURCE   Derived from initial Secretariat forecasts of industrial exports, and of trade in manufactures subject to the TCR.

NOTE   15 per cent of the 1/3rd of *moins-value* allocated to national development projects (= 110.4m. Fr.) is retained for reserve or other purposes.

budgetary revenue in the case of Upper Volta, 1.3 per cent for Mali and 1.4 per cent for Niger. Ivory Coast's net contribution was equivalent to about 6.3 per cent of the value of its total industrial exports to the Community and for Senegal the corresponding figure was 7.5 per cent.

In the event, the initial estimates proved to be over-optimistic and the sums initially available for discretionary compensation were much smaller. Recognition of the limited contribution which could be made to the promotion of balance by FCD subsequently led the Heads of State at their meeting at Bamako in October 1978 to agree to establish an additional instrument of economic cooperation in the shape of a solidarity fund – le Fonds de Solidarité et d'Intervention pour le Développement de la Communauté Economique de l'Afrique de l'Ouest (FOSIDEC). The object of FOSIDEC is to promote the economic development of member states and to contribute to the regional balance of the Community by financing loans, guarantees for loans, grants participations and Community studies. In its activities FOSIDEC is required to give priority to the least developed member states. For the initial two-year period 1977–78 FOSIDEC was financed by capital contributions from member states amounting to 5000 million fr. CFA. Subsequently, FOSIDEC is to receive aggregate annual contributions of 1500 million fr. CFA. The establishment of FOSIDEC equips CEAO with financial institutions for compensation and development comparable in scope to those of the ECOWAS Fund for Compensation, Cooperation and Development. If it is permitted to function in the spirit of its objectives, it could provide a useful supplement to the resources otherwise available for promoting the development of the least developed members of the group, although the extent of the priority to be enjoyed by these members in the operations of FOSIDEC has not been specified.

The operations of FCD itself would have been much larger during the initial quinquennium than in fact they were but for the treatment accorded to trade between Senegal and Ivory Coast, much of which took place free of duties, under an existing bilateral agreement dating from 1971. A decision of the heads of state in 1973 excluded effectively this bilateral trade from the creation of *moins value* or compensation payments during the period in question, although it was included in the base used for determining relative contributions to FCD. This arrangement was not extended on its expiry on 1 January 1979. From that date onwards, trade between Senegal and Ivory Coast will have resulted in *moins value* and compensation payments, to the extent that preferences are granted under the TCR. If, upon the incorporation of this trade into the TCR system, the previous arrangements had otherwise continued, the amounts available for redistribution through FCD to the least developed members would have become much greater. However, with the integration of this previously excluded trade into the Community's compensatory operations (at the insistence of the least developed members), a revised basis was adopted for dealing with that part of FCD's receipts (one-third in all) which, not being automatically applied to compensation for revenue losses, is available in principle to support discretionary redistributive payments. The effects of the changes are not yet clear, but, since Ivory Coast and Senegal have become eligible for payments from this source, this factor is likely to limit the benefits which the least-developed countries might otherwise have received from discretionary transfers although these could still be substantial. It is clear, however, that the effect of CEAO's fiscal arrangements during the first five years has been to compensate Niger, Upper Volta, Mali and Mauretania to the extent of more than 100 per cent of their calculated revenue losses.

Any assessment of whether these or any other similar arrangements could be viewed as equitable must obviously depend not merely on their purely *fiscal* or financial effects, but also on their *economic* implications, for it is the latter which will determine the resulting distribution of the burdens and the benefits.

If this kind of fiscal compensation arrangement is judged solely in terms of the extent to which it resolves the problem of the static costs of trade diversion, a major consideration must be how the prices of the products enjoying preferential treatment are affected as a result of the preferences accorded.

If export prices rise fully to reflect the tariff preference, exporting countries would not lose real income, but might lose budget revenue through their need to make provision for the fiscal transfers. The rise in the taxable incomes of exporters, if accessible, would operate to some degree to offset this. Those countries which are net importers, on the other hand, would require substantially full compensation for revenue losses if their public revenues (and real national incomes) were not to be reduced by preferential trade, as compared with their positions under a non-discriminatory tariff (whether this is the appropriate *anti-monde* for evaluating the costs and benefits of an integration arrangement is, however, debatable).

If, perhaps more realistically, it is assumed that the prices of exports do not rise by the full amount of the preference, either in the short or long run, then exporting countries would bear some of the real, as well as the fiscal, burden of compensation and, on the other hand, the 'static' argument for providing importing countries with full compensation in respect of preferential imports would fall away.

In the case of CEAO, such comparisons require further qualification since compensation payments and receipts are related to a purely theoretical and lower measure of preference which is calculated by reference to import duties other than the *droit de douane*. Yet the bulk of the Community's imports come from the EC, whose products are now subject to that levy to varying extents. The basis of calculation specified will tend to benefit net exporting countries at the expense of net importing countries. Upper Volta is a special case because its revenue losses were calculated by reference to an import duty tariff which implicitly included internal indirect taxes until the implementation of the fiscal reforms to be discussed in the concluding section.

In a broader perspective, other considerations may also become important, if not indeed decisive. Preferential trade arrangements such as these do not merely result in the reallocation of a given volume of trade, but also in trade expansion, which indeed is a major rationale for market integration. If, in an exporting country, existing production is not merely sold at a higher price but in addition output is also expanded, its gains may exceed the value of the preferential margin, because of the resulting expansion of output and employment. Similarly, if, for an importing country, the relevant alternative to importing from a partner is not to import from the rest of the world but to produce the good domestically, the opportunity cost of imports, even in real income terms and still more perhaps in terms of broader public objectives foregone, may well exceed the aggregate value of the preferential margin. To take these factors into account would involve an attempt to evaluate the overall costs and benefits of integration. This cannot be undertaken merely by looking at the impact effect of a particular arrangement on national income, but would also have to take into account a multiplicity of ends of public policy, including the creation of a more balanced economic structure, modernisation and economic stability.

At the stage presently reached by CEAO however, it is unlikely that many of these broader considerations are relevant. The Community's trade and customs arrangements have not yet seriously impaired the domestic autonomy of any of its least-developed members, principally because levels of tariff protection are not yet uniform and also because the degree of intra-Community preference accorded to partners through the TCR is, in any case, entirely a mattter for negotiation. From this perspective, at least up to 1979, CEAO's fiscal arrangements might be said to represent a not unsatisfactory arrangement for its least developed members. If tariffs and other policy instruments become harmonised, however, an entirely different situation could be created.

PROGRESS AND PROBLEMS

Eight years have elapsed since the Treaty of Abidjan came into force. What progress has been made during this period towards the implementation of the provisions of the Treaty and the attainment of general Community goals and what are the principal problems now confronting the Community?

In the basic field of customs, substantial progress has evidently been made towards implementing the Treaty's provisions. A common customs and statistical nomenclature has been adopted and those provisions of the Treaty relating to the allocation of revenues of a conventional customs union type appear to be operating satisfactorily. Although a CET is not yet in sight, agreement has been reached on the introduction of a simplified and harmonised structure for customs duties and other indirect taxes. Subsequently, each member state agreed to adopt a uniform *droit de douane* of 5 per cent and a single supplementary fiscal import duty, so bringing the total effective import duty up to the level of the charges previously imposed in diverse form. This measure of simplification clears the way for the ultimate unification of the supplementary fiscal duty, which would then produce a CET.

The measures for trade expansion, involving the duty-free circulation of most *produits de cru* and preferential treatment for industrial products originating in the area, have also been largely implemented and a substantial amount of intra-group trade is being undertaken. Although it is not possible to estimate how much is due to the Treaty provisions, it is unlikely that intra-group trade in manufactures between Ivory Coast and Senegal on the one hand and the less developed members on the other would have been anything like as great without the trade preferences which have been adopted.

The related objective of eliminating quantitative restrictions upon intra-group trade has not, however, been fully attained so far. It seems that with the possible exception of Upper Volta, which appears to have implemented the Agreement in letter and spirit, each member state has operated some trade restrictions in defiance of the provisions of the Treaty and subsequent decisions. The restrictions in question usually take the form of import certificates, which are claimed not always to be freely issued. Restrictions of this kind have been particularly prevalent in the textile industry where excess capacity exists. Ivory Coast, Senegal, Mali and Niger have all imposed restrictions in this case. Restrictions are not limited to textiles, however, and have also been imposed on other manufacture including confectionery and pneumatic tyres.

In the field of *produits de cru*, some restrictions are also operated. A particularly contentious instance is Ivory Coast's practice of limiting green coffee exports and of charging higher prices for the exported product than is charged to domestic processors.

The expansion of intra-Community trade in manufactures has evidently been greatly facilitated by the fiscal compensation arrangements which effectively relieve the less developed states of the real costs of trade diversion. One of the supposed merits of the particular device adopted is that by avoiding any direct link between compensation payments and preference margins received by any state, it should overcome an obvious constraint to trade liberalisation negotiations. The fact remains, however, that Ivory Coast and Senegal finance the bulk of the required contributions and are aware of it. In considering the accession of new products to the TCR regime, therefore, the additional fiscal costs falling on those countries can hardly fail to enter into their calculations, and this appears, at times, to have led to a reluctance on the part of each of those countries to agree to the inclusion of certain products into the TCR system.

With respect to the products which do receive preferences, however, it may be concluded that since the less developed members are effectively compensated for the full cost of trade diversion (and more in the initial five years), and since also the obligations and constraints imposed upon the development policies of these states are so far minimal, it is unlikely that they are disadvantaged by the trade liberalisation provisions of the Treaty. At the same time the two major exporters derive net benefits in terms of an expansion of real domestic income, although probably at some budgetary cost.

Whether the resulting pattern of trade properly reflects the competitive advantages of the respective producers (subject to the necessary distributional constraints imposed by the member states) is difficult to judge. In terms of 'revealed comparative advantage' as reflected in market performance in non-preferential third markets, both Ivory Coast and Senegal clearly enjoy productive superiority over their neighbours. In part, however, that performance reflects a variety of distortions which are produced by investment incentive legislation – as does the performance of those countries in the Community itself.

Systematic evidence on relative costs of production for all countries of the group is lacking, but for Ivory Coast, Senegal and Mali some material is available from an IBRD study (Balassa, 1978) on incentives and resource costs in the early seventies in those countries. In suggesting that Senegal and Ivory Coast differ in their respective productive efficiencies in different sectors, but that, unsurprisingly, both are superior to Mali, this study provides confirmation of the potential gains to be derived from integration despite the frequent similarities to be found in the resource-base of member countries.

The emergent pattern of specialisation in the CEAO, of course, is likely to be influenced not only by the factors discussed already, but also by the policies of transnational enterprises which operate in several countries, in part (as in textiles) through interlocking financial participations. Where transnationals operate in several countries, they are perhaps in a position to operate more international specialisation on lines of production in the interests of cost minimisation, while still effectively meeting the demands of national policy, than could wholly independent producers. This outcome does not appear to have occurred to any marked extent, however. Indeed, in most sectors of industry there is a noticeable replication of plants (sometimes belonging to the same transnational enterprise) each of which operates on a smaller scale and on a less specialised basis than would otherwise be appropriate. In this way, it may be that some of the advantages of regional integration, which derive from the exploitation of scale economies, are being dissipated. Uneconomic replication has certainly occurred in textiles (despite the interlocking links of many of the enterprises involved), batteries, pharmaceuticals and plastics. To a degree, this result must reflect constraints imposed by government policy, but it appears also to reflect the importance of the risk factor. The purely national markets of the smaller countries are usually too small to permit them, should a disruption of the Community occur, to absorb the output of a large plant limited to a narrow range of intermediate or final products.

If the achievements of CEAO are apparent, its limitations are equally so. The Community has grown out of an orthodox trade liberalisation bloc and its significant achievements are still largely confined to this sphere, despite the declared intention of its member states to broaden their cooperation and to establish an economic community. There has been a marked lack of progress in giving effect to the measures of positive integration which were foreshadowed in the Treaty. Indeed, even with respect to the basic objective of establishing a uniform degree of external tariff protection in the area, progress has been slow.

In that particular respect, a CET is to be established within 12 years of the coming into force of the Treaty, i.e. by January 1985. Preparatory measures already adopted include: the introduction of a common tariff and statistical nomenclature; the simplification of the indirect tax systems and the adoption of a uniform *droit de douane* of 5 per cent. The time taken to complete even these relatively uncontroversial and largely technical changes does not suggest that it will be easy to attain a CET by 1985.

The immensity of this task invites consideration of a more limited alternative approach to tariff harmonisation, namely to concentrate effort on securing a CET only for those products in which trade is currently significant or capable of becoming so in the near future. This approach would substantially limit the range of required negotiations, but could yield many of the benefits of a CET. The Community would retain the appearance of a free trade area to the extent that many external tariffs might differ, but uniformity would exist for items of Community origin which are significantly traded in the region. This step could be coupled with an agreement requiring tariffs to be harmonised also (a) on the products of any newly established industries as a precondition of their eligibility for the TCR regime and (b) on crucial imported intermediate inputs. A sectoral or designated product approach to trade liberalisation of this kind is, in general, open to the objection that it may entail serious allocation distortions for a regional economy. In CEAO, however, the limited extent of inter-industry linkages suggests that for the moment little weight need be given to this consideration until industrial development and internal integration have been carried a good deal further.

However, an important object of adopting a CET – even if limited to certain designated products – is to provide a uniform measure of protection to Community industries, thus promoting an optimal allocation of resources in the region. This objective cannot be assured unless fiscal incentives are also harmonised, since it would otherwise remain open to any member to alter unilaterally the measure of protection effectively afforded by a given external tariff. The Treaty in fact provides that its members will seek to harmonise fiscal incentives, and proposals were to have been submitted to the heads of state within two years of the coming into force of the Treaty, but this has not been done. An external study of incentive laws has been undertaken, but scarcely furnishes a basis for action. Incentive harmonisation is in any event a highly sensitive policy area. So long as the Community's activities remain so restricted, a comprehensive CET is unlikely to be acceptable to all members, unless at the same time a substantial degree of national autonomy is preserved with respect to fiscal incentives.

From these points of view, an increasingly apparent deficiency of the Community lies in the absence of any formulated industrial policy. Indeed, until some preliminary agreement has been reached on basic issues of industrial policy, it is difficult to see how constructive advances can be made with respect to either tariffs or fiscal incentives, since at Community level incentive policy must reflect industrial policy and give effect to it. So far, some preliminary consideration has been given to the issues involved in drawing up a statute for multinational enterprises (one result of which may be to narrow the concept of originating products) and also to the issues involved in regional industrial development, but a detailed study of industrialisation policy options has not yet commenced. Meanwhile, industrial developments continue to be initiated which largely replicate existing developments elsewhere, often in sectors such as that of textiles which Mauretania is about to enter, where surplus capacity already exists. Developments such as these underline the need to give urgent attention to the feasibility of industrial co-ordination if the production and cost-advantages of regional integration are not to be dissipated.

As for the fields of agriculture and transport – the latter notably ill-adapted to serve intra-Community trade – it is difficult to discern any notable contributions of a specifically Community, as opposed to a purely national, character which have been made within these sectors of activity. However, one promising development is that a number of regional institutions – mainly in the field of higher education and research – have finally reached the stage of detailed feasibility studies, and external financing for them has been negotiated on a Community basis.

The issues discussed to this point are specific to CEAO. There are evidently other matters which arise from the broader context of the operations of CEAO, and of certain of its members, which deserve mention in any appraisal of the prospects of the bloc.

Regional economic integration is necessarily to some extent an inward-looking policy. For the least-developed members of the CEAO there is probably no practicable alternative to such a policy for a long time to come, if they are to accelerate industrialisation and to promote a more balanced economic structure without incurring excessive costs. The situation is possibly otherwise for the Ivory Coast, which has a strong record of industrialisation behind it in the past twenty years and which has already developed a diversified, if limited, export trade in

West Africa outside CEAO. If policy reappraisals were to induce Ivory Coast to adopt a more outward-looking policy, in the interests of maintaining and accelerating its industrial growth, the required changes in the structure and level of its tariffs and incentives might well not be compatible with the needs of CEAO. At the very least, the adoption of such a policy might induce Ivory Coast to give less weight in future to the maintenance of its links with CEAO. If that were to happen, the cohesion of CEAO could be in doubt.

At a broader level, a major question mark overhanging CEAO concerns its relations with the emergent bloc of ECOWAS, to which all of its members also belong. This is acceptable so long as their obligations to CEAO do not actually conflict with those towards ECOWAS. The ultimate objectives of the two groups are indeed similar, although their approaches in certain respects differ. Until recently, however, there appears to have been little coordination between the two institutions, and despite the overlapping national membership of relevant bodies in the two at technical and political levels, measures in particular fields have sometimes been shaped by one organisation without taking adequate account of existing or projected measures in the other. For instance, the tariff nomenclatures recently adopted by each group are similar but not identical; their fiscal compensation provisions are similar in objectives and administrative procedures, but are not identical in content, and are not immediately compatible; rules of origin are not identical. These differences must constitute an obstacle to the assimilation of the operations of the two groups.

A question which clearly cannot be avoided is whether there can be a continuing role for CEAO if ECOWAS is successful. It seems entirely reasonable to suppose that even if ECOWAS makes good progress, there could still be an enduring role for CEAO in fostering a more intimate form of cooperation amongst the smaller group than could be envisaged in ECOWAS for many years to come, if at all. To make this possible, however, certain modifications would in due course be required in CEAO in several fields, including compensation and trade liberalisation, or alternatively exceptions or waivers from compliance with the Lagos Treaty would have to be sought.

Meanwhile, the odds against any early implementation of the Treaty of Lagos are such that the interests of the member-states of CEAO are unlikely to be served by postponing further attempts to advance towards more effective integration amongst themselves. It remains to be seen whether CEAO's principal members, beset as they now are by increasingly pressing domestic economic problems, will be inclined to try to impart a further impetus to the economic integration of the group, except for reasons of zonal political stability. The external intervention experienced by several West African states in the concluding stages of 1980 would, however, make it unsurprising if the political factor were in future to play a much more supportive role in underpinning the evolution of the group.

But even without new initiatives, however motivated, CEAO could survive, for its flexible techniques of cooperation – unlike those used in some other blocs – do not appear to depend for their stability on the adoption of further measures of policy harmonisation. But the price of a failure to embark on further measures of effective integration would clearly be a much diminished scope for exploiting its potential gains.

NOTES

1. The countries initially involved were Benin, Ivory Coast, Niger, Upper Volta (four of the five members of the Council of the Entente States), Mali, Mauretania and Senegal (the three members of OERS). Togo (the fifth member of the Entente), a former French Trust Territory and traditionally favouring a policy of free trade, was not a member of the institutions established within this framework. However, it has been represented by an observer at some of their proceedings. Benin, which had signed the Treaty, decided to withdraw from CEAO in 1973 but like Togo, asked for and obtained the status of an observer member.

9 The Caribbean Community
Kenneth O. Hall

BACKGROUND

The Caribbean Community (CARICOM) comprises twelve Commonwealth Caribbean countries: Antigua, Barbados, Belize, Dominica, Grenada, Guyana, Jamaica, Montserrat, St Kitts-Nevis-Anguilla, St Lucia, St Vincent and Trinidad and Tobago. The Bahamas, though not a member of the community, participates in many of its activities and other Caribbean countries such as Surinam, Cuba, and Haiti participate on an *ad hoc* basis in specific areas. The Treaty of Chaguaramas establishing CARICOM in 1973 is the most recent stage of a long history of efforts to promote political unity, economic integration and other forms of cooperation between the member countries. Two broad categories of efforts have been made in the past. The first, which was aimed primarily at political unity and pursued by the British government since the early period of settlement in the seventeenth century, culminated in the West Indies Federation in 1958. The Federation lasted only four years and collapsed in 1962 (Mordecai, 1968; Wallace, 1977). One of the main purposes of the Federation was the creation of an infrastructure which was thought at the time to be the essential prerequisite of independence as it was felt that none of the islands individually had the capability of assuming the responsibilities of independence unilaterally (Proctor, 1956). With the collapse of the Federation, however, Jamaica and Trinidad became independent in 1962 and by 1980 all the countries except Montserrat, Belize and Antigua had become independent. Antigua and Belize are expected to become independent by 1982.

The collapse of the Federation did not end the efforts at cooperation but inaugurated a new thrust with the Caribbean governments themselves taking the initiative. This stage was dominated by issues of economic integration. The Caribbean Free Trade Association (CARIFTA) was established in 1968 to promote free trade among the member countries (Brewster and Thomas, 1967; Caribbean Community Secretariat 1971; Demas, 1976; McIntyre, 1965). Although it was relatively successful in freeing trade between the countries and stimulating a greater volume of exports especially in manufactured products, by 1972 CARIFTA was generally seen as inadequate to meet the needs of economic integration among the member states. It was then decided that a more comprehensive scheme of economic integration was essential to achieve the purposes of economic development for the region (Caribbean Community Secretariat, 1972).

CARICOM then is an outgrowth of this long period of cooperation and to that extent it reflects the legacies of those efforts (Hall and Blake, 1978). Like its predecessors, CARICOM is intended to overcome the specific limitations of small developing island states as well as the constraints on development characteristic of all developing countries (Demas, 1974a). In general, the Caribbean region is characterised by under-development, fragmentation and a high degree of external dependence. CARICOM is a very small area with a population of just over five million people (see Table 9.1 for basic statistics) and a total GDP of 7688 million US dollars. In specific economic terms, these countries have high rates of unemployment ranging from 20 to 50 per cent, and a high concentration of export commodities with petroleum, bauxite, alumina and sugar accounting for 87 per cent of CARICOM's export earnings. Furthermore there are few linkages within and between the different national economies, with foreign ownership and control playing a dominant role in sectors such as manufacturing and tourism (Beckford, 1975; Girvan and Jefferson, 1971).

Although all the countries share these common characteristics there is a considerable disparity in resource endowments and stages of economic development between the twelve members. For this reason CARICOM is divided into two groups of countries, the more developed countries (MDCs) of Jamaica, Trinidad and Tobago, Guyana and Barbados and the less developed countries (LDCs) comprising the other eight members. Together the MDCs have over 90 per cent of the land area, account for over 87 per cent of the population and labour force and 90 per cent of the technical and managerial skills. They also have all the known significant mineral resources such as oil, gas and bauxite as well as the best of the agricultural land (Farrell, 1977). The economic rationale of CARICOM has therefore had to pay special attention to the traditional gains of economic integration but has also placed priority on developmental objectives as well as on the equitable distribution of the gains (Blake, 1976; Caribbean Community Secretariat, 1973).

The objectives of CARICOM and the areas in which it pursues activities, therefore, reflect both the historical traditions of close cooperation in economic and non-economic areas as well as a desire to promote development through a strategy of economic integration. It pursues activities in three broad areas: economic integration, functional cooperation and coordination of foreign policies. Its specific objectives are (Article 4, Treaty of Chaguaramas, 1973):

(a) the economic integration of the Member States to the establishment of a common market regime (hereinafter referred to as 'the Common Market'), in accordance with the provisions of the Annex to this Treaty, with the following aims:

   (i) the strengthening, coordination and regulation of the economic and trade relations among member states in order to promote their accelerated, harmonious and balanced development;
   (ii) the sustained expansion and continuing integration of economic activities, the benefits of which shall be equitably shared taking into account the need to provide special opportunities for the less developed countries;
   (iii) the achievement of a greater measure of economic independence and effectiveness by its member states in dealing with third countries, groups of states and entities of whatever description;

(b) the coordination of the foreign policies of member states and
(c) functional cooperation, including:

   (i) the efficient operation of certain common services and activities for the benefit of its people;
   (ii) the promotion of greater understanding among its people and the advancement of their social, cultural and technological development;
   (iii) activities in the fields specified in the schedule and referred to in Article 18 of this Treaty.

To carry out these objectives it has set up a number of institutions such as the Heads of Government Conference, the Common Market Council,

TABLE 9.1 *Basic indicators for CARICOM countries (latest year available)*

	Less developed countries (LDCs)			
	Antigua	*Dominica*	*Grenada*	*Mont-serrat**
1977				
Rate of unemployment (per cent estimated)	20.0	23.0	15.0–20.0	4.7
1974				
Population (thousands)	69.8	76.2	107.6	11.6
GDP at factor cost (m. US $)	55.9	27.9	36.0	6.3
GDP per capita (US $)	801.0	366.0	335.0	537.5
Agriculture as per cent of GDP	6.9	37.8	24.9	16.0
Exports as per cent of GDP¶	45.7	32.0	23.8	19.3
Imports as per cent of GDP ¶	85.7	61.8	50.8	60.2
Agricultural exports (% of total goods exports)	1.5	93.0	98.6	80.1
Tourism (% of total exports)**	21.6	14.3	10.1††	89.3
Tax revenue (% of GDP)	15.8	23.7	15.6	17.2
Area (square kilometers)	441.6	787.4	344.5	102.3
Population density (persons per square kilometer)	158.1	96.8	312.3	113.4
Arable land (square kilometers)	267.9	219.5	240.2	23.7
Arable land per capita (hectares)	0.38	0.29	0.22	0.20
1971				
Investment as % of GDP	19.3	29.2	26.4	28.7
Public investment (as % of total investment)‡‡	21.0	60.8	74.8	60.2

n.a. = not available.

NOTES   Except for calculations of GDP at factor cost, GDP per capita, and agriculture as a percent of GDP, the ratios are calculated from data at current market prices.

  * Except for the data on agricultural exports, the latest available data for Montserrat are for 1971.
  † The data are for 1971, except the data on population and agricultural exports, which are for 1974. The 1971 population figure was, however, used to estimate the 1971 GDP per capita.
  ‡ For 1971.
  § For 1972.
  ‖ The 1972 population figure was used to estimate the 1972 GDP per capita.
  ¶ Export and import data for the LDCs exclude nonfactor services.
  ** Total exports comprises exports of goods and tourism.
  †† Includes hotels only.
  ‡‡ For the LDCs, it is the ratio of public capital expenditure to gross capital formation, so that the ratio may be somewhat higher than the actual share of public investment in total investment.

SOURCE   Statistical Appendix and World Bank country reports.

TABLE 9.1 (*continued*)

LDCs (cont.)		More developed countries (MDCs)					
St Kitts	St Lucia	St Vincent	Belize†	Barbados	Guyana	Jamaica	Trinidad and Tobago
13.5	18.0	18.0	4.7	7.7‡	12.8‡	11.3‡	22.0‡
46.8	108.0	91.0	136.0	241.0	791.0	2 008.0	1 070.0
26.4	54.2	34.1	68.9	185.8§	403.2	2 271.6	953.2§
564.0	502.0	375.0	550.0	777.0§‖	510.0	1 131.0	910.0§‖
30.4	20.6	21.4	15.3	12.4§	30.5	7.8	4.7§
31.2	25.3	13.2	20.0	67.5§	40.6	36.8	38.3§
57.0	74.6	65.9	48.0	91.0§	55.3	45.7	46.8§
48.0	83.4	98.2	82.5	61.7	62.1	19.5	4.2
28.6	34.3	51.5	n.a.	61.5‡	n.a.	19.4‡	14.1‡
21.6	18.5	26.6	12.3	22.3‡	29.0	22.5‡	14.9‡
352.2	616.4	384.0	22 966.0	429.9	215 000.0	11 424.0	5 128.0
132.9	175.2	237.0	5.9	560.6	3.7	175.8	208.7
217.9	480.9	158.4	8 740.0	300.0	31 500.0	4 880.0	1 688.5
0.47	0.45	0.17	6.43	0.12	3.98	0.24	0.16
46.9	48.1	38.8	30.1	24.6	19.4	26.1	29.0
57.7	15.6	63.1	11.1	17.4	35.5	26.0	19.2

the Administrative and Technical Secretariat and a number of ministerial institutions as well as some associate institutions such as the Caribbean Development Bank (CDB) and the University of the West Indies (Geiser *et al.* 1976; Hall and Blake, 1978; Pollard, 1976).

ACHIEVEMENTS AND PROBLEMS

As the objectives which have been outlined above suggest, CARICOM does not fit easily into the standard classifications of different stages of economic integration. Officially it provides for a common market, yet it is clear that two of the three main areas of its activities are not primarily economic although in the context of the Caribbean they are considered as crucial complementary activities if the purely economic objectives are to be achieved. Furthermore the purely economic objectives do not make it easy to classify CARICOM as a free trade area, a customs union, a common market, an economic community or an economic union. In effect it is a hybrid to the extent that elements of all these standard stages are included (Demas, 1974b).

Turning to the common market, provision is made for trade liberalisation, a common protective policy, establishment, services and capital, the coordination of economic policies and development planning and a special regime for the LDCs. Assessment of the progress of economic integration achieved since its inception can best be done by outlining the detailed provisions of these various measures and an examination of the stages achieved in their implementation.

Trade liberalisation is by far the most specific provision of the CARICOM Treaty which stipulates that member countries should remove all duties and other import barriers to trade. By the time CARICOM itself was established in 1973 considerable progress had already been made in that direction. 90 per cent of intra-regional imports between the MDCs and over 80 per cent by the LDCs had been freed of all trade barriers (McIntyre, 1976a, 1976b). The remarkable progress in this area has not been sustained, however, as Jamaica and Guyana imposed quantitative restriction and licensing of intra-regional goods which had the effect of limiting the freedom of trade. Apart from the imposition of quantitative restrictions there have also been complaints by some countries that price controls and the activities of state trading corporations have effectively restricted trading (Republic of Trinidad and Tobago, 1979).

The controversy over these issues has not been effectively resolved although some improvements were made in 1979 when Jamaica increased its quota of intra-regional goods. However, as both Guyana and Jamaica officially declared that their actions were prompted by balance of payments problems rather than by any intention to infringe and restrict trade, it is unlikely that the disputes will disappear in the near future as both countries continue to experience severe balance of payments problems (Girvan, 1977; Ramsaran, 1978).

An important aspect of trade liberalisation deals with the question of common market origins. Two criteria have so far been used. One provides that goods wholly produced in the common market would qualify for free entry into member states. The other is the value added criterion by which goods qualify as a result of a certain amount of value being added in the member states. The experience of the value added criterion which is the principal one used indicates considerable difficulties in that it is difficult to police. More important, it is possible for a manufacturer merely to increase his profit margin to satisfy the minimum value added requirement. These practices have created considerable controversy and have led to complaints that countries have violated both the spirit and the letter of the treaty. Even greater controversy has arisen over the basic materials list which permits certain imported materials to be treated as of CARICOM origin after undergoing very simple processing. The disputes arising from these practices led the common market council in 1977 to adopt a new origin system based on a process criterion by which goods, in order to qualify for free trade treatment, would have to undergo specific processes. Apart from removing the controversy associated with the value added criterion, the new origin system was intended to encourage the greater use of regional raw materials in the manufacture of goods. Unfortunately the new origin rules have not yet been implemented resulting in a considerable amount of uncertainty and scepticism (Caribbean Community Secretariat, 1980).

The liberalisation of trade resulted in a significant expansion of intra-regional trade. Intra-regional exports increased from EC 86 million US dollars in 1967 to EC 222 million US dollars by 1972 and EC 709 million US dollars in 1976. Intra-regional imports increased from EC 96 million US dollars in 1967 to EC 242 million US dollars in 1972 and EC 715 million US dollars in 1976. The figures indicate that the annual rate of growth of intra-regional trade has been consistently higher than the rate of growth for total trade. Equally important is that intra-regional trade as a percentage of total trade increased during the period. It increased from 5 per cent in 1967 to 10.3 per cent in 1973 and although it fell to 7.3 per cent in 1974, by 1976 it had recovered to 8.3 per cent (Caribbean Community Secretariat, 1980; McIntyre, 1976b). The available data suggest that the intra-regional trade was of both a trade diversion and a trade creation character. The impact of this expansion in trade on various sectors does, however, show considerable disparity. The dynamism for intra-regional trade was primarily in fuels and manufactures. Between 1972 and 1976 CARICOM markets absorbed more than 50 per cent of the region's export of manufactures. In 1975 alone 82 per cent of the total manufacturing export went to CARICOM markets. On the other hand the share of food in intra-regional trade dropped from 28 to 20 per cent between 1967 and 1974.

Apart from the disproportionate percentage of manufactures in regional trade, the geographical distribution indicates that the MDCs were the principal beneficiaries where their share of intra-regional trade amounted to 96 per cent.

Unlike trade liberalisation which has for the most part been implemented, the common protective policy consisting of the common external tariff (CET) and a regime for regional quantitative restrictions has not so far been effectively implemented. It is still considered neither common nor very protective. In practice there are four separate tariffs, the CET for the MDCs, the tariffs for the Eastern Caribbean Common Market countries, the Belize Tariff and the Montserrat Tariff. A certain commonality existed between the four separate tariffs in 1973 and it was stipulated that a phasing in of all the tariffs should begin in 1977 and end in 1981. Although the tariff was restructured into a single column tariff to satisfy external factors, the phasing in has not yet commenced. Eastern Common Market Caribbean countries have decided that they were unprepared to proceed with the phasing in process until they had decided which product would be eligible for higher protection.

In addition the unit of account in which specific rates of duty in the CET among the MDCs was fixed in 1973 has since been eliminated due to the abolition of an official price for gold. Currency fluctuation between member states has consequently meant that no harmonisation of the rates of duty exists at the moment. With regard to the regional quantitative restrictions little or nothing has so far been done to determine which products should be included. In effect the common protective policy has so far not created a framework within which regional production could be given the necessary protection that it was intended to provide.

One of the normal expectations of economic integration is that ultimately there would be the unification of the market for factors of production. CARICOM has provisions under the broad heading of establishment, services and movement of capital. The treaty does not, however, contemplate the free movement of workers and capital. It does commit governments to an examination of ways and means to introduce a scheme for the regulated movement of capital. At the same time it was expected that there would be greater movement of resources than had been the case prior to the treaty. Pursuant to that expectation agreement has been reached on the establishment of a regime of CARICOM enterprises which would permit the establishment of regional companies in certain priority areas which would have the authority to draw capital from different member states (Caribbean Community Secretariat, 1980). Some countries have also given preferential treatment to the nationals of CARICOM countries over nationals of non-CARICOM countries in respect of the establishment of economic enterprises and the establishment of services (Republic of Trinidad and Tobago, 1979).

The question of freedom of movement of persons has not received technical examination and no effort has been made to remove the barriers. This issue has long been a very controversial one in movements of Caribbean integration. Some countries have always advocated freedom of movement while others have very strong reservations, fearing that they would become the recipients of large amounts of unskilled labour which would merely increase their already high unemployment. At the policy level regional technicians have favoured a cautious approach on the assumption that removal of the barriers to free movement of the factors of production including technical personnel would accentuate the tendencies towards polarisation and disparities already so evident in CARICOM. Some of the LDCs are already complaining about the braindrain of skilled and professional people who have migrated to some of the MDCs. It remains to be seen then to what extent CARICOM, through the regime of CARICOM enterprises, will be able to effectively mobilise factors of production and at the same time avoid some of the sensitive political issues which have plagued the whole issue of free movement of factors.

Although trade liberalisation and its effects have tended to dominate CARICOM up to this point, the main benefits of the economic integration in CARICOM were expected to derive from the coordination of economic policies and development planning. Most of the technical studies had concentrated on the complementary development of key productive sectors, agriculture, natural resources, industry and tourism.

At the macro-level very little progress has been made to integrate the productive sectors of the individual economies. CARICOM has approached the issue on a sector by sector basis rather than with the use of a grand macro-economic perspective plan. Thus there is no provision for major regional planning and regional programmes are seen as additions to, rather than as substitutes for national sectoral programmes. At the institutional level the multi-national enterprise has been used as the mechanism for implementation. These enterprises will not, however, undertake the entire regional production but will seek to promote the development of production in member states and operate in a manner similar to management and service companies. The first of these measures was the establishment of the Caribbean Food Corporation (CFC) in 1977 (Hall and Blake, 1976). The corporation is owned by CARICOM governments and has powers to establish branches and subsidiaries in member states in collaboration with member governments or the private sector to produce, process, and distribute food. The CFC has its headquarters in Trinidad and is in the process of recruiting its staff. It is anticipated that the CFC would, over a period of ten years, replace the more than EC $1 billion of food importation in the region in the five categories: meat and livestock, fish, fruit and vegetables, cereals and pulses and animal feeds. Although no investments have so far been made, technical work has been done on project identification in some of these sectors and it is anticipated that some of these projects will be undertaken soon.

In addition to the CFC several proposals have been made for the joint development of natural resources. These include the regional corn/soya-bean project in Guyana involving the governments of Guyana, St Kitts-Nevis-Anguilla and Trinidad and Tobago; the corn/soya-bean project in Belize; and the aluminium smelter project based on bauxite/alumina from Guyana and Jamaica and natural gas from Trinidad to be owned jointly by the three governments. Only the Guyana project has so far been implemented.

In the area of industrial programming progress has been much slower than in agriculture. Substantial technical work has been done on the pulp and paper and the cotton and textile industries but the institutional framework has not reached the point where these studies can be implemented. Efforts are now being made to undertake a technical study similar to that which was used in the regional food plan.

Beyond the expectation that CARICOM would implement complementary production structures, it was also anticipated that there would be greater harmonisation and coordination of economic policies in the specific areas of fiscal incentives to industry, intra-regional and extra-regional double taxation, monetary payments and exchange rate policies and the ownership and control of regional resources, as well as external economic policies. In general, the arrangements do not really contemplate formal convergence of these policies. Nevertheless a long tradition of consultation already exists in some of these areas such as banking and the frequent intra-regional meetings provide opportunities for informal contacts of ministers and officials.

An agreement exists on harmonisation of fiscal incentives to industry but this has not been extended to other areas. There is also a double taxation agreement between the LDCs and one between the LDCs and the MDCs as a group. Recently an agreement was also arrived at for the creation of a Caribbean traveller's cheque. Two of the most important instruments of monetary cooperation have been the clearing facility operated by the monetary authorities and the balance of payments mutual support facility. Under the clearing facility the monetary authorities extend and receive credit which has been extended from three to six months. The facility has been expanded from 20 million US dollars in 1973 to 40 million US dollars in 1977 and 80 million US dollars in 1978. The mutual balance of payment facility was established in 1976 for extension of balance of payment support up to 60 million US dollars in SDRs. Although the facility has not been formally used, balance of payment support of 80 million US dollars was extended to Jamaica by the governments of Barbados, Guyana, Trinidad and Tobago in 1976. Apart from this facility a special emergency fund was created by the MDCs to provide budgetary support to the LDCs. Beyond these specific facilities, little has been done in the other areas of monetary policy.

In the external sphere the treaty does not provide for uniform economic relations with the outside world and the individual countries continue to negotiate economic agreements with third countries on a bilateral basis. In 1975, the heads of governments established a set of procedures of consultation between member governments when they plan to enter into such agreements. Despite the continuation of bilateral economic arrangements with third countries CARICOM has made considerable progress in the development of joint actions and coordinated approaches in their economic relations with some external economic issues. In their negotiations with the EC, CARICOM negotiated as a group. They have adopted similar approaches in their negotiations with Canada and Mexico. It is now also the general practice at international meetings such as UNCTAD, GATT and IMF for the CARICOM countries to coordinate their work and appoint a single spokesman for the group.

One of the main features of the CARICOM arrangement was the establishment of a special regime for the LDCs. Three sets of measures were included (Blake, 1976):

(a) Measures to facilitate LDC exports to the Common Market;
(b) Measures to promote a greater flow of resources into the LDCs; and
(c) Measures to confer greater benefits to the LDCs in certain policy coordination instruments.

In the first category the LDCs are given preferential treatment to promote the export of their goods to the MDCs by reduction of the percentage of the local value added for LDC goods entering MDC markets (a reduction from 50 to 40 per cent). The LDCs are also allowed to provide export subsidies for their export to the MDCs and can impose quantitative restrictions and quotas on MDCs' goods entering their markets.

In the second category the LDCs have a longer time within which to phase into the CET. They can provide longer tax holidays and other fiscal incentives to industry and have a more favourable tax treatment under double taxation agreements. The CDB and the Caribbean Investment Corporation (CIC) are the main instruments through which greater amounts of resources could be transferred to the LDCs. It was informally agreed that the bulk of the soft loans and grants of the CDB would go to the LDCs while the CIC would receive contributions from government and private sources in the MDCs to be used as equity capital in industries in the LDCs.

Despite the existence of these measures it is generally agreed that the LDCs have not been significant beneficiaries of the integration process (Caribbean Community Secretariat, 1977; Godwin and Lake, 1977). Their share of intra-regional trade has declined while very few industrial enterprises have been established in them in spite of the special arrangements. Even in the area of agricultural production in which they were expected to have comparative advantage, the arrangements have not stimulated increased agricultural productivity and problems with the marketing arrangements have tended to place them at even greater disadvantage. Despite the improvements in the CDB's performance since 1975 it is still generally agreed that the volume and quality of resources reaching the LDCs from these two sources are inadequate. For this reason the LDCs have been complaining bitterly in recent times about their adverse position in the integration process and have adopted a negotiating posture that they will not agree to a 'deepening' of the integration process until more effective measures have been adopted to counteract the existing polarisation of economic activities and secure a more equitable distribution of the benefits of integration (Axline, 1978).

ASSESSMENT AND PROSPECTS

Assessment of the progress toward economic integration is one of the most problematic areas of integration studies. In part this derives from the difficulty of identifying a set of criteria which can be sufficiently operationalised as instruments of measurement. This has resulted in a tendency for most integration movements to be measured in terms of their approximation to theoretical models which often do not reflect the practical situation. This is particularly true of integration movements among developing countries where far fewer theoretical formulations have been made than for developed countries. In CARICOM these difficulties are compounded by the multiplicity of objectives, the areas of activities and the absence of a precise time-table within which those objectives are to be achieved.

Notwithstanding these difficulties it is possible, however, to say that CARICOM has not lived up to the expectation of its founders. This is perhaps the only common feature of the assessments made about CARICOM in the published literature, statements by technicians in the organisation, politicians, the regional press and the public at large. This conclusion is borne out by the recent appointment of a 'blue ribbon' committee headed by William Demas, President of the CDB and a former Secretary-General at CARICOM Secretariat,[1] by the Common Market Council to review the functioning of the integration movement and to take recommendations for its improvement in the decade of the 1980s. The very appointment of such a high powered committee, the members of which had all been closely associated with the establishment of the present arrangements, strongly suggests that the initial momentum which was responsible for the transition from CARIFTA to CARICOM has now for the most part dissipated and new measures are required. More important, the terms of reference of the committee cover nearly every area in the economic movement. They include areas which have so far not been implemented as well as new problems and issues such as energy and balance of payment problems which are now thought to be so urgent that the movement can make no further progress without coming to grips with them.

Whether the general atmosphere, as reflected in the appointment of this committee and its comprehensive terms of reference, justifies the predictions that CARICOM is in a stage of crisis facing imminent collapse is difficult to determine. Whatever criteria are used, including the objectives and their attainment, the scope and implementation of decision or theories of developmental integration, it is clear that CARICOM is now at a point of stagnation. Furthermore, measured by its own objectives of integrating the economies of the Caribbean, stimulating economic activities in key areas and reducing the external dependence of the region, it appears that the existing arrangements have not been able to produce the desired results (Axline, 1978; Hall and Blake, 1978; Ramsaran, 1978; Sackey, 1978).

The main debate then surrounding the assessment is really over causes of non-performance as well as predictions about the future based on analysis of those causes. Two schools of thought, with different variations, appear to have emerged in the debate over CARICOM's achievement and its future. There is a neo-functionalist school closely identified with the Secretariat and many regional technocrats who see CARICOM as essentially sound and offering an opportunity for the solution of regional problems through cooperation and integration (Blake, 1979; Demas 1976, 1978; McIntyre, 1977). For them there is a considerable commonality of problems and the long history of cooperation between the countries and constructive achievements will ultimately outweigh the specific difficulties arising from the process of integration. The current difficulties tend to be viewed less as fundamental problems incapable of amicable resolution than as the natural problems associated with closer integration. Their view is that development of the Caribbean is a long term operation and the benefits of integration are unlikely to be realised in the short run; thus the current problems provide the stimulus for further advancement and greater involvement rather than an opportunity to abandon the process. In the opinion of the neo-functionalist some of the current problems are attributable primarily to the international economic crisis and their impact on individual countries through the form of high interest rates, balance of payments difficulties and unemployment. The immediate issue is to find solutions to those pressing short term problems while maintaining the long term view that regional integration is still a viable strategy to achieve the objectives of economic development and reduction of external dependence. The appointment of the Committee referred to above is in keeping with this outlook. As neo-functionalists they assume that greater cooperation and integration is a gradual process which will respond both to the internal dynamics of greater contact as well as to the ability to take account of new developments. Their strategy involves making maximum use of internal and external developments to provide momentum for the achievement of their goals.

The second school, associated more with the structuralist and developmental school and represented primarily by the academic community, see economic integration as a rational strategy only to the extent that it can provide a basis for collective self-reliance through complementary production structures and a reduction of external dependence (Brewster, 1977; Farrell, 1977; Lewis, 1976; Thomas, 1977, 1979). In their view the structure of CARICOM offers very few opportunities and at best is little more than a free trade association which will never overcome the development problems of the Caribbean and which in fact increases the dependence on external sources. The difficulties in CARICOM are viewed not as temporary but fundamental. CARICOM, in their view, was designed for and can only benefit those countries with an industrial base and within those countries the industrial and commercial classes who are closely allied with foreign capital. The conflict between the LDCs and the MDCs over the distribution of benefits is not accidental but a direct consequence of the structural limitations of the regional integration movement. In the future then CARICOM can only stagnate or fail as the internal contradictions become more and more evident.

From whatever point one looks at it, it would appear that the prospects for CARICOM are not very hopeful and indeed several factors provide little ground for overwhelming optimism. Compared to 1973 there is no doubt that the internal dynamism which propelled the movement to its present stage is either in abeyance or lacking. Mention might be made of three developments. First is the absence of close political cooperation that characterised the period in 1973, especially between the leaders of Trinidad and Tobago, Jamaica, Guyana and Barbados. Given the fact that so much of the momentum was provided by the heads of government of these countries and the fact that they have provided the most important thrust for the movement to date, the failure to convene a general heads of government conference since 1975 is damaging, if not necessarily fatal.

A second factor is the severe and prolonged economic problems being experienced in Jamaica and Guyana. These have forced both countries to resort to restrictions on intra-regional trade. Quite apart from the difficulties this state of affairs has created for the trading regime in CARICOM, the crisis has meant that both countries are pre-occupied with solutions to their own problems and are hardly in a position to be involved in any new and major initiative. This must also be seen in the context where the LDCs have been complaining that the benefits of integration so far have not been equitably distributed and they will not be prepared to adopt new measures to further the integration process unless tangible and concrete benefits can be derived. It is questionable whether any major developments can be made towards implementing the objectives of CARICOM in the near future. This is especially important in a context where most of the provisions in the treaty were imprecisely formulated on the understanding that they would be negotiated and implemented over time. It is very unlikely that the package of benefits which were negotiated in 1973 could now be repeated.

The third issue worth mentioning is the question of ideological pluralism which has to some extent determined the development programmes of different countries. In Jamaica, under democratic-socialism, and Guyana, under cooperative socialism, there has been considerable state intervention in the ownership and operation of the economy. In Trinidad and Barbados, on the other hand, private initiatives are still favoured in external and internal trade. In both Jamaica and Guyana, foreign exchange allocations tend to be based on developmental policies in which certain goods are regarded as essential. This is also likely to affect the issue of foreign investment where some countries feel that the solution to their economic problems does not lie in unrestricted foreign investment whereas others with limited capital of their own and smaller markets are much more likely to favour unrestricted foreign investments. Thus differences in economic philosophy and increasingly sharp divisions which have emerged will make the task of maintaining even what has so far been achieved very difficult.

The prospects for CARICOM are not entirely determined by the internal factors but are also linked with external developments. As in other integration movements external factors could either stimulate the process towards greater integration or could have an adverse effect tending towards disintegration. In CARICOM the external factor is particularly important in view of the high degree of dependence on the outside world. External factors were clearly a major motive for the formation of CARICOM in 1973 with the decision of the British government to join the EC and the consequent need of the Caribbean governments to re-negotiate their trading agreements with the EC.

The role of external factors in the future is likely to be even greater, as more and more countries are forced to look outside for solutions to their economic problems. In doing so they tend to be regarded as individual countries and the new groups into which they become involved such as SELA, the Group of 77, the Caribbean Group for Co-operation in Economic Development, have objectives similar to CARICOM and could therefore be competitive or treat individual members not as part of a regional integration movement but as individual entities. For example, the EC, while making some allocations for regional programmes, provides the bulk of its assistance to individual countries and to that extent it is questionable whether economic integration offers a more effective strategy in dealing with international economic issues than individual development. This issue is likely to be more important in the near future as more and more of the LDCs become independent and as individual countries have to seek external solutions to their own economic problems. To a large extent then CARICOM could either become a conduit for external assistance or could be seen as an obstacle to the effective exercise of national sovereignty. Already there has been considerable controversy over the relations between some countries and other third world countries as over the aluminum/bauxite project when agreements between one country and a non-CARICOM country are seen in direct conflict with regional commitments. In brief, the policies pursued by external agencies and countries in the future will, to a large extent, influence CARICOM's viability.

NOTE

1. The members of the Committee include William Demas, President of the Caribbean Development Bank and former Secretary-General of CARICOM Secretariat; Arthur Lewis, Princeton University and former President of the Caribbean Development Bank; Alister McIntyre, Director of Commodities Division, UNCTAD and former Secretary-General of CARICOM Secretariat; S. S. Ramphal, Commonwealth Secretary-General and former Foreign Minister of Guyana; Vaughn Lewis, Director of the Institute of Social and Economic Studies; Edwin Carrington, Deputy Secretary-General, ACP Secretariat and former Director of Trade and Integration, CARICOM Secretariat; Charles Skeete, Director of the Inter-American Development Bank; G. Arthur Brown, Deputy Administrator, UNDP; Kurleigh King, Secretary-General, CARICOM Secretariat.

10 The Latin American Free Trade Association

M. H. J. Finch

INTRODUCTION

In February 1960, seven Latin American countries signed the Treaty of Montevideo to bring into being the Latin American Free Trade Association (LAFTA – Spanish acronym ALALC). They included the three largest economies of the region (Argentina, Brazil and Mexico) as well as Chile, Paraguay, Peru and Uruguay. In 1961 Colombia and Ecuador joined, and with the accessions of Venezuela (1966) and Bolivia (1967) the Area comprised the whole of South America – except for Guyana, Surinam and French Guiana – and Mexico (see Table 10.1 for basic statistics). In its early years the LAFTA arrangements appeared to function well. Nonetheless, by 1967 the scheme had entered the period of stagnation and crisis which it was never able to overcome. In 1969 it was necessary to extend the target date for achievement of regional free trade, while a group of member countries initiated a more ambitious programme of sub-regional integration as the Andean Pact (AP). Successive attempts to renegotiate the Treaty of Montevideo failed, and in 1980 LAFTA finally expired, to be replaced by the Latin American Integration Association (LAIA – Spanish acronym ALADI).

The central concern of this chapter must be to offer an account of the reasons for the failure of the LAFTA scheme. To do so, it is necessary to examine in the first section the motives and circumstances leading to LAFTA in the late 1950s. In the second section the structure and limitations of the Treaty are examined. In the following sections the achievements of LAFTA in its early years, and the reactions to its crisis, are examined. Finally the nature of its failure and the causes of it are diagnosed, and the prospects for regional integration schemes in Latin America are tentatively suggested.

TABLE 10.1   *Size characteristics of LAFTA countries 1978*

	Population (millions)	*Area (thousand km²)*	*GNP (thousand million US $)*	*GNP per capita (US$)*	*Manufacturing* industry as % of GDP*
Argentina	26.4	2767	50.4	1 910	33
Bolivia	5.3	1099	2.7	510	13
Brazil	119.5	8512	187.6	1 570	25
Chile	10.7	757	15.1	1 410	21
Colombia	25.6	1139	21.8	850	22
Ecuador	7.8	284	6.9	880	15
Mexico	65.4	1973	84.4	1 290	24
Paraguay	2.9	407	2.5	850	16
Peru	16.8	1285	12.4	740	26
Uruguay	2.9	176	4.7	1 610	23
Venezuela	14.0	912	40.7	2 910	17

* 1975
SOURCES   World Bank, *World Development Report*, 1980; UN, *Statistical Yearbook*.

ANTECEDENTS AND NEGOTIATIONS

It is of fundamental importance to an understanding of the successes and failures of LAFTA to recognise that the movement leading to the Treaty was not unified in pursuit of a common objective. There were in fact two projects under negotiation in the late 1950s whose aims and methods were not wholly consistent, on the basis of which a compromise integration scheme was fashioned. External pressures also contributed to the shape of the final project. While the signing of the Treaty of Rome in 1957 lent urgency to the creation of a Latin American trade bloc, the negotiations had also to take into account the membership of GATT of some of the participating countries, the opposition of the IMF to a proposed scheme for regional payments, and the initial hostility of the US government to the emergence of an exclusive Latin American trading system.

The first integration project was developed within the UN Economic Commission for Latin America (ECLA) as a relatively ambitious attempt to overcome what were perceived as major obstacles to the sustained development of the Latin American economies. Although the need for some form of Latin American Regional Market (LARM) was foreshadowed in ECLA's first *Economic Survey of Latin America* in 1949, it was not until the mid-1950s, following the creation of a Trade Committee in 1955, that detailed study began. By then the impetus of the early stages of import-substituting industrialisation in the region had begun to wane, and payments problems were increased by deteriorating terms of trade after the Korean War. It was ECLA's view that the intensification of intra-Latin American trade was required to overcome the terms of trade problem and to widen the 'domestic' market beyond the limitations of 'twenty watertight compartments' in order that the regional industrialisation process might progress to include the manufacture of consumer durables and capital goods.

The task of elaborating proposals for a system of regional trade preferences was given to a working group (of the Trade Committee) on the LARM. Its deliberations during 1958–9 were conducted in the context of a commitment in principle made by the nations of the region during 1957 to set up a Latin American Common Market (LACM). The proposals of the working group were presented in 1959 and envisaged the eventual creation of the LACM, to be preceded by a ten-year stage during which trade between member countries would be substantially freed of tariff restrictions. Liberalisation would proceed at a slower pace for agricultural commodities, and for manufactured consumer goods, where the likelihood of trade creation would provoke an unacceptable level of disruption. Other proposals included preferential treatment for member countries at a less advanced stage of development, a system of credit and technical assistance to promote exports and new industries, and a regime to permit two or more countries to reduce trade restrictions on a non-extensive basis in order to promote their industrial complementarity. The proposals clearly aimed to promote import substitution on a regional rather than national basis, with the emphasis on trade liberalisation as the vehicle, rather than the possibility of regionally-planned industrialisation. There were no recommendations concerning regional infrastructure or a regional development bank. However, a regional payments regime, already the subject of a second study group of the Trade Committee, was proposed.

Although it had been intended to draft an integration scheme on the basis of these proposals, the appearance of a second integration project in 1959 complicated the situation. Less concerned with future industrialisation than with the shrinking level of existing intra-regional trade which they dominated, the four Southern Cone countries (Argentina,

Brazil, Chile and Uruguay) had in 1958 begun to study ways of stimulating increased mutual trade. Largely by the use of bilateral agreements involving the discriminatory application of trade and exchange controls, these countries had in the 1940s and early 1950s developed an important mutual trade in primary commodities. On the basis of this the share of total Latin American exports going to other Latin American countries had increased from less than 6 per cent pre-war to almost 10 per cent in the post-war decade (ECLA 1957, Tables 33, 34). After 1955, however, the deteriorating balance of payments situation of the four countries and the greater leverage of the IMF caused a retreat from bilateralism and with it the level of trade declined. The problem to which the group of experts of the four countries addressed themselves in 1958 was therefore to devise a formula consistent with GATT membership which would allow the recovery of former reciprocal trade levels.

The solution which was reached, and presented to the ECLA Trade Committee meeting in Panama in May 1959 alongside the working group's project, was also a scheme for a free trade zone. It received a cooler reception than its competitor, largely because as a sub-regional scheme it threatened the achievement of a regional common market, and the Panama meeting endorsed the proposals of its working group. Nonetheless, the initiative lay with the southern group of countries. Having a limited, urgent and short-term objective in view, and a formula which they believed to be adequate, they were determined to press ahead. However, the scheme was not exclusive, and in the succeeding months a number of other Latin American countries expressed their intention to join the scheme which would evidently proceed with or without them. ECLA's reservations were thus undermined, and the project was modified somewhat by principles adapted from the working group scheme, notably on industrial complementarity agreements, treatment of less advanced members, and escape clauses. But the essential mechanism of trade liberalisation adopted in the Treaty of Montevideo was that of the Southern Cone project, and reveals the narrow commercial rather than developmental objective of its origins. 'The Latin American Free Trade Association thus came into being as a hybrid: it was an emergency solution to immediate problems affecting a nucleus of its members, but in order to transcend this limited purpose it was adapted to form the first stage in the movement towards a common market' (Finch, 1973). That fact is an important if incomplete explanation of LAFTA's failure.

STRUCTURE

The ambiguous origins of the Montevideo Treaty are reflected in the gulf between the rhetoric of its preamble and its formal provisions. The former speaks of 'efforts to establish, gradually and progressively, a Latin American common market', and of 'the desire to pool their efforts to achieve the progressive complementarity and integration of their national economies on the basis of an effective reciprocity of benefits' (ECLA 1962, p. 57). In practice the contracting parties did little more than commit themselves to future rounds of negotiations. Trade liberalisation was to occur via two mechanisms. The first was by annual negotiations of national schedules which listed commodities on which the member countries separately made concessions applicable to all other members. The second, the common schedule, listed the commodities on which regional free trade was to be progressively established in four rounds of negotiations occurring at intervals of three years. Though concessions on the common schedule were to be irrevocable, those on national schedules could be withdrawn. Other safeguard clauses existed to protect 'specific productive activities of vital importance' (article 23) or countries experiencing balance of payments difficulties. Agricultural imports by member countries might be limited to the volume needed to meet a deficit in internal production. Chapter VIII of the Treaty indicated the special treatment, including the granting of tariff concessions which would not be extensive to other member countries, available to countries at a relatively less advanced stage of economic development, a designated status immediately granted to Paraguay and (in anticipation of membership) Bolivia. There was provision also for agreements on industrial complementarity within industrial sectors.

Although such agreements came to assume increasing importance in LAFTA's second decade, the central provisions of the Treaty concerned trade liberalisation through the two schedules. Here the scheme's ancestry in the Southern Cone project was clearly evident. The pace of liberalisation was to be determined by an arithmetical formula. Each country was to make tariff concessions to other members annually on commodities traded in the previous three-year period, by an amount equivalent to 8 per cent of the weighted average tariff applicable to non-member countries. The limitations of this national schedule approach are worth emphasising. It involved negotiations on a commodity-by-commodity basis, and the character of these negotiations was essentially bilateral. The multilateral requirement of an integration scheme consistent with Article 24 of GATT was met by making the national schedule concessions extensive to all member countries, but this did not create a regional market in any commodity (since there was no reason why more than one member should reduce tariffs on a particular commodity), while it did allow any two countries to stimulate trade between themselves (on the assumption that the country negotiating a concession from another member would be at least as likely as any other to be able to take advantage of it).

Whereas national schedule concessions were in principle likely to be long drawn-out and tedious in negotiation but relatively easy to make, the common schedule required all the member countries to agree a list of commodities on which they were prepared to eliminate tariffs irrevocably. At each round of negotiations 25 per cent of the aggregate value of regional trade was to be freed, such that by the conclusion of the fourth round in 1973, 'substantially all' of (existing) regional trade would be free of tariff duties. The free trade area would thus be completed in a transition period of twelve years from the implementation of the Montevideo Treaty in 1971.

The ruling principle in the liberalisation process was to be that of reciprocity of concession and benefit, the latter defined (article 13) in terms of 'the expected growth in the flow of trade between each Contracting Party and the others as a whole'. Logically, therefore, measures designed to correct a lack of reciprocal benefit – and indeed those to protect the relatively less advanced members, and the general escape clauses – were almost entirely concerned with the pace of trade promotion and liberalisation, and neglected completely the possibility of direct encouragement to new or existing economic activity. The only suggestion of an industrial programme, the regime for agreements on industrial complementarity, was no more than an umbrella under which private sector groups might negotiate commercial concessions within industrial sectors. LAFTA had no regional 'plan' of its own, nor mechanisms for harmonising the plans or policies of its members, nor development bank to finance projects of regional interest.

Integration was sought by the Treaty signatories for mostly ill-defined reasons, and the Treaty itself had the advantage of demanding no automatic commitment from its members. The Southern Cone countries saw it as an instrument to revive a limited trade in traditional commodities, and Mexico was anxious to diversify its export markets (Schmitter and Haas, 1964). Governments were persuaded to adopt the LAFTA scheme by the perceived need to follow the EC example, and by ECLA's advocacy of it. The role of technocrats, trained and influenced by ECLA, was probably crucial (Mitchell 1967). In no case does the initiative for trade liberalisation appear to have come from the private sector. Indeed, while ECLA envisaged the scheme as the first stage towards a regional common market which would enhance the industrialisation process, it was precisely private sector manufacturing industry which adopted the most strongly negative attitude. In the three countries of greatest industrial development a larger, regional market offered little benefit, while for the intermediate group of countries in which a high-cost, highly protected manufacturing sector had developed in the previous decade, the private sector perceived the likelihood that losses would far outweigh gains (Vaitsos, 1978; Finch 1973).

IMPLEMENTATION 1961–7

The events of 1967 may be taken to mark the watershed in LAFTA's fortunes. Up to 1967 some progress was made in the promotion of regional trade (see Tables 10.2, 10.3 and 10.4) and the timetable for trade liberalisation was generally adhered to, though there were also calls for the reform of the organisation. From 1967 onwards LAFTA experienced continuous crisis, for which the search for a solution was finally to prove fruitless.

TABLE 10.2   *Intrazonal Exports of LAFTA Countries 1961–77 (million US \$, fob, 3-year averages)*

	1961–3	1964–6	1967–9	1970–2	1973–5	1976–7*
Argentina	154.9	245.4	328.7	405.1	827.2	1176.9
Bolivia	3.8	4.5	13.8	42.3	116.1	167.4
Brazil	84.9	175.9	202.8	355.2	889.4	1343.0
Chile	43.8	57.6	96.7	124.5	314.2	529.8
Colombia	7.6	21.6	37.3	93.3	179.0	244.8
Ecuador	7.2	12.9	15.6	27.6	121.0	315.6
Mexico	21.3	51.3	68.7	117.0	235.0	343.2
Paraguay	10.5	17.4	16.9	23.0	46.3	62.8
Peru	45.4	64.3	47.2	71.1	149.8	198.9
Uruguay	9.8	19.3	22.2	33.3	94.0	135.1
Venezuela	150.4	141.2	159.0	145.1	222.1	510.5
Total	**539.6**	**811.4**	**1008.9**	**1437.5**	**3194.1**	**5028.0**

* 2-year average

SOURCES   LAFTA; J. W. Wilkie and P. Reich (eds), *Statistical Abstract of Latin America*, vols 19 and 20 (Los Angeles, UCLA Latin American Center Publications, University of California, 1978, 1980).

TABLE 10.3   *Share of intrazonal exports of LAFTA countries 1961–77*
(%, 3-year averages)

	1961–3	1964–6	1967–9	1970–2	1973–5	1976–7*
Argentina	28.7	30.2	32.6	28.2	25.9	23.4
Bolivia	0.7	0.6	1.4	2.9	3.6	3.3
Brazil	15.7	21.7	20.1	24.7	27.8	26.7
Chile	8.1	7.1	9.6	8.7	9.8	10.5
Colombia	1.4	2.7	3.7	6.5	5.6	4.9
Ecuador	1.3	1.6	1.5	1.9	3.8	6.3
Mexico	3.9	6.3	6.8	8.1	7.4	6.8
Paraguay	1.9	2.1	1.7	1.6	1.4	1.2
Peru	8.4	7.9	4.7	4.9	4.7	4.0
Uruguay	1.8	2.4	2.2	2.3	2.9	2.7
Venezuela	27.9	17.4	15.8	10.1	6.9	10.2
Total	**100**	**100**	**100**	**100**	**100**	**100**

* 2-year average
SOURCE   as Table 10.2.

In 1961 exports of the nine LAFTA member countries to each other were valued at 299 million US dollars; their mutual trade represented 6.0 per cent of their total trade. Both the value and the proportion were at the lowest levels of any year in the previous decade (Dell, 1966, p. 219). With the inclusion of Venezuela and Bolivia, to facilitate comparison with later years, intra-regional exports in 1961 totalled 488 million US dollars (6.7 per cent of total exports). By 1967 the trade had grown to 850 million US dollars (8.5 per cent of the total), and in fact these figures represented slight reductions on those for 1965–6. The major decline in participation was experienced by Venezuela, not surprisingly, since Venezuelan oil exports had not been subject to the difficulties of the Southern Cone countries in the 1950s (and Venezuela was not yet a member). The combined participation of Argentina, Brazil and Chile rose from 51 per cent to 62 per cent, and of Mexico from 2 per cent to 7 per cent. Mexican exports contained manufactured goods in a much higher proportion than those of the other countries, but the trade of the region – even of the largest and most advanced exporter, Argentina – continued to be dominated by traditional primary products.

That the major share of the gains should be experienced by the three largest Southern Cone countries, in the form of an enlarged but mainly traditional trade, is consistent with the origins of the LAFTA scheme. So too is the manner in which the pace of trade liberalisation declined. In

TABLE 10.4 *Proportion of intrazonal exports and imports in total exports and imports of LAFTA countries 1961–77 (3-year averages)*

		1961–3	1964–6	1967–9	1970–2	1973–5	1976–7*
Argentina	X	13.1	16.3	22.2	22.3	25.8	24.7
	M	12.5	21.7	23.3	20.9	21.4	24.4
Bolivia	X	4.8	3.4	7.7	18.5	29.4	35.4
	M	13.5	10.1	13.3	23.5	32.7	37.0
Brazil	X	6.3	11.1	10.4	11.1	11.7	12.1
	M	14.6	20.5	13.2	9.2	7.2	10.4
Chile	X	8.3	7.9	9.9	12.2	17.5	26.2
	M	18.1	25.6	26.4	24.2	21.9	29.9
Colombia	X	1.8	4.1	6.7	12.2	13.4	11.3
	M	3.1	7.9	8.7	9.9	11.1	12.1
Ecuador	X	6.5	9.6	9.3	11.6	18.5	23.3
	M	7.1	8.5	11.4	13.2	14.1	11.5
Mexico	X	2.8	5.2	6.3	8.7	8.6	9.1
	M	0.6	1.8	2.3	3.3	5.3	4.3
Paraguay	X	30.2	33.4	34.6	32.0	29.4	27.3
	M	24.4	27.2	23.9	26.3	44.2	45.1
Peru	X	8.6	9.2	5.9	7.4	9.5	13.1
	M	9.4	11.8	16.0	16.0	15.4	25.7
Uruguay	X	6.0	10.4	12.4	15.4	25.9	23.9
	M	21.4	31.5	27.8	33.6	34.4	32.2
Venezuela	X	5.9	5.4	5.1	4.7	4.5	5.6
	M	2.0	2.7	3.0	3.9	5.8	7.2
Total	**X**	**7.0**	**8.9**	**9.6**	**11.1**	**13.0**	**13.5**
	M	**9.2**	**12.1**	**11.7**	**10.9**	**10.5**	**13.1**

* 2-year average
X exports
M imports
SOURCE as Table 10.2.

the first two rounds of national schedule negotiations, in 1961–2, the member countries recorded a total of 7593 tariff concessions in respect of zonal imports. Compared with the Treaty requirement of an 8 per cent reduction in the regional tariff for each country, the first round achieved an estimated average 25 per cent reduction, and the second a further 15 per cent. This was clearly the easy stage in liberalisation, in the sense that many of these tariff concessions were irrelevant in terms of the trade they generated: Ecuador in fact led the way with 23 per cent of concessions granted but absorbed only 1–2 per cent of intra-regional imports. A further sense in which early liberalisation was easy was that this was precisely what the Southern Cone countries had designed their scheme to achieve, i.e. the limited granting of mutual concessions to promote trade in traditional commodities. Correspondingly, a further 42 per cent of the 1961–2 concessions were made by Argentina, Brazil and Chile, and it is probable that the concessions were responsible for a substantial part of the growth of regional trade. But after 1962 national schedule concessions became more difficult to make, with only 1800 added in the following four years.

In 1964 the first round of negotiations on the common schedule fell due. It was decided in advance that although inclusion of a commodity on the common schedule was irrevocable, it was not necessary to activate any part of the common schedule until 1973, and thus the establishment of regional free trade in any commodity might be postponed until then. This prevarication only partially cleared the way for the first common schedule, which took seven months of 1964 to agree. The commodities included in it were primarily agricultural, notably bananas, cacao, coffee and cotton. However, to minimise the dislocation which free trade in agricultural commodities might be expected to provoke, it was agreed that the escape clause contained in article 23 of the Treaty, permitting members to restrict regional imports which had 'serious repercussions' on domestic activities, might be invoked after 1973. Thus the liberalisation principle was further weakened.

The stresses imposed on the LAFTA system by the need to agree the first common schedule also revealed a more important source of conflict, expressed particularly by countries outside the ranks of the 'big three', concerning the very nature of the integration process. Broadly speaking, they argued that trade liberalisation was not enough. The concessions they were able to win, however, amounted to little more than differential treatment in the pace of liberalisation. Ecuador and Paraguay, already having the status of relatively less developed countries, received such additional concessions in 1963 and 1964, and there were moves to extend loans, credit and technical assistance to them. More significant, however, was the dissatisfaction of the 'intermediate' group of countries, particularly Uruguay, Chile and Colombia. All three had substantial deficits in their zonal trade. Need for special treatment for countries with inadequate market size, especially to stimulate new activities, was agreed in 1963, and in 1964 Resolution 100 was adopted as (in effect) the condition for the approval of the common schedule by the intermediate group. The Resolution, had it been implemented, would have transformed LAFTA. It called for wide-ranging measures to secure economic policy coordination among the member countries, with provision for regional investment planning in industry, agriculture and infrastructure, leading to an association of complementary economic structures within a customs union. Such an ideology of regional integration could make little appeal to the three dominant countries, and it was this fact which was to lead directly to the meeting of the Andean Pact (AP) countries in Bogotá in 1966 and the eventual formation of the sub-regional scheme for the AP. Uruguay was left to secure admission to the category of relatively less developed countries, in 1967.

Disenchantment with the achievement of LAFTA was by no means confined to the governments of the smaller countries. ECLA, whose formal status *vis-à-vis* LAFTA was that of adviser on technical matters, continued to press for a more ambitious programme of integration. Its former Executive Secretary, Raúl Prebisch, participated in a high-level study group which in 1965 called for an extended LACM – incorporating the Central American Common Market (CACM) – to be achieved during a transition period of ten years by across-the-board tariff reductions (in contrast with LAFTA's commodities approach) and the gradual establishment of a common external tariff (CET). Industrial groups were identified whose characteristics made them particularly appropriate for integration agreements, the role of the Inter-American Development Bank as a source of finance was to be enhanced, and the political authority of the integration scheme was to be increased.

Inevitably the proposals found no substantive support within an increasingly divided LAFTA. Curiously, however, some of them were echoed in an agreement made by American heads of state meeting in Punta del Este in April 1967. The presidents agreed on the aim of a LACM, to be achieved during the transition period 1970–85 and involving the convergence of LAFTA and the Central American Common Market (CACM). This decision was so much at odds with the existing condition of LAFTA and devoid of concrete proposals for the attainment of the objective that it was impossible to translate it into any kind of realistic programme.

The impossibility indeed became manifest within months rather than years. In 1967 the second round of the common schedule was due for negotiation. Since the importance in regional trade of commodities included in the first schedule had fallen to 23 per cent in the base period 1963–5, the target for the second round was 27 per cent of trade in that period. Two commodities, crude oil (15 per cent) and wheat (13 per cent), would have met the target, but encountered opposition because of the dependence their inclusion would create on Venezuela and the competition to high cost oil production in some countries; and because it might endanger domestic wheat production and supplies of PL 480 wheat from the USA. An alternative list of 100 commodities was also rejected. Negotiations on the second common schedule were abandoned in late 1967, resumed in 1968, and finally terminated with no agreement. Quite apart from the failure to convert LAFTA into a more meaningful instrument for regional integration, the member countries had now defaulted on the central Treaty provision for trade liberalisation.

PARALYSIS 1967–80

Following the *impasse* of 1967–8, the year 1969 was largely devoted to a process of assessment of LAFTA. The outcome, at the end of 1969, was the Caracas Protocol, a document which substantially modified the terms of the Montevideo Treaty and gave a second decade of half-life to the scheme. The negotiations were not encouraging for the future: 'as deliberations proceeded, commitments were weakened or diluted, exceptions and safeguards . . . augmented and strengthened, and by the end of the meeting everything had been conditioned by everything else and put off to some hazy, uncertain future' (*Comercio Exterior de México*, 16, 2, 1970, p. 16). The main provisions were these: firstly, the transition period for the establishment of free trade, due to terminate in 1973, was extended to 1980. Secondly, common schedule negotiations were suspended for five years, and the date for implementing regional free trade in the commodities included in the first common schedule was left to be decided. Thirdly, the extent of annual tariff reductions to be granted by each country on its national schedule was reduced from 8 per cent of the average tariff to third countries to 2.9 per cent. Fourthly, in what was termed an 'Action Plan', studies on conditions for the establishment of a LACM were to be undertaken in the four years to 1973; and on the basis of these studies, collective negotiations would begin in 1974 on the future of LAFTA and the LACM.

In spite of the optimistic rhetoric with which the Caracas Protocol was presented, and which continued to be heard (though with diminishing frequency) during the 1970s, the Protocol represented the near-collapse of the LAFTA scheme. In effect, the member countries decided to mark time. The Protocol corresponded most closely to the interests of the largest members, in confining LAFTA (and markedly weakening it) to an organisation for trade liberalisation and promotion, while relegating other decisions to further study and seemingly endless negotiation. Thus in addition to the annual ordinary conferences, meetings were held during 1974 and 1975 to attempt to restructure the LAFTA mechanism in line with the second phase of the Action Plan, but without success. 'One clear-cut idea emerged from these meetings: there was no possibility whatever that the eleven members would agree on any matter of importance' (Baldinelli, 1977). In 1975 Chile ratified a protocol of 1966 and thus brought into existence a permanent council of ministers of foreign relations, almost a decade after it had been intended to create it. This briefly raised the expectation that the greater direct involvement of member governments might raise LAFTA from the state of stagnation and frustration into which it had sunk. However, the Council did not hold its first meeting until August 1980 when, with the Caracas Protocol due to expire at the end of the year, its function was to agree the form of LAFTA's successor.

The complete failure of LAFTA in the 1970s to overcome the problems which were manifest in the second half of the 1960s should not be taken to mean that nothing was achieved in the 1970s, nor that alternative modes of economic integration were not explored. Regional trade continued to increase, with exports exceeding 10 per cent of global exports for the first time in 1969, and rising sharply in the mid-1970s to average 13.5 per cent in 1976–7. Valued at current prices, intra-zonal exports reached 1 billion US dollars in 1968 and averaged 5 billion US dollars in 1976–7. A substantial part of this export trade – probably about 50 per cent – took place in commodities which were not covered by LAFTA concessions, and the LAFTA arrangements were therefore only one factor in this expansion. Inevitably, in view of the Caracas Protocol, the national schedule programme was of greatly reduced significance in the 1970s. With 11 018 national schedule concessions negotiated by the end of 1969, the following decade saw the net addition of only 224. Moreover, a substantial proportion of these concessions did not give rise to any trade flows at all. In 1968 García Reynoso indicated that of 614 tariff concessions granted on manufactured goods, only 24 had in fact been used (*Comercio Exterior de México*, 14, 1, 1968, p. 15). A variety of explanations for the non-utilisation of concessions has been adduced, including non-tariff trade barriers, regional transport costs, lack of information to producers and exporters on the availability of concessions, and insecurity engendered by the impermanence of concessions and changing margins of preference resulting from the lack of a CET. The existence of unproductive tariff concessions within LAFTA, and the desire of some countries (particularly those forming the AP) to see them eliminated in LAIA, makes the re-negotiation of national schedule concessions an urgent task of the transition from LAFTA in 1980.

One aspect of LAFTA which showed considerably more dynamism in the 1970s than in the 1960s was the number of complementarity agreements concluded. The regime of industrial complementarity is a facility passively offered to industrial groups in member countries, and implies no national (still less supranational) industrial programming. It provides for tariff reductions applicable to industrial sectors, or to the international operations of a single industrial company. The regime was not fully structured until 1964, when a significant departure from the original design was incorporated: those countries not wishing to participate in a complementarity agreement no longer enjoyed the tariff concessions of the agreement under most-favoured-nation treatment. This change undoubtedly accelerated adoption of the regime, but there were other causes too, notably their increasing use by multinational corporations to diversify markets within Latin America and in some cases to organise production on a regional basis.

The first agreement, dealing with trade in electronic data-processing equipment, was in fact negotiated by IBM in 1962. Subsequent agreements concerned sectors producing electronic valves (General Electric, Philips and RCA), domestic electrical apparatus and communications equipment – the latter two in 1966. Thus the early adoption of the scheme was slow, but in the following six years a further 16 agreements were concluded, and five more were added during 1976–8. By 1979, over 3500 (non-extensive) tariff concessions had been negotiated under the scheme, in a range of industrial sectors including chemicals and petrochemicals, electrical generation and transmission equipment, glass products and office equipment. The automotive industry is a significant absentee from the list. Only one of the 25 agreements has been signed by more than five countries, whereas 17 have been signed by only two or three countries. Argentina, Brazil and Mexico are the only countries to be signatories of at least half of the agreements. The relative gains made by the industrial complementarity scheme, during a period when the trade liberalisation programme was at a standstill, tended to increase the influence of the private sector particularly via the industrial sectoral meetings organised by LAFTA. In addition it has been argued by Raddavero (1978) and others that multinational corporations have been the main beneficiaries of the complementarity scheme.

Clearly the scheme has been one factor in the growth of intrazonal trade in manufactures, though it is doubtful whether its significance was very large compared with the reorientation of economic policy in many countries at the end of the import substitution era towards frequent exchange rate adjustment and the granting of export incentives. The expansion of the regional market for regional manufactured goods was a basic objective of the LAFTA scheme, particularly on the part of its proponents within ECLA, and the share of manufactures within LAFTA trade has increased sharply, from 11 per cent in 1960 to 40 per cent in 1970 and 42 per cent in 1973 (ECLA data in *Comercio Exterior de México*, 21, 6, 1975, p. 190). The significant fact is, however, that in spite of the rapid growth of this trade, exports of manufactured goods by LAFTA countries to non-LAFTA markets were growing more rapidly. The participation of the regional market in regional manufactured exports was thus falling, from 36 per cent in 1968 to 27 per cent in 1973 (de Vries, 1977). Compared with the attractions of developed country markets during the generally expansive period 1968–73, measures promoting regional trade could only exert a modest pull. It is noticeable, however, that the proportion of total regional exports to total exports by LAFTA countries turned sharply upward in 1974, suggesting that one effect of international recession was to induce greater utilisation of regional market opportunities. The three largest member countries accounted for 79 per cent of intrazonal manufactured exports in 1973 (*Comercio Exterior de México*, 21, 6, 1975, p. 190), and in all three cases a high proportion of their regional exports consisted of manufactures (Argentina 49 per cent, Brazil 57 per cent, Mexico 72 per cent). However, the dependence of these countries on the regional market for manufactures varied widely, with Argentina most closely linked (53 per cent of total manufactured exports), Brazil with 26 per cent, and Mexico with only 11 per cent. Moreover, against the trend for LAFTA as a whole during 1968–73, Argentina increased the regional share of its manufactured exports in this period (de Vries, 1977).

FRAGMENTATION

Disenchantment during the period of LAFTA's crisis was directed at LAFTA itself, rather than at possibilities of effective economic integration. Hence a reaction to the crisis was to seek alternative and more appropriate modes of integration or cooperation. The most important of these was the movement initiated in Bogotá in 1966 and confirmed in 1969 when five Andean countries signed the Cartagena Agreement creating the AP. With the subsequent accession of

Venezuela, the group emerged as a sub-regional scheme – the desirability of sub-regional integration had been approved by the American chiefs of state in 1967 – of far greater ideological coherence and equality of development levels among member countries than LAFTA. Since the AP is the subject of the next chapter, it is only necessary here to indicate the significance of the scheme for LAFTA.

In general terms, and in spite of the formal compatibility of the two schemes, there can be little doubt that the emergence of the AP further debilitated an already ailing LAFTA. The AP has consistently maintained that its objective is to accelerate the achievement of a LACM by a sub-regional integration process more suited to the condition of its members. Nonetheless the effect of the AP scheme was to slow down progress within LAFTA, since its members were obviously reluctant to grant new trade concessions within LAFTA which were inconsistent with its own across-the-board liberalisation scheme and more particularly with its sectoral industrial development programme. Indeed, in 1974 the AP countries were authorised to cancel certain existing national list concessions in favour of preferential treatment to their two less developed members, Bolivia and Ecuador, and at the same time to withdraw national list concessions on products as and when they were affected by sectoral industrial programmes. But beyond such discrepancies between the two schemes, the true significance of the AP was that it represented a different ideology of integration – in which industrial development was of the essence – pursued by a group of countries whose predominantly democratic, reformist character contrasted with the neo-liberal economic philosophies of the military or autocratic regimes of Brazil, Argentina, Uruguay and Paraguay. The decision of Chile after the *coup* of 1973 eventually to withdraw from the AP reflects the group's well-defined ideological character.

A second major reaction to the crisis of LAFTA has been the growth of bilateralism among the countries (other than Mexico) not involved in the AP. The remaining four countries had been engaged (with Bolivia) since 1967 in negotiations for economic cooperation and the joint exploitation of the River Plate Basin, an organisation formalised by treaty in 1969. This background, and the degree of ideological conformity of the countries' regimes in the 1970s, have served to promote bilateral arrangements among the group. As early as 1967 a sub-regional agreement was drafted to promote industrial complementation between Brazil and Argentina. However, the traditional rivalry of the two dominant South American nations, which became acute in the early 1970s over competing proposals for the joint exploitation with

Paraguay of hydro-electricity resources, has inhibited any such development. The practice of bilateralism has in fact been extended furthest by Uruguay in its relations with its two large neighbours, based on its eligibility within LAFTA as a relatively less developed country to receive tariff concessions which were not extensive to third countries. With Argentina, major infrastructural projects promoting the physical integration of the two countries were accompanied by an Economic Cooperation Agreement in 1974, and in 1980 proposals for customs union status between the two countries were proceeding. In 1975, Uruguay signed a Treaty of Friendship, Cooperation and Trade with Brazil. In both cases the non-extensive concessions granted by Uruguay to the bilateral partners contravened the most-favoured-nation principle, and required retrospective authorisation in LAFTA Resolution 354.

A third development in the field of integration traceable to the inadequacies of LAFTA was the creation, from an initiative by Mexico, of the *Sistema Económico Latinoamericano* (SELA) in 1975. In both structure and objectives, SELA represents a clear departure from previous attempts at regional integration. Among its 26 members in 1980 were nations of the English-speaking Caribbean as well as of Central and South America. Cuba is a member. Its mode of operation is flexible and pragmatic: the general requirement in other schemes of unanimity and a clearly defined framework are discarded. The two central objectives of the scheme are the creation of a forum within which the nations of the region can define common positions, particularly on commercial questions, for presentation to global organisations, and the promotion of economic cooperation within the region. There is no formal trade liberalisation programme, and therefore no inconsistency with LAFTA membership.

The first objective was formerly served by the Special Coordinating Commission for Latin America (CECLA), a body created in 1963 as an off-shoot of the Organisation of American States, whose principal declaration was the Consensus of Viña del Mar which defined a markedly independent posture for Latin America in relations with the USA. However, CECLA functioned in a largely *ad hoc* manner without a permanent secretariat, whereas SELA offers a firmer institutional base. Thus common positions were agreed during 1979 on relations with the USA and the EC, and consultation meetings were in process with regard to the UNDP, UNIDO and UNCTAD. A cooperation agreement with Spain has been signed.

The second objective of SELA is largely organised through the creation of action committees with the participation only of those countries which choose to participate. Among those to be created have been a Committee for the Reconstruction of Guatemala (formed in 1976 with 16 members following an earthquake), and committees on fisheries, foodstuffs, capital goods and tourism. SELA also proposes the formation of multinational companies owned by public or private groups within the region, and the first of these, Multifert, began operations in the marketing of fertilisers in 1980.

PROSPECTS AND ASSESSMENT

Whereas SELA appeared by 1980 to be well established with a number of new action committees proposed for formation, the Treaty of Montevideo (as amended by the Caracas Protocol) was due to expire at the end of the year. The negotiation of the Treaty of Montevideo 1980, setting up LAIA, was not due merely to the normal difficulties of terminating the life of an institution. Although LAFTA offered no further possibility of advance, it had helped to promote an important increase in regional trade, not only by tariff concessions but also through the LAFTA Payments System (created in 1965) and the Santo Domingo Agreement of 1969 by which multilateral support was made available to member countries undergoing payments difficulties. Just as established interests had helped to bring the LAFTA process to a standstill, so new interests promoted by LAFTA could not permit the LAFTA achievement to be undone.

There were thus two central tasks for 1980: to devise an alternative framework of integration to succeed LAFTA, and to decide the future of the tariff concessions not all of which had generated any trade and which are a potential obstacle to the AP sub-regional integration in particular. The objective of LAIA is defined as the eventual achievement of a LACM, to be reached gradually and progressively but without a timetable or quantitative targets. Promotion of mutual trade and economic complementarity and cooperation are stated as the means by which the objective is to be achieved. A new principle is embodied in the Treaty, that of a minimum regional margin of preference relative to tariff levels applicable to third countries. But the primary instrument of the new scheme, the negotiation of commercial and complementarity agreements, adopts the flexibility of SELA in that they are to be binding only on those countries which choose to enter them. Three categories of economies, advanced, relatively less developed (Bolivia, Ecuador and Paraguay), and intermediate, are recognised, with appropriate provision for the latter two. The fate of the existing concessions was to be determined in intensive negotiations to be concluded in the near future, with the expectation that the great majority would be reconfirmed without extensive bargaining.

Although the recurrent theme of a LACM has surfaced once more, it is difficult to see in the formation of LAIA much more than a holding operation. The flexibility of the new scheme may permit new initiatives, but LAIA has to contend with the fact that its members have sought alternative solutions to their problems in the previous decade, and that these orientations are unlikely to be substantially shifted by the emergency creation of LAIA. Rather, the tendency towards subregional groupings is likely to be strengthened. In spite of the adoption of pluralism as a key principle of LAIA, there are deep ideological divisions within the region, as was made clear by differing reactions of Southern Cone and the AP countries to the military *coup* in Bolivia in July 1980. LAIA has nothing to offer which might overcome those divisions.

The obvious judgement to make on LAFTA is that it failed. Before accepting too readily that view, it is as well to recall the limited and specific objective of the Southern Cone group for which it was created and which was more or less satisfactorily met: the renewal of traditional trade flows. That objective, and indeed a more extensive process of trade liberalisation, did not meet the aspirations of the smaller, less developed member countries. Even so, the non-automatic, commodity-by-commodity approach, coupled with the specification of quantitative liberalisation targets, inevitably led the scheme into an *impasse*.

The Treaty of Montevideo was thus an inappropriate vehicle either for trade liberalisation or for economic integration to promote development. Underlying that difficulty were the gross disparities in economic size of the eleven nations, and the failure to arm the principle of reciprocity of benefit with weapons adequate to ensure that the disparities, especially in industrial development, did not grow larger. The divisive effect of an unequal distribution of benefit accentuated the disagreement over the objective which LAFTA should pursue. This led to the formation of sub-regional units possessing more coherent and positive ideological identities than that of LAFTA. Finally, while the design of the LAFTA scheme and the disparity of its membership may be regarded as responsible for its failure, it should also be borne in mind that regional trade had occupied only a marginal place in the total foreign trade of the region before 1960, and no place at all in the prevailing import-substitution strategies of the post-1930 period. The merits of the technocratic, developmentalist dream of a regional common market thus bore little relationship to the political economy of the region in 1960; they remained unproven at the time of writing.

11 The Andean Pact

Ali M. El-Agraa and David E. Hojman

INTRODUCTION

The general historical background to the Andean Pact (AP) and the basic statistics of its member nations form an integral part of the previous chapter. The reader is therefore advised to consider this chapter as a natural extension of that on LAFTA. Also, because of this, the chapter is very brief.

MEMBERSHIP AND AIMS

The AP was formed in 1969 with the signing of the Cartagena Agreement by Bolivia, Colombia, Ecuador, Peru, Venezuela and Chile as a result of these countries' dissatisfaction with LAFTA. Chile withdrew in 1976; Bolivia contemplated withdrawal in 1980 but that turned out to be simply a threat. As the statistical data given in Chapter 10 clearly show, the member countries of the AP are at an intermediate level of development in relation to the members of LAFTA as a whole. Because of this, Bolivia and Ecuador, like Paraguay in LAFTA, are accorded special status in the AP – see below.

The aims of the AP can be stated briefly. The members pledge themselves to pursue industrial development of the 'region' through joint programming to achieve, among other objectives, the following:

- (i) greater expansion, specialisation and diversification of industrial production;
- (ii) maximum utilisation of resources available to the 'region';
- (iii) stimulation of greater productivity and more efficient use of factors of production;
- (iv) advantageous exploitation of economies of scale; and

226

(v) equitable distribution of the benefits derived from economic integration.

Since the members' dissatisfaction with LAFTA was basically due to the uneven distribution of the gains attributable to economic integration, the AP pledges itself to 'equity of distribution' and commits itself to this aim by acceding to the principle of 'equality of membership'. This is to be ensured through the provision of an 'industrial planning programme', a 'code for foreign investment', etc. and through according special treatment to Bolivia and Ecuador since, if market forces were to operate freely these countries, being the least developed members of the AP, could be completely by-passed particularly with regard to investment in plant and capital equipment, i.e. the natural tendency would concentrate industry in the areas where industrialisation had already commenced (see Brown, 1961; El-Agraa, 1979a; El-Agraa and Jones, 1981, Chapter 5).

The AP has a comprehensive integration programme which includes the Inter-regional Trade Liberalisation Programme, the Industrial Programme, the Programme for the Harmonisation of National Policies, the Common External Tariff (CET) and certain mechanisms to generate financial cooperation and technical assistance.

INSTITUTIONS

The main institutions responsible for the running of the AP are the Commission and the Junta. The Commission comprises two representatives from each member state (the official voting delegate and one alternate) and is responsible for keeping a close watch on national positions, determining common policies, coordinating development policies and furthering regional goals. It is also responsible for acting as a watch-dog on the administrative and technical operations of the Junta and for initiating modifications to the Cartagena Agreement. The Junta is the secretariat and plays an active role in planning regional industrial development and supervising the trade liberalisation programme.

In addition, there is the Andean Development Corporation (Corporación Andina de Fomento, CAF) which is responsible for the economic integration of the member countries in terms of national specialisation and equitable distribution of investment within the 'region', taking into consideration the need for 'effective action to benefit the relatively less developed' members of the scheme. The CAF is free to operate in several countries and is therefore international in character.

BOLIVIA AND ECUADOR

The AP countries adopted their ambitious scheme because they were adamant that they could 'maintain their national sovereignty only if they preserved a definite equality among themselves' (Vargas-Hidalgo, 1979). This equality, we have seen, takes the form of counteracting the 'natural' process whereby development is concentrated in the regions which are already more developed than the rest of the area. Hence the agreement on the industrial planning programme, the foreign investment code, etc. Of greatest importance, however, are the special treatment granted to Bolivia and Ecuador, the least developed members of the AP, within the programmes specified in the previous section and the advantages accorded to them in the AP's institutions: for example, special voting procedures and special treatment within the CAF – the objective of the CAF is to enhance the economic integration of the group 'in the context of rational specialisation and an equitable distribution of investment within the area, *taking into consideration the need for effective action to benefit the relatively less developed countries'* (the italics are not in the original CAF charter).

Hence the AP is distinctively ambitious in that it is (together with the Central American Common Market before it) practically unique, in the global experience of economic integration among a group of developing nations, for pledging its members to this even and harmonious development process.

PROGRESS IN MAJOR FEATURES

The AP has several features and space limitations do not permit an adequate consideration of them all. We shall therefore briefly discuss only the most significant.

INTRA-REGIONAL TRADE BARRIERS

The Cartagena Agreement distinguishes between three commodity groups: (a) imported goods, (b) goods produced in all member nations and (c) the remainder. Intra-AP tariffs on (a) have been completely eliminated while the dismantling of tariffs on (b) is postponed pending negotiations on production rationalisation. (c) constitutes 60 per cent of the AP tariff schedule (3000 items in a list containing 5000); these tariffs were reduced to a maximum of 100 per cent in 1971, with a further 10 per cent per annum reduction until 1976 and 6 per cent per annum thereafter. Hence, the maximum tariff on (c) in 1980 was 26 per cent. This means that tariffs on (c) should be completely eliminated by 1985 except for those of Bolivia and Ecuador which are accorded more time for adjustment as part of the 'special treatment' clause.

Non-tariff barriers on intra-AP trade were eliminated at the start of the 'automatic' intra-AP trade liberalisation programme (*Comercio Exterior*, 1980).

The automatic dismantling of intra-AP trade barriers was accompanied by an eleven-fold increase in intra-area trade during 1969–80 (see Table 11.1) and this has frequently been advanced as evidence of the success of the AP. Given the qualifications stated in Chapter 3 and in El-Agraa (1980, Chapter 5), it would be naive to accept this proposition particularly when most of the increase was in favour of Chile (between 1971 and 1975) and Chile is no longer a member of the AP.

THE CET

The CET is very important particularly for a group of developing countries since it determines the degree of effective protection afforded to local industry.

The CET should have been established in 1980. However, successive meetings during that year were to no avail due to the differing positions of the member nations: Peru wanted a rate not exceeding 40 per cent but was willing to accede to the Colombian proposal of 60 per cent; Ecuador and Venezuela wanted no less than 80 per cent (*America Latina Informa Semanal* 5/12/1980).

It is pertinent to ask: why these differing positions? The answer is simple and requires consideration of three inter-related issues: the protection afforded to import-substituting industrialisation, anti-inflationary policies and oil exports (more generally, availability of foreign exchange). The combined effect of these factors is different for each country and therefore it should not be surprising that each nation has a particular stance with regard to the CET since it occupies a particular and differing role within each nation's general strategy. More specifically, Ecuador and Venezuela (the AP oil exporters – see Table 11.2) have the lowest inflation rates (see Table 11.3) of the group;

TABLE 11.1(a)　*AP total and regional exports (US $m)*

	Total export		Regional exports		Ratio of regional to total exports		
	1971	1978	1971	1978*	1971	1975	1978
Bolivia	181.1	641.0	17.1	21.4	0.094		0.033
Chile	994.0	2 472.7	27.2	–	0.027	0.069	
Colombia	748.0	3 221.4	76.6	366.8	0.102		0.114
Ecuador	237.3	1 532.0	19.1	73.8	0.080		0.048
Peru	887.0	1 933.1	26.8	143.7	0.030		0.074
Venezuela	3 092.0	9 173.4	53.4	186.4	0.017		0.020
AP†	5 145.4	16 500.9	193.0	792.1	0.038		0.048

TABLE 11.1(b)　*AP traditional and non-traditional regional exports (US $m), growth rates and country shares*

	Regional exports		Annual growth rate (%)	Country shares (%)	
	1969	1978		1969	1978
*Traditional**					
Bolivia	3.2	16.6	20.1	11.9	10.4
Colombia	5.4	63.7	31.5	20.1	40.0
Ecuador	5.3	26.6	19.6	19.7	16.7
Peru	12.6	42.0	14.3	46.8	26.4
Venezuela	0.4	10.3	43.5	1.5	6.5
AP	26.9	159.2	21.8	100.0	100.0
Non-traditional					
Bolivia	0.1	4.8	35.3	0.3	0.8
Colombia	20.9	303.1	34.6	59.5	47.9
Ecuador	2.2	47.2	40.6	6.3	7.5
Peru	4.7	101.7	40.7	13.4	16.1
Venezuela	7.3	176.1	42.4	20.8	27.8
AP	35.1	632.9	37.9	100.0	100.0
Both					
Bolivia	3.3	21.4	23.1	5.3	2.7
Colombia	26.3	366.8	34.0	42.4	46.3
Ecuador	7.3	73.8	28.9	12.1	9.3
Peru	17.3	143.7	26.5	27.9	18.1
Venezuela	7.7	186.4	42.5	12.4	23.5
AP	62.0	792.1	32.7	100.0	100.0

* excluding petroleum and petroleum derivatives.
† excluding Chile.

SOURCE　Inter American Development Bank, 1976, 1977 and 1979.

TABLE 11.2   *AP net exports of petroleum and petroleum derivatives (US $m)*

	1973	1974	1975	1976	1977	1978	1979*
Bolivia	48.9	163.9	114.5	112.6	67.4	44.1	40.1
Colombia	61.7	106.4	75.6	−74.3[†]	−50.5	−104.4	−360.0
Ecuador	207.1	607.8	515.9	565.2	484.1	520.6	909.1
Peru	−46.3	−175.3	−202.2	−217.0	−234.0	169.0	672.0
Venezuela	4458.3	10731.0	8324.1	8757.0	9088.8	8627.6	13558.0

* Estimates
[†] a negative sign means net imports.

SOURCE   Inter American Development Bank, 1979.

TABLE 11.3   *AP annual variation in the consumer price*
index (%)

	1976	1977	1978	1979
Bolivia	4.5	8.1	10.4	19.7
Colombia	20.4	32.9	17.9	24.4
Ecuador	10.7	13.0	11.7	10.2
Peru	33.5	38.1	57.8	66.7
Venezuela	7.7	7.7	7.2	12.3

SOURCE   Inter American Development Bank, 1979.

Venezuela has a relatively developed but highly inefficient industrial sector facing an insufficient national market and chronic recession; Ecuador is less industrialised and now wants to use the income from oil to carry out an accelerated industrial development programme; Peru has been self-sufficient in oil only since 1978 and also has the highest inflation rate within the AP, hence massive subsidisation of industrial imports or inflationary protection afforded to domestic industry are not policies that Peru will willingly accede to.

DECISION 24

Decision 24 is concerned with the treatment of foreign investment. Originally, only a maximum of 14 per cent of profits could be remitted abroad, but this was later increased to 20 per cent (Decision 103 of 1976). The Decision also stipulates that foreign companies are allowed to operate until 1989 in Colombia, Peru and Venezuela and until 1994 in Bolivia and Ecuador – foreign firms must then turn either 'national' by selling locally 80 per cent of their shares or 'mixed' by becoming 51 per cent or more locally owned. Other clauses state that banking and insurance, the media, marketing, transport and public services are reserved for national companies.

However, there are some exceptions: (a) in Bolivia and Ecuador foreign investment is allowed for a longer duration in mining, oil, forestry and agriculture; (b) investment by international agencies such as the IADB is exempt from Decision 24; (c) foreign companies which sell more than 80 per cent of their total output outside the AP are also exempt; (d) a company can be declared 'mixed' if the local government owns at least 30 per cent of its shares.

In addition to these provisos it should be pointed out that some member nations seem to apply regulations much harsher than Decision 24 while others would be prepared to welcome any foreign investment particularly where it is not forthcoming (e.g. Peru).

Broadly speaking, external loans have continued to increase but direct foreign investment has fallen abruptly since 1975. The total decline in direct foreign investment between 1975 and 1978 for the AP was 700 million US dollars – see Table 11.4. Since Chile withdrew from the AP in 1976 it would seem that the decline can be partly attributed to that factor not only because of the reduced market size of the AP but also because of the possible future instability of the Pact which is a very important consideration for any foreign investor.

TABLE 11.4 *Private direct investment (US $m), selected Latin American countries*

	1970	Period peak (if not 1978)	1978
Bolivia	− 75.9	53.4 (1975)	11.6
Brazil	131.0		1 885.5
Chile	41.0	49.8 (1975)	− 8.2*
Colombia	39.0		60.1
Ecuador	88.6	161.6 (1971)	39.9
Mexico	323.0	678.2 (1974)	529.6
Peru	− 70.0	315.7 (1975)	25.0
Venezuela	− 23.0	417.7 (1975)	67.6
AP†	− 41.3	917.3 (1975)	204.2
Latin America	908.1		3 475.1

* 1977.
† Excluding Chile.

SOURCE Inter-American Development Bank, 1976, 1977, 1979.

THE SECTORAL PROGRAMME OF INDUSTRIAL DEVELOPMENT

Before the formation of the AP most member countries operated national import-substituting industrialisation programmes. The object of the Sectoral Programme of Industrial Development (SPID) was to rationalise industrialisation by allocating plants in such a way that optimal utilisation in the context of even development is ensured. What is happening in reality is far removed from this noble ideal. For example, in the car and metal-working SPIDs production was allocated to member countries where production facilities were already in existence! Indeed allocations were easier to make on a 'regional' basis only with regard to industries that did not exist at all within the AP and little has actually materialised here. By mid-1980 production was in progress in more than 60 per cent of units assigned and this involved 65 firms (*Comercio Exterior*, June 1980). However, these firms had come into existence well before the SPID!

In short, the notion of equal distribution of industry has been greatly undermined. This is because of the varying levels of structure (or development) of the countries concerned and the inability of those most lacking in structure (the relatively less developed) to exert any influence on decision-making in the face of resistance to the closing of existing plants (for fear of reductions in employment levels). Hence the pledge of equal distribution of production plants for 'even' development remains simply a 'pledge'!

CONCLUDING REMARKS

It is evident that the task the AP set itself is quite ambitious and is, arguably, unique with regard to its objective of balanced, even and equitable development. The discussion in this chapter clearly demonstrates the erosion of this ideal in the face of the harsh reality that those who 'have' will resist any pressure on them to part with what they have even when they 'pledge' themselves to the contrary. Therefore, instead of repeating what is stated in other chapters, one should note that a recipe for success necessitates answering convincingly the set of questions at the end of Chapter 7.

Vargas-Hidalgo (1979) stresses that the uneven distribution of costs and benefits is due not simply to the existing economic structure of the members and their differing national needs but also to the inevitable politicisation of the issues since they are resolved by governments on political criteria, not according to pure technical economic guidelines. Moreover, he urges us to realise that two other factors have contributed to the present *impasse*. One of these is a set of problems peculiar to the AP: the non-compliance of its members with group decisions and the lack of a uniform application of decisions. In this respect, he concludes that the establishment of an AP 'court of justice' may be of vital importance. The other factor is the withdrawal of Chile from the AP. Here he proposes that future researchers should study the problem of 'how Chile's continuing participation in four important Decisions . . . will affect the proper functioning of the system'. These Decisions concern the AP multinational corporations, the avoidance of double-taxation, internal transportation by highway among member nations and an inter-regional highway network.

In conclusion, therefore, one should stress that the *impasse* in the internal relationships of the AP is the consequence of the unequal distribution of costs and benefits, the politicisation of integration issues and the incompatibility of national policies.

POSTSCRIPT

The AP is now virtually defunct: the Bolivian government, who threatened withdrawal in 1980, is no longer recognised by the other members of the group and, in early February 1981, the president of Ecuador announced that in view of the border disputes with Peru, he could no longer consider Ecuador to be a member. If this withdrawal by Ecuador is genuine, the AP is effectively restricted to Peru, Colombia and Venezuela, a situation which is unworkable – see below.

One could argue that the demise of the AP was inevitable given the earlier withdrawl of Chile and the general nature of the membership since, with the single exception of Decision 24, there is nothing original about the AP. The concern with equal distribution of benefits and the Sectoral Industrial Programmes had already been anticipated by the Central American Common Market (CACM) – see next chapter, and the AP does not seem to have learnt very much from the CACM experience. Even in the case of Decision 24, the number of loopholes is now so great as to make it somewhat ineffective.

It would seem that the AP was always unworkable: the duplication of inefficient plant before economic integration had gone too far to justify it as an instrument of industrialisation, so the main benefit which could have been achieved through economic union was net trade creation; this would have benefited the relatively more developed member countries only, hence it was never a real option.

Finally, one could argue that lack of political will and the absence of adequate policy instruments are a major factor in the demise of the AP.

12 The Central American Common Market

Victor G. Bulmer-Thomas

ORIGINS OF THE CENTRAL AMERICAN COMMON MARKET (CACM)

The Central American Republics of Costa Rica, Nicaragua, El Salvador, Guatemala and Honduras have a tradition of union, both of the political and economic kind. Ruled as one territory by Spain under the *Audiencia de Guatemala* in the colonial epoch, they continued as one nation for the first twenty-one years of independence (1821–42). There followed a century of attempts at political (and sometimes economic) union among sub-groups of the five republics (Karnes 1961), before the final, successful movement towards economic integration began in the 1950s.

Despite the rhetoric, it is doubtful whether the tradition of union has really been of much benefit in the most recent integration experience. Although the CACM has survived despite the intense ideological differences among its members, this is due more to the perceived sharing of mutual benefits than to traditions of union; furthermore, it is significant that the one country (Honduras), which considered itself to be a net loser from integration, could not be persuaded to remain a member despite appeals to the powerful union myth and in fact left the market in 1970.[1]

The prime mover in the preliminary drive towards integration in the 1950s was the Economic Commission for Latin America (ECLA). Awareness of this fact is important for a true understanding of the CACM, because ECLA thinking was at that time dominated by the model of '*desarrollo hacia dentro*' – import-substituting industrialisation (ISI). The size of the individual republics, in terms of GDP, income per head and population (see Table 12.1), made it clear that industrialisation

TABLE 12.1   *Basic data for the CACM*

	1950	1960	1970	1978
Costa Rica				
Population (thousands)	801	1 171	1 730	2 111
GDP per head ($)	235	368	568	1 640
Share of industry in GDP (%)	12	12	19	18
Share of agriculture in GDP (%)	46	37	23	20
El Salvador				
Population (thousands)	1 856	2 612	3 534	4 354
GDP per head ($)	182	218	291	706
Share of industry in GDP (%)	14*	15	20	16
Share of agriculture in GDP (%)	53*	32	27	27
Guatemala				
Population (thousands)	2 791	3 765	5 270	6 621
GDP per head ($)	132	277	361	917
Share of industry in GDP (%)	12*	13	16	16
Share of agriculture in GDP (%)	33*	28	27	26
Honduras				
Population (thousands)	1 369	1 883	2 640	3 439
GDP per head ($)	131	181	280	529
Share of industry in GDP (%)	9	13	14	16
Share of agriculture in GDP (%)	55	44	32	28
Nicaragua				
Population (thousands)	1 057	1 477	1 830	2 395
GDP per head ($)	173	227	424	894
Share of industry in GDP (%)	10*	16	18	21
Share of agriculture in GDP (%)	44*	24	24	25

* Taken from M. Monteforte Toledo, *Centro America: Subdesarrollo y Dependencia*, (Mexico City: instituto de Investigaciones Sociales, 1972) Chs IV and V.

NOTE   GDP calculated in current prices and converted to dollars at official exchange rate; 'industry' is defined as mining and manufacturing, while 'agriculture' includes forestry and fishing.

SOURCE   United Nations, Statistical Yearbook; United Nations, Monthly Bulletin of Statistics.

could only be carried out at the regional level, otherwise high-cost, inefficient plants would be duplicated across the isthmus.

The initial efforts towards economic integration were hampered by the fact that the traditional export-orientated model ('*desarrollo hacia afuera*') was working well in the wake of the commodity boom brought about by the Korean war. This soon changed, however, and by the mid-1950s, the world price of Central America's traditional exports (coffee, bananas, cacao, sugar)[2] had begun a secular decline which continued through most of the 1960s. The result was a surge of interest in the ISI model and there followed in quick succession a series of treaties, culminating in the General Treaty on Economic Integration signed at the end of 1960 by Guatemala, El Salvador, Honduras and Nicaragua with Costa Rica signing two years later. It is this treaty which established the CACM[3] and which falls due for renewal in 1981.

Judged by the orthodox tenets of customs union theory (Viner, 1950), the CACM could hardly be other than a failure. In the absence of a significant industrial base before union for all but non-traded manufactured goods,[4] trade creation was expected to be slight; trade diversion, however, was likely to be significant because the dominant source of imports was low-cost goods from third countries. Furthermore, the conditions suggested in the literature (Lipsey, 1960) for a successful union just did not exist in Central America; pre-union intra-regional trade was negligible (2–3 per cent of total trade for most of the 1950s) and none of the five economies could be regarded as competitive with each other, except in the case of primary products which were in any case effectively excluded from the General Treaty.

We have already seen, however, that industrialisation was one of Central America's major objectives in forming the CACM. Consequently, even within the context of the orthodox theory and assuming net trade diversion, the CACM could be judged a success if the social utility attached to the collective consumption of industrial activity should exceed the welfare loss associated with net trade diversion (see Johnson, 1965, and Chapter 2, pp. 14–19).

There are, however, additional reasons why Central American policy-makers could afford to ignore the likelihood of net trade diversion (quite apart from the cynical observation that much of the welfare loss would be sustained by the politically powerless consumers!). First, the assumption that trade creation is welfare-improving rests crucially on the assumptions of fixed external terms of trade and full employment. If the domestic resources freed by trade creation cannot find employment or can only do so in the export sector at the expense of a deterioration in the terms of trade, then trade creation may reduce welfare.

Secondly, trade diversion is only welfare reducing if factors of production are valued at their social opportunity cost. If, in the presence of un- or under-employment, resources can be attracted to the high-cost industrial activities without loss of output elsewhere (particularly in the export sector), then trade diversion can bring improvements in welfare. The principal distorted factor prices in Central America are labour and foreign exchange and this has profound implications for measuring the net benefits realised by the CACM, as we shall see below.

Thirdly, even if trade diversion leads to a fall in output in the (traditional) export sector, this need not matter if there is an improvement in the external terms of trade. With Central America an important supplier in several world markets for traditional exports (particularly bananas), this was a real possibility and enabled policy-makers to view the CACM as a means to reduce dependence on the external sector, improve the terms of trade and achieve industrialisation at one and the same time.

The fact that the CACM, therefore, was likely to be net trade diverting did not trouble policy-makers unduly. However, it had one important implication which was not adequately perceived at the time. If a union is, on balance, net trade creating, the balance of payments and the distribution of net benefits between members are not likely to be serious problems; with trade creation, the balance of payments deficit of one member in intra-regional trade should be matched by a surplus in trade with the rest of the world, while net trade creation ensures that consumers throughout the region benefit, if not in equal proportions.

The same is not true of a trade diverting union. Here the distribution of net benefits (assuming these are positive) is all important and can to some extent be identified with surpluses in intra-regional trade, because the principal means by which trade diversion improves welfare is through an increase in domestic production and intra-regional exports (see below). Consequently, there must be adequate means in a trade diverting union to ensure that benefits are more or less equally distributed and this was not the case in the CACM.[5]

The CACM achieved an initial success, which led many observers to herald it as a model of its kind (Wionczek, 1972). The first difficulty the CACM encountered was the loss of government revenue consequent upon the combination of net trade diversion and prohibitively high tariffs on imports from third countries. This resulted in the San José Protocol, ratified in 1967, a desperate and ill-conceived measure which allowed countries to bolster government revenues by imposing a surcharge of 30 per cent on the common external tariff (CET). The next crisis occurred with the '*guerra inutil*' between El Salvador . and Honduras in 1969,[6] which led to Honduras' departure from the CACM in the following year. Since then, the CACM has virtually stagnated despite various high-level attempts to revive it, but its survival now depends on renewal or renegotiation of the General Treaty in 1981.

In what follows, we concentrate on the achievements and failures of the CACM, the controversial role played by multinational companies (MNCs) and the prospects for a revived market. First, however, it is important to examine the instruments by which the CACM was brought into being and their effectiveness for achieving the region's objectives.

INSTRUMENTS OF INTEGRATION

We have seen in the preceding section how the CACM was formed to meet the objective of rapid industrialisation of the region subject to a mutual sharing of the net benefits expected from its formation. Industrialisation in turn was expected to bring with it rising incomes and a decreased dependence on the rest of the world. The instruments of integration must therefore be examined in this context.

The industrialisation objective was pursued through the freeing of trade within Central America subject to a CET on third countries. The freeing of trade was effectively restricted to industrial products[7] and was carried out quickly and efficiently; as soon as the General Treaty went into effect, 74 per cent of all items listed in the tariff schedule entered intra-regional trade free of all restrictions and this figure had increased to 94 per cent by the end of 1966 (see Hansen, 1967). The remaining items not subject to free trade[8] accounted for only 5 per cent of the value of intra-regional trade by the end of the decade. Where tariffs were reduced over a period of years, this was done automatically and no doubt accounted for the CACM's great success in this area – a lesson not lost on those responsible for the Cartagena Treaty setting up the Andean Pact.

Before union, the Central American republics imposed different tariff rates on imports from the rest of the world; the adoption of a CET required the harmonisation of the tariff structure. The result was (pre-union figures in brackets) the following average nominal tariff rates by type of good: consumer goods 82.5 per cent (64 per cent); raw materials and intermediate goods 34.4 per cent (30 per cent); building materials 32.2 per cent (30 per cent) and capital goods 13 per cent (12 per cent) (see Hansen, 1967, p. 27). In fact, these figures are somewhat misleading, because – as a result of generous incentives (see below) – firms were often able to import their intermediate and capital goods requirements duty free.

The general picture, however, is clear. The CET raised the nominal rate of protection on consumer goods (thereby causing 'trade suppression') and lowered the nominal rate of protection on other goods (thereby causing 'external trade augmentation'). Trade suppression involves a switch from low-cost to high-cost sources of production and is therefore exactly like trade diversion, while external trade augmentation encourages imports from the lowest-cost source and is therefore like trade creation. Because external trade augmentation was so substantial, it was claimed by some economists that the CACM was on balance net trade creating (see Wilford, 1970). Although this is an exaggeration (see Willmore, 1975/6), external trade augmentation remains important and is one reason why the region's dependence on the rest of the world has not declined.

The combination of free trade within the region, together with almost prohibitive tariffs on consumer goods and low tariffs on other goods brought about a dramatic decline in government revenue from trade taxes. The latter have traditionally been the major source of tax revenue in Central America (see Wilford, 1978) and the problem was to some extent anticipated. As a result, the republics reached agreement in 1962 on uniform fiscal incentives for industrial development, the aim being to prevent a competitive reduction of the tax rates applied to the newly established industries.

Unfortunately, the agreement was never ratified;[9] the result has been wasteful competition among the countries to provide the most generous incentives to new firms (see Joel, 1971) and a progressive deterioration in the public finances of all the republics. In an effort to restore fiscal health, the San José Protocol was signed (see above) and indirect taxes on sales were introduced or increased on a national basis, but the result was far from satisfactory.

In the preliminary discussions before the formation of the CACM, the weaker industrial members (Honduras and Nicaragua particularly, but Costa Rica also to a smaller extent) expressed their fears that the freeing of intra-regional trade would lead to a concentration of new activity in the stronger industrial countries (Guatemala and El Salvador). Honduras was especially vocal (see Delgado, 1978) about the need for mechanisms which would ensure relatively equal distribution of the benefits from industrialisation; at the same time, it was recognised that Central America was too economically small to support more than one firm in many industrial sectors; with several firms in these sectors, as ECLA repeatedly stressed, the potential cost-savings through economies of scale would be dissipated.

The result was the Régime for Central American Integration Industries, signed in 1958 by all countries. The Régime is one of the more remarkable features of the CACM and has been studied in depth (cf. Cohen Orantes 1972); the firm[10] receiving status as an integration industry would receive duty free treatment on its inputs while being guaranteed free access to the regional market; at the same time, the same products produced by firms not accorded integration industry status would be subject to trade taxes within the region. The Régime therefore conferred a virtual monopoly position on any firm lucky enough to receive its benefits, although in return it would be subject to price and other controls.

By locating firms equitably among the member countries, it was hoped to achieve balanced industrial development in the region. Unfortunately, only two firms have received benefits under the scheme[11] and the scheme went into abeyance soon after the foundation of the CACM. It has often been claimed (cf. Vaitsos, 1978) that the USA killed the Régime because of its ideological opposition to enforced monopolies. This, in fact, is not so; the Régime was effectively destroyed by the signing of the General Treaty, which established free trade on a *product* basis (thereby leaving little room for protection by *plant*), although it is also true that El Salvador and Guatemala, who stood to gain most by unrestricted free trade, were not unhappy to see the Régime lapse.

Deprived of its principal mechanism for ensuring an equal distribution of benefits, the CACM was left with only a number of minor instruments for achieving this objective. These included the Central American Bank for Economic Integration (CABEI), whose lending policy does in fact favour the less industrialised members (see Cline, 1978, Table 17) and the Regional Secretariat (SIECA), which has laboured hard, if unsuccessfully, to secure a more equitable sharing of benefits.

Many regional organisations, other than SIECA and CABEI, have been set up in an effort to promote economic union in Central America. The most important of these is the Central American Economic Council, which consists of the ministers of economy of the respective countries, but mention should also be made of the Central American Institute for Industrial and Technical Research (ICAITI), whose establishment in 1956 showed an early awareness of the need for the transfer and adaptation to Central American conditions of advanced country technology. There is also a monetary clearing house, which enables the bulk of intra-regional trade to be settled in domestic currencies.

A casual visitor to Central America today, returning after an absence of thirty years, would probably be most struck by the improvement in transport and communications. Although these are a precondition for successful integration, it is also legitimate to view them as instruments of integration. The Pan-American Highway, linking many of the major industrial centres, was completed just in time for the inauguration of the CACM and has proved most beneficial in allowing countries to take advantage of the incentives which intra-regional free trade offered.

SUCCESS AND FAILURE IN THE CACM

The most tangible evidence of the CACM's success has been achieved in the field of intra-regional trade. From the negligible levels recorded in the 1950s, intra-regional trade has risen to great importance (see Table 12.2); the CACM's share of total Central American trade rose rapidly from 6 per cent in 1960 to nearly 25 per cent in 1968. From then on the share has tended to fall away, suggesting that 1968 (the last 'normal' year of operation of the CACM before the war between El Salvador and Honduras) was a critical turning-point in the market's fortunes.

The increase in the proportion of intra-regional trade has been achieved primarily at the expense of the USA. In the 1950s, the USA accounted for 60–70 per cent of exports and imports by value; these shares were reduced to 33 per cent and 39 per cent respectively by 1968, since when the shares have stabilised. Some countries, however, notably El Salvador and Guatemala, have *increased* their dependence on the USA in the last decade both as a market for exports and as a source of imports (see Table 12.2).

The CACM, therefore, has in general reduced the geographic concentration of Central American trade and geographic concentration has often been cited as a source of export instability (cf. Soutar, 1977), which in turn has been claimed to be prejudicial to economic growth.[12] Furthermore, since trade within Central America is almost exclusively in manufactured goods, the CACM has reduced the importance of primary products in total exports – a further cause of export instability, as some claim.

Although the relationship between export instability and economic growth is a controversial one, the impact of the CACM on export instability is an empirical question, which can fairly easily be settled. We are therefore fortunate to have a recent study (Caceres, 1979), which examines the total variance of exports over the 1962–73 period using a portfolio model. The results, however, suggest that on balance the CACM has *increased* export instability[13] and the explanation is not

TABLE 12.2   *Central America: external transactions (m. US $)*

	1950	1960	1970	1977
Costa Rica				
Exports (fob)	56.0	86.0	231.0	798.0
% to CACM	0.6*	2.9	19.9	21.0
% to USA	65.7*	52.3	42.5	31.3
Imports (cif)	46.0	110.0	317.0	1026.0
% from CACM	0.4*	3.2	21.7	15.9
% from USA	60.1*	46.8	34.8	35.2
El Salvador				
Exports (fob)	68.0	117.0	228.0	973.0
% to CACM	3.3*	11.0	32.3	16.3†
% to USA	82.1*	35.1	21.4	32.3
Imports (cif)	48.0	122.0	214.0	942.0
% from CACM	9.0*	10.5	28.4	23.2†
% from USA	59.9*	42.9	29.6	29.4
Guatemala				
Exports (fob)	79.0	117.0	299.0	1160.0
% to CACM	1.7*	4.3	35.5	24.4†
% to USA	76.6*	55.6	28.3	33.1
Imports (cif)	71.0	138.0	284.0	1084.0
% from CACM	1.0	5.6	22.9	9.5†
% from USA	64.5	46.0	35.3	39.3
Honduras				
Exports (fob)	65.0	63.0	179.0	504.0
% to CACM	6.2*	12.9	10.6	8.5
% to USA	77.8*	57.4	54.6	49.2
Imports (cif)	33.0	72.0	220.0	581.0
% from CACM	3.7*	7.4	24.9	12.3
% from USA	71.6*	56.1	41.5	42.9
Nicaragua				
Exports (fob)	27.0	63.0	179.0	627.0
% to CACM	2.0	4.5	26.3	21.2
% to USA	45.5	40.3	33.2	23.6
Imports (cif)	25.0	72.0	198.0	755.0
% from CACM	2.5	3.9	25.3	21.6
% from USA	65.1	52.7	36.5	28.8

* Taken from J. B. Nugent, *Economic Integration in Central America* (Baltimore: Johns Hopkins University Press, 1974) Table 1-1. Figures refer to 1953.
† Taken from *Consejo Monetario CentroAmericana Boletin Estadistico*, 1977.
NOTE   Honduras is treated as a member of the CACM even in 1977.
SOURCE   United Nations, *Yearbook of International Trade Statistics*.

hard to find. The principal determinant of any one member's intra-regional exports is the value of their trading partners' traditional exports. The variance of the latter is positively correlated for most pairs of countries, so that extra- and intra-regional exports tend to move together.

Apart from the pattern of trade, the CACM has brought a further structural change in the form of the increased share of industry in GDP. As Table 12.1 makes clear, this has risen from the 'floor' level of 9–14 per cent in 1950 to an average of 18 per cent in 1978 with all countries (even Honduras) benefiting to some extent. We may also note for further reference that the industrial share tended to peak around 1970, suggesting again that the CACM has stagnated since then.

Given that the CACM was conceived as a mechanism for rapid industrialisation, it is safe to assume that much of this increased share was due to regional integration. The same cannot be said of the acceleration of the rate of growth of GDP (see Table 12.3), which also coincided with the foundation of the CACM. Various attempts (cf. McClelland, 1972; SIECA, 1973 and Nugent, 1974) have been made to isolate the contribution of the CACM to the annual growth rate of GDP, ranging from a 'high' of 1.6 per cent to a 'low' of 0.6 per cent per annum. The methodologies employed in these studies, however, leave a lot to be desired (see Lizano and Willmore, 1975).

When net welfare benefits are defined by orthodox customs union theory, it is possible for regional integration to promote an increase in the rate of growth of GDP with negative welfare benefits (net trade diversion). This is an unsatisfactory state of affairs and it seems preferable to postpone discussion of the CACM's impact on growth

TABLE 12.3 *Real rates of growth of GDP (annual averages); per capita rates of growth in brackets (%)*

	1950–5	1955–60	1960–65	1965–70	1970–75	1975–78
Costa Rica	7.4(3.5)	4.8(1.1)	3.9(0.2)	6.9(3.8)	6.4(3.9)	6.9(4.3)
El Salvador	4.5(1.8)	3.9(1.2)	7.7(4.2)	4.3(0.7)	5.3(2.3)	5.7(2.7)
Guatemala	2.3(−0.9)	5.3(2.2)	6.2(3.1)	5.9(3.1)	5.9(2.9)	7.0(4.0)
Honduras	4.1(1.0)	4.4(1.3)	4.8(1.7)	4.8(1.7)	2.9(−1.0)	8.1(4.3)
Nicaragua	8.3(5.5)	2.3(−0.8)	8.2(5.2)	4.0(1.5)	5.9(2.5)	1.7(−1.9)

SOURCE For the period 1950 to 1965, data taken from R. Hansen, *Central America: Regional Integration and Economic Development* (Washington DC: National Planning Association, 1967) table II. For the period 1965–78, data taken from United Nations, *National Accounts Yearbook*.

until we have observed its net welfare impact according to the non-orthodox interpretation outlined earlier.

Part of the interest in industrialisation in the 1950s stemmed from the need for an alternative to agriculture as a source of employment generation. In order to evaluate the impact of the CACM in this respect, it is necessary to know the proportion of the increment in output which can be attributed to integration; from this, on the basis of employment elasticities, the number of jobs created directly in industry can be estimated, as well as the indirect employment effects (if input–output tables are available).

This approach is used in a major study of employment in Central America (see Frank, 1978), where it is estimated that some 3000 new manufacturing jobs were created directly every year by integration from 1958 to 1968 and 2500 new jobs from 1968 to 1972. When indirect employment effects are taken into account,[14] these figures increase to 4200 and 3500 respectively, with between 50 per cent and 66 per cent of the indirect job creation occurring in the urban economy itself.

Whether these increases are significant or not depends, of course, on the impact of integration in providing employment for those entering the labour force over the same period. The study estimated that for every 100 workers entering the labour force, between 10 and 14 found jobs which were due to the CACM (i.e. these jobs would not have been available if a customs union had not been formed). This is by no means a negligible impact, although it must be remembered that the study is somewhat partial because it ignores the impact of integration on working conditions in the agricultural sector.[15]

We may now turn to the principal concern of this section – measurement of the social costs and benefits of integration. As stated earlier, the formation of the CACM would be expected to lead to net trade diversion and this is confirmed by a number of studies (see Willmore, 1975/6). However, with a changing tariff structure *vis-à-vis* the rest of the world pre- and post-union and with distortions in factor markets, net trade diversion is unlikely to give a satisfactory guide to net welfare benefits. This conclusion is strengthened when dynamic considerations are taken into account.

In an illuminating analysis of costs and benefits in the CACM, Cline (1978) has attempted to remedy some of the major deficiencies in the orthodox theory and his results are presented in Table 12.4. Cline continues to treat trade creation and diversion as leading to welfare gains and losses respectively, but notes that these effects will be compounded by those of external trade augmentation and trade

TABLE 12.4   Costs and benefits (static and dynamic) of integration in CACM 1972 in '000 US $

	Costa Rice	El Salvador	Guatemala	Honduras	Nicaragua
(A) *Static costs (−)* *and benefits (+)*					
Trade creation	+1 933	+446	+1 802	+1 748*	+3 061
Trade diversion	−3 475	−2 943	−3 787	−1 970*	−2 473
External trade augmentation	+60	0	+551	+416*	+234
Trade suppression	−1 870	−8 435	−4 375	−1 671*	−2 263
Labour opportunity cost	+1 876	+9 269	+10 231	+1 210*	+1 912
Economies of scale	+1 932	+1 228	+1 977	+254*	+986
Foreign exchange savings	+16 292	+36 324	+39 810	+5 547*	+17 463
Industry intermediate effects	−3 668	−2 345	−2 934	−1 226*	−2 441
Sub-total	+13 080	+33 544	+43 275	+4 308*	+16 479
(B) *Dynamic net benefits*	+1 673	+1 640	+16 583	+11 019	+23 161
Total	+14 753	+35 184	+59 858	+15 327	+39 640
Ratio, share in gains/ share in population	0.78	0.94	1.03	0.55	1.80

* Refers to 1968.
SOURCE   derived from W. R. Cline, 'Benefits and Costs of Economic Integration in Central America', in W. R. Cline and C. Delgado (eds), *Economic Integration in Central America* (Washington DC: Brookings Institution, 1978) Tables 5, 6, 7 and 16.

suppression; in terms of these four criteria, as Table 12.4 shows, the costs of integration far exceed the benefits and this is true of all member countries. It is particularly interesting to note the importance of trade suppression as a result of setting the CET on consumer goods at a rate far exceeding the pre-union average for the five union members.

The study then goes on to take account of factor price distortions; the increased domestic production in country 'A' made possible *both* by trade creation in country 'B' *and* trade diversion in country 'A' attracts factors of production at rates assumed to be well above their social opportunity costs. In the case of labour, the difference between the market wage and the shadow wage gives rise to a welfare benefit which is based on the net increase in output; this gain is estimated in Table 12.4 using a shadow wage varying from $93 per annum in El Salvador and Honduras to $340 in the case of Costa Rica.[16] This welfare gain proves to be substantial for Guatemala and El Salvador.

The next static gain considered in Table 12.4 relates to the economies of scale effect. With factors valued at social opportunity cost, a 1 per cent change in all inputs leading to a $(1 + x)$ per cent change in output will generate a welfare gain of $(x/1 + x)$ per cent of the change in output. Estimates of economies of scale in Central American industry must be considered rather crude, but there is some evidence (Williams, 1978) to suggest that, where constant returns do not prevail, increasing returns are the rule rather than the exception. These estimates are responsible for the scale effects in Table 12.4.

Trade diversion, by locating production within the region of goods which were previously imported from the rest of the world, tends to improve the extra-regional balance of payments. A net trade-diverting customs union, therefore, will save on foreign exchange and the savings can be considered as leading to a welfare benefit if the shadow price of foreign exchange exceeds the market rate. Using a variety of approaches to calculating this shadow price,[17] the study then estimates the welfare benefit and finds (even with a shadow price only 25 per cent above the market rate) a massive gain (see Table 12.4).[18]

The 'dynamic' effects of integration are hard to measure, but are usually considered to be important. There is the impact which integration has on foreign capital flows (i.e. in attracting funds which – in the absence of union – would not have come) as well as the impact which structural transformation might have in raising utility for a risk-averting nation. An attempt is made to measure these effects in the study referred to above, and is included in Table 12.4 under the rubric 'dynamic effects', although it must be admitted that the methods of estimation are somewhat unreliable.

The 'static' gains from integration represent 1.9 per cent of the region's GDP in 1972. Adding in the 'dynamic' gains, this figure rises to about 3 per cent, which is very substantial and helps to account for the relatively robust nature of the CACM, despite the political upheavals which afflict the region. Although one cannot extract the increase in GDP attributable to the CACM precisely from these figures, it is clear that it could have been important. Indeed, if the 'static' gain is spread over the 1960–72 period and added to the 'dynamic' gain, it suggests a 1.2 per cent rise in the annual growth rate above what it would otherwise have been.

According to Table 12.4, all countries have enjoyed net welfare benefits from the CACM, although the distribution is very unequal. Honduras' share of 'static' net benefits is about 4 per cent, far less than her share in population or Regional GDP (see Table 12.1), while El Salvador and Guatemala – as was suspected from the outset – have been the principal beneficiaries.

The position changes somewhat when 'dynamic' benefits are

considered; Honduras' share of these benefits is closer to 20 per cent while El Salvador and Costa Rica appear to benefit very little. When both benefits are added together, we can observe how the benefits are shared relative to population shares (see last line in Table 12.4). Honduras still benefits least, but Nicaragua does best (thanks to 'dynamic' benefits, which brought a great flow of investment to Nicaragua and which it is claimed would not have occurred in the absence of integration).

It would be easy to criticise the methodology employed in the construction of Table 12.4 and no doubt other investigators, using slightly different assumptions, could come up with very different results. The most suspect gain, in this context, is likely to be that due to the foreign exchange savings, which dominates all other 'static' gains (losses) and prevents the CACM from being net welfare reducing on 'static' criteria.[19]

Despite this, the important point to note is that, in the context of distorted factor prices, the extra output made possible by integration can have welfare improving effects. Although first-best policy is no doubt the removal of the underlying distortions, this may not be possible in practice; in that case, integration among countries is an important second-best policy for welfare improvement and Table 12.4 suggests that the gains could be substantial.

THE CAUSES OF THE CACM'S FAILURE

Although the CACM has survived, its second decade cannot be regarded as a success. The most obvious sign of failure has been the departure of Honduras, but by general consensus the market has lost its dynamism. Intra-regional trade has been declining as a proportion of total trade, the rate of growth of GDP in several countries has fallen and the industrial share of GDP has been rising only in Honduras and Nicaragua.

To the architects of the CACM, the last point is perhaps the most serious. Industrialisation was to be achieved by import substitution at the regional level, but this industrialisation appears not to have been carried beyond the 'easy' stage of consumer goods production. The result is that the growth in industry is now tied by and large to the growth of real disposable income in the region with the possibility of above proportional growth determined by the size of the income elasticity for consumer goods.

Consumer goods output – in the absence of regional intermediate and capital goods production – is very import-intensive and this is confirmed by input–output analysis for Central America (Bulmer-Thomas, 1979). The direct and indirect requirement for imported intermediate and capital goods inputs to satisfy a given level of consumer goods output is a *potential* stimulus, in the form of high backward linkages, to further industrialisation through a deepening of the import substitution process. That it has not taken place demands some explanation.

High backward linkages are an inducement to invest in supplying industries; the inducement, however, is only a necessary condition, since it does not take into account the profitability of new production. In the context of the CACM, the two most important determinants of profitability are market size and the effective rate of protection (ERP). Indirect evidence[20] suggests that market size was not the prohibitive factor, so analysis must focus on the ERP.

The ERP for an activity measures the protection received by its net output, i.e. the amount by which value added in the protected situation exceeds the value added that would be achieved under free trade. The higher the ERP, *ceteris paribus*, the more resources will be pulled into an activity and vice versa. In Central America, high tariffs on consumer goods imports combined with low or zero tariffs on other goods suggest that the ERP for consumer goods production will be very high, while that for intermediate and capital goods industries will be very modest.

There have been a number of studies of the ERP in Central America and, fortunately, they reach a common conclusion. The only one of these to use an actual input–output table (Bulmer-Thomas, 1976) is restricted to Costa Rica, but – given the use of a CET – the results should not differ too much among the member countries.[21] Table 12.5

TABLE 12.5 *Average effective rates of protection for Costa Rica, Corden Estimate* (%)

	1965–7	1968–9	1970–1	1971–4
All manufacturing	65.9	78.8	65.9	98.6
Intermediate goods	32.1	39.9	32.1	49.5
Capital goods	32.3	49.1	32.3	58.8
Consumer goods	81.8	95.7	81.8	120.2
Agriculture and exported processed food	−2.5	−3.6	−2.5	n.a.

n.a. = not available
SOURCE V. G. Bulmer-Thomas, 'The Structure of Protection in Costa Rica—a new Approach to Calculating the Effective Rate of Protection', *Journal of Economic Studies*, Vol. 6 (1976) Table 3.

shows that the ERP on consumer goods output has been high and rising and is between two and three times higher than that found in other industries.[22]

If industrialisation through a deepening of import substitution is ruled out by the structure of protection, it is tempting to ask why further industrialisation could not be pursued through export promotion of those consumer goods industries in which the CACM has a comparative advantage *vis-à-vis* the rest of the world. The answer is again provided by the structure of protection, although this time in a slightly different form; when an industrialist considers the merits of exporting relative to home (regional) sales, he is concerned with the proportionate difference between net output[23] in the two markets. If home net output is greater, there can be said to be a bias against exports and the bias is an increasing function of the difference between the two output measures.

When considering exports to the rest of the world, the Central American industrialist can expect to lose the protection he enjoys on his output, while at the same time continuing to pay above world prices for his inputs (both domestic and imported). The result is that net output in third markets is likely to be smaller than net output under free trade with the result that anti-export bias will exceed the ERP for any activity. Indeed, this is in general confirmed by empirical studies (Bulmer-Thomas, 1979), with the result that net output on sales to the rest of the world is on average about 50 per cent of that achieved on sales within the CACM.

Further industrialisation, therefore, either through a deepening of import substitution or through exports to the rest of the world appears unlikely without radical changes in the market's structure; the analysis so far, however, does not explain why industrialists did not form a pressure group sufficiently powerful to push successfully for the necessary changes.

Traditionally, industrialists have been marginal in Central American politics with political power (even in Costa Rica) concentrated above all in the hands of those with landed interests. The initial drive towards industrialisation was supported by these groups and indeed many of them invested heavily in new industries, the most spectacular example being that of the Somoza family in Nicaragua. For such investors, however, the correct comparison is not between the profitability of one type of industry over another, but between the marginal rate of return in industry as against the return in agriculture. In this calculus, world prices for primary products are all important and it is no surprise to find that the stagnation of the CACM in the early 1970s coincided with a sharp increase in the price of Central America's traditional exports, reaching its climax with the coffee boom of 1975–7.

The attachment of many industrialists, therefore, to industrial development is skin-deep. The rate of profit on existing industry is generally thought to be high (cf. Cline and Rapoport, 1978a), but the profits will be reinvested outside industry if the rate of return on non-industrial investment justifies it. The result is that the power of industrialists to speak and act as a group is very limited and the most obvious example is provided by their recent failure to prevent the government of Costa Rica from lowering tariffs unilaterally in an effort to reduce inflation.

The failure to evolve a framework within which further industrialisation could proceed must be considered as a major cause of failure in the CACM. Apart from the weakness of industrialists as a pressure group, it can also be explained by the lack of supra-national agencies with sufficient authority to galvanize member governments into concerted action. Although SIECA (the regional secretariat) has performed excellently at a *technical* level and has offered its own blueprint for the future success of the CACM (the so-called Rosenthal Report, see SIECA, 1973), it has not exerted much political influence.

The SIECA plan called for institutional changes, including a council of ministers and a permanent committee similar to the EC Commission; the proposals were agreed in principle by the ministers of finance and economy, as well as the presidents of the Central Bank, and a high-level committee (*Comité de Alto Nivel* – CAN) was set up to review the proposals. The CAN studied the proposals for two years and in 1976 presented the region's governments with a draft treaty which was never adopted, the main reason being the opposition of governments to the implied erosion of national sovereignty.

None of the explanations of the causes of failure so far given justify the departure of Honduras. Following the war with El Salvador, Honduras declared herself willing to remain in the CACM, provided that a new treaty could be signed which gave her preferential treatment in such things as tariff and fiscal policy. The proposals proved unacceptable to El Salvador and Honduras left the CACM at the end of 1970. Significantly, she has reiterated her determination to stay outside the CACM despite the signing of a peace treaty with El Salvador in October 1980.

Honduras' departure was mainly effected by the strong feeling that she was not benefiting as much as the other countries from membership, a feeling that is confirmed by Table 12.4. Subsequently, she signed a series of bilateral trade treaties with the other CACM countries (except El Salvador), which have undoubtedly worked in her favour and in recent months she has even extended the scope of these treaties (particularly with Guatemala) to greater advantage. It is perhaps not surprising, therefore, that Honduras has shown no inclination to rejoin the CACM.

THE ROLE OF MULTINATIONAL COMPANIES

Prior to the formation of the CACM, there was virtually no investment by multinational companies (MNCs) in Central American industry, direct foreign investment being restricted mainly to agriculture, transport, communications and public utilities (see Rosenthal, 1973). The CACM changed this picture completely and, since 1960, there has been a marked increase in direct foreign investment (see Table 12.6), most of which has been earmarked for investment in industry (see Willmore 1976, Table 12.1). As a consequence of the rise in direct foreign investment, the repatriation of profits has increased in importance and now represents an important debit in the current account of the balance of payments.

The role of MNCs attracted by the CACM invites analysis, because they have been singled out by many economists (cf. Vaitsos, 1978) as a destabilising force leading to *disintegration* of the market. Furthermore, the new revolutionary government in Nicaragua has made it clear that its continued participation in the CACM depends on restructuring the

TABLE 12.6 *Direct foreign investment in CACM Annual flows (m. US $)*

	*Estimated book value at end 1959**	*Direct foreign investments*			
		1960	*1970*	*1975*	*1978*
Costa Rica	73.2	2.4	26.3	69.0	47.0
El Salvador	43.0	4.4	3.1	13.1	23.3
Guatemala	137.6	16.8	24.6	80.0	127.2
Honduras	115.5	7.6	8.3	7.0	13.1
Nicaragua	18.9	1.7	15.0	10.9	7.0

* Taken from G. Rosenthal, *The Role of Private Foreign Investment in the Development of the Central American Common Market*, mimeo, Guatemala, 1973, p. 86 (in millions of dollars).

SOURCE United Nations, *Yearbook of National Accounts Statistics*; International Monetary Fund, *International Financial Statistics*.

market in a way that no longer works principally in the interests of the MNCs (as Nicaragua claims).

That the formation of the CACM was the crucial incentive for investment by MNCs cannot be doubted; out of 155 foreign manufacturing subsidiaries setting up after integration, only ten established plants in more than one country (see Vaitsos 1978, note 151), suggesting that market size was the all-important determinant of investment flows. Much of this investment, as was noted earlier, simply would not have come at all had it not been for regional integration.

The performance of MNCs in CACM can be summarised as follows: most of them eschew local participation, restricting it at best to a minority stake (Rosenthal 1973); foreign firms tend to be larger than their domestic counterparts in terms of number of employees and control about 30 per cent of industrial production; direct foreign investment, however, is unevenly distributed across the industrial spectrum, being most heavily concentrated in activities such as tyres, glassware and chemicals.

In a statistical test on 33 pairs of foreign and domestic firms in Costa Rica, each pair being matched for size and product mix, Willmore (1976) found no statistically significant difference for the two types of firm other than that MNCs employ relatively more administrative personnel, export a greater proportion of their output to the CACM and employ a *lower* capital–output ratio.

This is hardly the sort of evidence with which to build a case against the MNCs, so we must look elsewhere for an explanation of the hostility they have generated. The net welfare gain associated with direct foreign investment will be determined principally (cf. MacDougall, 1960) by the proportion of net output retained in the country through taxation; this proportion has been exceptionally low in Central America and figures are available (Cline and Rapoport, 1978b) to show that in a majority of industries the proportion of profits tax exempted has varied from 70 per cent to 100 per cent.

This, however, only shows that the net gain is likely to have been small. In order to demonstrate a welfare loss, we have to suppose that direct foreign investment has introduced distortions in individual markets sufficient to outweigh the potential net gain; this is not impossible and, indeed, it is most likely to arise when direct foreign investment takes place through acquisition of existing firms, thereby increasing sellers' concentration and reducing competition.

There is some slight evidence in support of this point of view (see Willmore 1976), but it cannot generally be sustained. In his monumental study of direct foreign investment, Rosenthal (1973) found that in the case of 299 MNCs' subsidiaries in Central America, only 46 had been established as a result of take-overs of domestic firms and in half these cases domestic capitalists retained a minority interest.

In one respect, however, direct foreign investment has or could lead to serious problems. The attraction of the CACM to the MNCs was the captive home market; such firms have no interest in sales to the rest of the world and, indeed, several cases have been found (Rosenthal 1973) where sales outside the CACM were specifically forbidden by the terms of the agreement between the subsidiary and head office. Such restrictions do not as yet have much force, but if policy in the CACM should turn more radically in favour of export promotion, it could prove awkward.

We are forced to conclude, therefore, that the hostile attitude to MNCs' investment in the CACM is largely misplaced. Although the net benefits associated with direct foreign investment are probably small, they are likely to have been positive rather than negative. In a restructured market, however, it is legitimate to expect the distribution of benefits to be more favourable to the CACM and we shall return to this point in the next section.

CONCLUSIONS

By general consent, the CACM is at present in crisis; as this chapter is being written (February 1981), negotiations on its future are being held, but it is conceivable that the General Treaty will not be renegotiated and yet another chapter in Central American union could be brought to a close. If, however, as seems more likely, the CACM continues, there are several alternative directions in which it could move and each of these warrants further discussion.

Whichever course is adopted, the negotiations will have to take account of the problems which the CACM encountered even in the decade of success (1960–70). The principal deficiency has been the unequal distribution of net benefits, which ultimately led to the departure of Honduras, but which also led to serious doubts in Costa Rica over continued membership. Because the CACM is on balance trade diverting (see Table 12.4), it is clear that net benefits can only be achieved if the increment in production made possible by integration is distributed fairly evenly across the isthmus; it is the extra production which makes possible the favourable welfare effects listed in Table 12.4

(e.g. economies of scale effect and foreign exchange savings).

The regional integration industries scheme was a bold attempt to answer the problem of equal distribution of benefits. It could be revived again, if the CACM takes the deepening ISI path outlined below, since this deepening will require the production of intermediate and capital goods, for many of which the market is only large enough to support one plant. On the other hand, it is more realistic to recognise that the scheme proved unwieldy with long bureaucratic delays in its implementation, so that alternatives need to be found. One possibility would be a regional investment allocation proportional to each country's imbalance in intra-regional trade.

The allocation of investment funds at the regional level assumes the existence of supra-national institutions, which at present (with the exception of CABEI) are not available. Such institutions imply a reduction in national sovereignty, which makes them very unpopular with member governments, but it is difficult to see how the CACM can be strengthened without them. For example, the ability of Central American republics to speak with one voice in international commodity agreement negotiations could prove of immense value, while the area's banana marketing agency (COMUNBANA) will never compete effectively with the multinationals unless policy is harmonised at a regional level.

A further weakness of the CACM even in its successful decade has been the fiscal crisis. The use of additional tariffs to 'solve' this crisis has simply brought further problems, since it has provided a stimulus to inflation and trade suppression (see Table 12.4). Indeed, several countries in recent months have made efforts to reduce tariffs and Costa Rica has even done so on a unilateral basis as part of its anti-inflation programme.

Since under trade diversion, imports are replaced by home output, it is logical to replace trade taxes by taxes on production or incomes from production. The main area for improvement is unquestionably taxes on corporate income, where collections (as opposed to tax rates) remain ludicrously low. This would also help to meet Nicaragua's demand that the CACM be restructured in a way which does not work principally for the benefit of MNCs.

A final weakness of the CACM, in the long-run perhaps the most important, has been the failure of pressure groups to emerge with sufficient authority to ensure the continuance and revival of the CACM. It has often been said that the CACM was the creation of '*tecnicos*', but it is also true that once in existence it generated interest groups among workers and industrialists, who have had very little influence on the CACM negotiations. Given the *realpolitik* of Central America, perhaps it is indispensable to restructure the market in a way which favours agriculturalists too. This could be done by freeing trade in agricultural products other than basic grains (to which a protocol already applies) or through regional price support policies for foodstuffs.

We now turn to the choices faced by the CACM's negotiators. The most obvious 'choice' is the break-up of the CACM and, in view of the civil war in El Salvador, political unrest in Guatemala and the socialist experiment in Nicaragua, this cannot be ruled out. In practice, however, break-up is likely to be followed by a series of bilateral trade treaties, which means that the CACM would continue much as it is; this would also be the outcome if the member countries simply chose to extend the life of the existing treaty.

Both of these options would ensure the continued stagnation of the CACM; in order to revive the former dynamism, the market must move in one of three ways, as the author has argued elsewhere (Bulmer-Thomas, 1979). The first policy is a further deepening of ISI through revisions to tax and exchange rate policies which increase the profit-ability of intermediate and capital goods production. The domestic resource cost per unit of foreign exchange saved from this policy, however, is likely to be very high and the social utility attached to additional industry would have to be very great to justify it. Furthermore, Cline (1978b) has shown that those sectors exhibiting the greatest potential for ISI tend to be those with the lowest ranking in terms of comparative advantage.

The second option calls for a massive redistribution of income in favour of the poor and middle income groups so as to stimulate production of labour-intensive goods. This can be called an indirect ISI policy, because it is implicitly assumed that the rich have the higher marginal propensity to import. Simulations based on this policy for other countries have suggested that the results are likely to be somewhat modest; the models on which these simulations are based have been criticised as misspecified (Lysy and Taylor, 1979), but there is as yet insufficient evidence to suggest that this is the way to revitalise the CACM; politically, of course, it is inconceivable at present.

The third option is a policy of export promotion. The consumer goods base constructed in Central America is a solid achievement, but its growth – in the absence of exports to the rest of the world – is too closely tied to the growth of regional real income. With a reduction in anti-export bias and a deliberate policy of export promotion, the way would be opened for specialisation by country according to comparative advantage. Economies of scale effects could be enjoyed, foreign trade would become less dependent on primary products, and there might even be beneficial employment effects if the potential exports turn out to be labour-intensive.

The author is in no doubt that the third option is the most viable. One of its merits is that it does not require long, protracted negotiations between member countries over the siting of new production facilities and the regional reduction in tariff levels (to reduce anti-export bias) is consistent with the region's anti-inflation policies. The distribution of benefits is largely determined by *national* export promotion policies and supra-national agencies, although desirable, are not essential. It does not of itself contribute to a solution to the fiscal crisis, but it is likely to strengthen the hand of industrial pressure groups.

A policy of export promotion does little to revitalise the CACM as such, but it has been argued all along that the CACM was essentially a means for industrialisation. If industry continues to expand and increase its share of GDP through a policy of export promotion rather than ISI, that reduces the CACM to the rather minor role of providing a sizeable home market from which exports can be launched, but the CACM is not an end in itself (unlike the EC) and to pass beyond the CACM is, in a sense, the greatest tribute which the member countries can pay it.

NOTES

1. It might also be argued that Panama's exclusion from the CACM owed something to its separate colonial and post-colonial experience, but this is not really so. Many attempts have been made to secure closer economic ties between the CACM and Panama, but the main stumbling block has always been the service-dominated nature of the Panamanian economy.
2. The list of traditional exports excludes cotton and beef, although these are now important sources of foreign exchange earnings for several of the CACM members. The reason is that these products were developed for the export market comparatively recently (since 1950) and are therefore regarded as non-traditional.
3. The General Treaty provided for free trade among member countries with a common external tariff, but does not countenance the free movement of labour or capital. It therefore established a customs union, not a common market, but the use of the latter term is so widespread, that it would be pointless to try and change it.
4. Before the CACM, the share of industry in GDP was approximately 10 per cent (see Table 12.1). This corresponds to the 'floor' level found in Chenery's cross-section work (Chenery, 1960) and is made possible by the

large number of manufactured goods (e.g. bread, bricks) which receive almost infinite rates of effective protection through high international transport costs.

5. In the 1950s, a great deal of attention was given to the equal distribution of benefits (see Delgado, 1978). The chief instrument conceived was the Regime for Central American Integration Industries, signed in 1958, which was intended to achieve a 'fair' spatial distribution of 'basic industries' among the five republics. Unfortunately, the freeing of trade on a *product* basis within the CACM, made possible by the General Treaty, effectively cut the feet from under the Regime, which relied on the adoption of a (temporary) monopoly by a particular *plant* (see above).

6. This war is often called the 'football war', because it occurred shortly after a soccer match between the two countries (see Cable, 1969). In fact, the origins of the war lie elsewhere (see Durham, 1979) and Central Americans prefer the term *'guerra inutil'* used in the text.

7. Agricultural products were in the main excluded from the General Treaty, although several years later an agreement was reached on free trade in basic grains (corn, beans, rice and sorghum).

8. The principal items excluded from the free trade provisions of the Treaty are cotton, coffee, sugar and various goods subject to a government monopoly, such as rum and ethyl alcohol, which remain important sources of tax revenue.

9. The main stumbling block between member countries over the agreement on uniform fiscal incentives was provided by Honduras' insistence on special treatment. The need for this was not denied by the other members, but the distance between what they were prepared to offer and what Honduras demanded proved too great (see Delgado, 1978, pp. 36–9).

10. In fact, the Régime distinguished whole sectors as 'integration industries', so that in principle the scheme could have applied to several firms in each industry; in practice, however, it was clear that it would only be used where a single plant (firm) was coterminous with the industry.

11. The two are a tyre factory in Guatemala and a caustic soda plant in Nicaragua.

12. Since this hypothesis was first put forward, it has been tested empirically with mixed results. MacBean (1966) found no evidence that export instability was inversely correlated with the rate of growth of GDP, whereas Yotopoulos and Nugent (1976) actually found a positive association. Other studies, however, notably Glezakos (1973), have found a negative correlation and there is an overwhelming feeling on the part of LDC policy-makers, enshrined in the proposals for a New International Economic Order, that export instability is harmful to growth.

13. The study in question, however, suggests that the CACM has had a stabilising influence in the case of Costa Rica and Nicaragua. In the case of the former, it is due to the counter-cyclical nature of the change in the value of traditional exports relative to the change in the other republics.

14. At the time the employment study was carried out, no input–output tables for Central America were available, so that calculations were performed on an adapted Colombian coefficients matrix. It should be noted that this is likely to bias upwards the measurement of indirect employment effects,

given the greater import-intensity of Central American over Colombian industry.

15. If, for example, the transfer of labour to industry results in the modernisation of agriculture through labour-saving technological change, the net gain in employment will be much more modest than the figures in the text. This line of reasoning is pursued in Reynolds and Leiva (1978).

16. The shadow price of labour (W^*) was estimated according to the formula:

$$W^* = W_R (1 - U_R)$$

where W_R is the rural wage rate and U_R is the rural underemployment rate. The latter varies from 58.3 per cent in the case of El Salvador to 14.7 per cent in the case of Costa Rica and is the main source of the difference in shadow prices by country.

17. The shadow price of foreign exchange is derived in three ways: through the tariff-based Harberger (1965) and Bacha and Taylor (1971) methods and through the solution to an econometric model for Central America (Siri, 1978).

18. The final 'static' gain (loss) listed in Table 12.4 is the 'industry intermediate effects'. The net gain in production in each sector gives rise to additional output and import requirements in each sector via input–output relationships; these requirements can then be converted to welfare gains (losses) through the three effects listed above: labour opportunity cost, economies of scale and foreign exchange savings. The reason why this effect appears in Table 12.4 with a minus sign is because the indirect requirements are mostly met by imports, which generate a loss of foreign exchange.

19. The formula used by Cline for the foreign exchange saving net welfare effect (BFE) is:

$$BFE = (f^* - 1)(DELTX + TS - TCCE - ETA)$$

where f^* is the shadow price of foreign exchange estimated as the premium over the market rate, $DELTX$ is the increase in exports to partners, TS is trade suppression, $TCCE$ is trade creation and ETA is external trade augmentation. According to this formula any saving in foreign exchange (through, for example, trade suppression) is converted to domestic currency via the shadow exchange rate; the domestic resources used in production, however, are not costless and must be evaluated at shadow prices before being deducted from the gross domestic currency equivalent of the foreign exchange saving to give the net welfare gain. This will only give the same result as the above formula in exceptional circumstances. This interpretation of BFE implies that the four terms in the brackets should be measured at world prices. If, in fact, domestic prices are used (as happened in Table 12.4), it will impart a bias to BFE according to the extent and size of trade taxes. For both these reasons, the estimates of BFE in Table 12.4 must be considered *maxima*.

20. Many feasibility studies, some by ECLA, have considered the possibility of establishing intermediate and capital goods industries and have in general concluded that the small market size need not be prohibitive.

21. In Rapoport (1978), similar results are found for Costa Rica, but the average ERP and its spread is estimated to be lower in the other republics.
22. The estimates presented in Table 12.5 are based on the Corden method, which lumps non-traded inputs with primary inputs as part of the protected net output. The Corden method therefore gives rather low estimates of ERP when compared with other methods which recognise non-traded goods as part of intermediate inputs.
23. In reality, he considers the proportionate difference in *profits*, but no satisfactory method has been developed for measuring the impact of protection on one primary input, so that the effect of protection is measured in terms of its impact on *all* primary inputs.

13 ASEAN and Overall Conclusions

Ali M. El-Agraa

In this chapter I wish first of all to make a few points about ASEAN, then to bring together the conclusions that emerge from the book as a whole and finally to prognosticate about the future of international integration.

ASEAN

As stated in Chapter 1, ASEAN consists of: Indonesia, Malaysia, the Philippines, Singapore and Thailand. These countries have very different histories, political structures, populations, cultures and economic organisations. Table 13.1 gives some basic statistics.

This book does not contain a separate chapter on ASEAN because, at this stage in its development, most of the aims and achievements of ASEAN can be briefly expressed in two main points:

TABLE 13.1(a) *Population, income, production and exports of ASEAN Countries*

			Real GDP growth			Exports	
		GNP	*(average annual*			*(Annual average*	
		Per	*growth per cent)*			*volume growth*	
	Population	*capita*			*(million*	*per cent)*	
	(millions)	*(US $)*			*US $)*		
	1976	*1976*	*1960–70*	*1970–76*	*1976*	*1960–70*	*1970–76*
Indonesia	135.2	240	3.5	8.3	8 547	2.0	8.2
Malaysia	12.7	860	6.5	7.8	5 707	8.9	4.3
Philippines	43.3	410	5.1	6.3	2 433	2.9	3.4
Singapore	2.3	2 700	8.8	8.9	6 585	4.2	14.1
Thailand	43.0	380	8.2	6.5	2 980	5.2	9.5

TABLE 13.1(b)   *Exports by industrial origin, broad groups, 1970 and 1975 (per cent of total exports)*

	Foodstuffs and raw materials (including processed)*		Basic metals†		Other heavy manufactures‡		Textiles and other manufactures	
	1970	1975	1970	1975	1970	1975	1970	1975
Indonesia	93.8	92.0	0.8	1.2	4.6	6.6	0.8	0.2
Malaysia	70.5	68.1	19.8	13.3	8.0	15.4	1.6	3.2
Philippines	94.4	82.2	1.2	1.7	3.2	5.3	1.2	10.7
Singapore	46.9	25.1	1.3	1.9	42.0	65.7	9.9	7.4
Thailand	80.9	74.1	11.8	5.1	1.8	12.0	5.4	8.7

* Products of agriculture; mining; food, beverages and tobacco processing; forestry.
† Mainly ingots of metals.
‡ Paper, chemicals, metal manufactures (including machinery and transport equipment).
SOURCE   S. W. Arndt and R. Garnaut, 'ASEAN and the Industrialisation of East Asia', *Journal of Common Market Studies*, Vol. XVII, no. 3 (1979).

(i) ASEAN was established in 1967 with the Bangkok Declaration but was inactive until February 1976 when the Treaty of Amity and Cooperation in South East Asia was signed in Bali creating a Secretariat in Jakarta and issuing a Declaration of ASEAN Concord containing the following programme of action on the economic front:

(a) 'Cooperation in basic commodities, particularly food and energy, specifically agreement by member states to give one another priority in supply in periods of critical shortage and in the acquisition of exports (presumably in periods of surplus)'.

(b) 'Industrial cooperation, specifically "to establish large-scale ASEAN industrial plants, with priority to projects which utilize the available materials in the member states, contribute to the increase of food production, . . . save foreign exchange and create employment" '.

(c) 'Cooperation in trade, specifically the establishment of "preferential trading arrangements as a long term objective . . . through rounds of negotiations subject to the unanimous agreement of member states" '.

(d) 'Joint efforts to improve access to markets outside ASEAN and joint approach to international commodity problems and other world economic problems'. (Arndt and Garnaut 1979, p. 198.)

(ii) Despite this vigour all that ASEAN has achieved so far is:

  (a) The establishment of a large urea plant (570 000 tonnes) in Indonesia but this had already been adopted as a national project by the Indonesian government.
  (b) Tariff cuts on a large number of items but their size is modest (10 % when the average tariff level is as high as 100 %) and are unlikely to have any significant impact on trade. In any case, the 'rules of origin' are such that much of the existing trade would fail to qualify for even these limited cuts!
  (c) On the second front, namely that of regional industries, progress appears to have been negligible.

It is therefore not surprising that Arndt and Garnaut (1979) made the remark that since 1976 there has been much useful talk but little practical action. However, ASEAN shows signs of developing into an important and permanent regional organisation. Hence any study of ASEAN would have to rely heavily on *potential* gains rather than the *actual* experience of the organisation. For this reason a separate chapter on ASEAN cannot be justified *at this moment in time*.

OVERALL CONCLUSIONS

One of the overall conclusions is that the so-called *types* of economic integration are appropriate only for textbook exposition purposes since they do not represent any single actual scheme. Even at the simple 'sectoral' level a degree of coordination and a minimum provision of certain institutional arrangements are needed to ensure proper and smooth functioning, for example the ECSC needed the High Authority. Also at the 'free trade area' level some administrative mechanism has to be incorporated to ensure the proper carrying out of 'rules of origin' in order to eliminate trade deflection. Hence cooperation in general and coordination of certain policies in particular are not matters strictly confined to 'economic unions' and higher levels of integration.

A second overall conclusion is that it is not entirely true that customs union theory suffers from *general* lack of applicability to the real world; this is only partially so. The theory suggests that the most likely benefits of economic integration are essentially those due to economies of scale. Economies of scale can come about in several ways, some of which are due to managerial and organisational efficiency so that plants do not have to be physically located in a concentrated area. Once allowance is made for several plants to manufacture the same product the location of such plants within an integrated area becomes of crucial importance. The experience of the EC, CMEA, EAC, etc. has clearly demonstrated that decisions regarding the location of industry have been the main source of frustration, hindering progress in some cases and leading to complete collapse in one instance. Hence, the theory does have some bearing on reality but this does not mean that it is entirely satisfactory because, despite my initial efforts (El-Agraa 1979, 1980; and El-Agraa and Jones, 1981, Chapter 6), it has not yet come to terms with unemployment and economic growth.

A third overall conclusion is that the term economic integration does not seem to mean the same thing for every type of scheme in existence. In advanced Western economies integration is about resource reallocation as determined by the law of comparative advantage defined basically in a *static* sense. For developing countries economic integration is about promoting or enhancing economic development and is advanced basically in terms of a *dynamic* infant-industry argument. In the socialist countries of Eastern Europe, integration is about production planning and plant location also defined in a context of dynamic development.

It is probably somewhat unfair to suggest that advanced Western economies are preoccupied with the static resource reallocation effects of integration since they do in fact *recognise* the dynamic effects and hope to achieve them. However, their predominant behaviour seems to be in contradiction to this recognition. For instance, most of the publicised discussion regarding the EC is conducted in terms of possible trade creation which is basically about replacing a participating nation's own expensive production by cheaper imports from a partner. In spite of this participants are outraged when they find that they are losing production in certain items accompanied by increased imports from a partner of the same item! One of my colleagues used to stress to his students that joining the EC means that British Leyland will 'go bust'. Of course, this is an over-exaggeration since what the theory suggests is that sections of British Leyland will have to cut back production or shut down altogether while other sections may get a boost. The point to stress is that the theory, despite its limitations, does point to possible redundancies in certain industrial sectors and to expansion in other sectors, but if redundancies are not acceptable then, in a fully-employed world, expansion is impossible. This argument is intuitively reinforced in a world of less than full employment: redundancies here will be vigorously resisted and expansion is impossible since unemployment is basically structural, i.e. the pool of unemployed labour does not contain the 'right' skills required in the expanding industrial sectors. In short, participants seem to enter into arrangements the possible gains from which they then proceed to actively undermine.

Related to the last issue is the point that although economic integration is pursued for wider economic aims, participants also seem preoccupied with their 'net contribution' to a central budget which pays for certain administrative tasks and, in certain instances, for carrying out certain policies. For example, in the EC *all* participants seem to want 'net receipts' in terms of contributions; this is a very peculiar demand given that the EC budget has to be balanced. Admittedly some members make unfair contributions but a situation where each participant makes nil net contribution does not make sense either. More generally, contributions have to be assessed in the wider context of economic gains and losses and must be discussed with reference to the terms of entry negotiated at the time of accession to the EC; unduly unfair contributions seem to reflect the short-sightedness of those who negotiated the accession treaties in the first place.

A very significant overall conclusion is that the global experience of economic integration has clearly demonstrated the ease with which *negative* integration can be achieved and the difficulties involved in making progress, if at all, in terms of *positive* integration. This should not be surprising, however, since the dismantling of tariff barriers and import quota restrictions is easy, particularly in a world where these have been gradually reduced through multilateral negotiations (the Kennedy and Tokyo Rounds conducted under the auspices of GATT) and the GSP (the Generalised System of Preferences) whereby certain industrial exports by developing nations are granted preferential treatment in certain advanced countries. Positive integration, on the other hand, is mainly about non-tariff barriers and here harmonisation is of paramount importance. However, harmonisation is a positive act which requires not only concerted action but also, in a number of areas, a certain degree of political commitment with implications for the sensitive issue of sovereignty as, for example, is the case in fiscal harmonisation, monetary integration and the coordination of employment policies.

PROGNOSTICATIONS

Finally, let me prognosticate about the future of integration. Haberler described the 1960s as the decade of integration. In this book we have discussed ten schemes of integration and have omitted almost twice as many. Those left out are very insignificant and the schemes covered encompass practically the whole world except for such large countries as Canada, China, India, Japan and the USA. Given that the basic justification for economic integration, particularly for developing nations, is in terms of increased size of market, it would seem that the prospects for further schemes are very limited. Of course there are prospects for higher levels of integration and for different rearrangements of groupings but these will not add significantly to the actual *number* of countries involved. Moreover, as the experience of the EC has clearly demonstrated, economic integration is very attractive when participants are experiencing high rates of growth because under such conditions even the 'regional problem' loses some of its importance. But in a stagnating world, particularly one suffering from stagflation, national interests will predominate in any discussion and will, therefore, cloud the issues. Thus, given these two considerations, it would seem that Haberler's statement is here to stay.

This, however, does not mean that the world has exhausted the possibilities for integration in the future. On the contrary, in terms of achieving *positive* integration the world is at an embryonic stage. Hence, the true challenges of integration are still to be faced and the day that one can look back and say that such a period was 'the decade of positive integration' should be awaited with extreme fascination.

Bibliography

America Latina Informa Semanal (London: Latin-American Newsletters) several numbers.

Arndt, S. W. (1968) 'On discriminatory versus non-preferential tariff policies', *Economic Journal*, vol. 78.

Arndt, S. W., and Garnaut, R. (1979) 'ASEAN and the Industrialisation of East Asia', *Journal of Common Market Studies*, vol. XVII, no. 3.

Axline, W. A. (1978) 'Integration and Development in the Commonwealth Caribbean: the politics of regional negotiations', *International Organization*, vol. 32, no. 4, pp. 953–73.

Bacha, E. and Taylor, L. (1971) 'Foreign Exchange Shadow Prices: A Critical Review of Current Theories', *Quarterly Journal of Economics*, vol. 85.

Balassa, B. (1962) *The Theory of Economic Integration*, (London: Allen and Unwin).

Balassa, B. (1967) 'Trade creation and trade diversion in the European Common Market', *Economic Journal*, vol. 77.

Balassa, B. (1974) 'Trade creation and trade diversion in the European Common Market: an appraisal of the evidence', *Manchester School*, vol. 42, no. 2, pp. 99–135.

Balassa, B. (1975) *European Economic Integration* (Amsterdam: North-Holland).

Balassa, B. (1978) 'Avantages comparés et perspectives de l'intégration économique Afrique de l'Ouest', unpublished.

Baldinelli, E. (1977) 'A New Road to Latin American Integration', *Comercio Exterior de Mexico*, vol. 23, no. 1, p. 21.

Banco Nacional de Comercio Exterior (1963) *La Integración Económica Latinoamericana*, Mexico.

Barker, T. S. (1970) 'Aggregation error and estimates of the UK import demand function', in K. Hilton and D. Heathfield (eds), *The Econometric Study of the United Kingdom* (London: Macmillan).

Barten, A. P., d'Alcantra, G., and Cairn, G. J. (1976) 'COMET, a medium-term macroeconomic model for the European Economic Community', *European Economic Review*, vol. 7, no. 1.

Bayliss, B. T. (1980) 'Competition and Industrial Policy', Chapter 6 of A. M. El-Agraa (ed.), *The Economics of The European Community* (Oxford: Philip Allan).

Beckford, G. (1976) *Caribbean Economy* (Mona, Jamaica: Institute of Social and Economic Research).

Behrman, J. N. (1972) *The Role of International Companies in Latin American Integration* (Lexington, Mass.: Heath).

Bergesten, C. F., and Krause, L. B. (eds) (1975) *World Politics and International Economics* (Washington D. C.: Brookings Institution).

Bhagwati, J. (1971) 'Customs Unions and Welfare Improvement', *Economic Journal*, vol. 81.

Binswanger, H. C. and Mayrzedt, H. M. (1972) *Europa Politik der Rest-EFTA Staaten*, Schultheses Poligraphischer Verlag, Zurich (Vienna: Wilhelm Braumüller)

Blake, B. (1976) *Anti-polarisation and Distribution Mechanism in CARICOM* (Georgetown, Guyana: Caribbean Community Secretariat).

Blake, B. (1979) *The Caribbean Community: An Assessment* (Georgetown, Guyana: Caribbean Community Secretariat).

Blankart, F. A. (1979) 'Interdépendance et Intégration', paper presented to a conference on 'la Suisse et la Communauté élargie: perspectives à long terme' held at the Battelle Institute, Geneva, November.

Brainard, L. J. (1980) 'CMEA Financial System and Integration', in P. Marer and J. M. Montias (eds), *East European Integration and East-West Trade* (Bloomington: Indiana University Press).

Brewster, H., and Thomas, C. (1967) *Dynamics of West Indian Integration* (Mona, Jamaica: Institute of Social and Economic Research).

Brewster, H. (1977) 'Focus on CARICOM: An overview of the Political Power', *Caribbean Contact*, July, vol. 5, no. 4, p. 14.

Brown, A. J. (1961) 'Economic Separatism versus a common market in developing countries', *Bulletin of Economic Research*, vol. 13.

Brown, A. J. (1972) *The Framework of Regional Economics in the United Kingdom* (Cambridge University Press).

Brown, A. J. (1980) 'Fiscal Policy: II The Budget', Chapter 12 of A. M. El-Agraa (ed), *The Economics of The European Community* (Oxford: Philip Allan).

Brus, W. (1979) 'Economic Reform and COMECON Integration in the Decade 1966–75', *Wirtschaft und Gesellschaft: Kritik und Alternativen*, (Berlin: Duncker and Humbolt).

Bulmer-Thomas, V. G. (1976) 'The Structure of Protection in Costa Rica – A New Approach to Calculating the Effective Rate of Protection', *Journal of Economic Studies*, vol. 3.

Bulmer-Thomas, V. G. (1979) 'Import Substitution v. Export Promotion in the Central American Common Market', *Journal of Economic Studies*, vol. 6.

Cable, V. (1969) 'The Football War and the Central American Common Market', *International Affairs*, October.

Caceres, L. R. (1979) 'Economic Integration and Export Instability in Central America: A Portfolio Model', in S. Smith and J. Toye (eds), *Trade and Poor Economics*, (London: Frank Cass).

Cairncross, Sir Alec et al. (1974) *Economic Policy for the European Economic Community: the Way Forward* (London: Macmillan).

Caribbean Community Secretariat (1971) *CARIFTA and the New Caribbean* (Georgetown, Guyana).

Caribbean Community Secretariat (1972) *From CARIFTA to the Caribbean Community* (Georgetown, Guyana).

Caribbean Community Secretariat (1973) *The Caribbean Community: A Guide* (Georgetown, Guyana).

Caribbean Community Secretariat (1973) *Treaty of Chaguaramas*, (Georgetown, Guyana).
Caribbean Community Secretariat (1977) *Review of the Special Regime for the LDCs* (Georgetown, Guyana).
Caribbean Community Secretariat (1980) *Developments in CARICOM since 1973* (Georgetown, Guyana).
Casson, M. (1980) 'The theory of foreign direct investment' International Economics Study Group, *Conference Proceedings* (University of Sussex).
CEAO (1973) *Traité Instituant la Communauté Economique de l'Afrique de l'Ouest*, (Ougadougon).
CEAO, *Journal Officiel*, various years (Ougadougon).
CEAO (1979) *Statistiques des Produits Agréés à la T.C.R.* (Ougadougon).
CEAO (1979) *Tarif d'Usage T.C.R.* (Ougadougon).
Chenery, H. B. (1960) 'Patterns of Industrial Growth', *American Economic Review*, vol. L.
Cline, W. R. (1978) 'Benefits and Costs of Economic Integration in Central America', in W. R. Cline and E. Delgado (eds), *Economic Integration in Central America* (Washington D.C.: Brookings Institution).
Cline, W. R. and Rapoport, A. (1978a) 'Industrial Comparative Advantage in the Central American Common Market', in W. R. Cline and E. Delgado (eds) op. cit.
Cline, W. R. and Rapoport, A. (1978b) 'Industrial Comparative Advantage: Supplementary Tables', Appendix F of W. R. Cline and E. Delgado (eds) op. cit.
Cohen Orantes, I. (1972) *Regional Integration in Central America*, (Lexington, Mass.: Lexington Books).
Collins, C. D. E. (1980) 'Social Policy', Chapter 15 of A. M. El-Agraa (ed.), *The Economics of the European Community* (Oxford: Philip Allan).
Comercio Exterior de México, monthly report on Latin American Integration.
Commission of the European Communities (1970) 'Report to the Council and the Commission on the realisation by stages of economic and monetary union in the Community', *Bulletin of the European Communities*, Supplement, no. 11 (The Werner Report).
Commission of the European Communities (1975) *Report of the Study Group 'Economic and Monetary Union 1980'*, Brussels, March (The Marjolin Report).
Commission of the European Communities (1977) *Report of the Study Group on the Role of Public Finance in European Integration*, 2 vol., Brussels, April (The MacDougall Report).
Commission of the European Communities (1980) *La Suisse et la Communauté*.
Cooper, C. A., and Massell, B. F. (1965a) 'A new look at customs union theory', *Economic Journal*, vol. 75.
Cooper, C. A., and Massell, B. F. (1965b) 'Towards a general theory of customs unions in developing countries', *Journal of Political Economy*, vol. 73.
Corden, W. M. (1972a) 'Economies of scale and customs union theory', *Journal of Political Economy*, vol. 80.
Corden, W. M. (1972b) 'Monetary Integration', *Essays in International Finance*, April, no. 93 (Princeton University).

Corden, W. M. (1977) *Inflation, Exchange Rates and the World Economy* (Oxford University Press).

Corner, D. C., and Stafford, D. C. (1977) *Open-ended Investment Funds in the EEC and Switzerland* (London: Macmillan).

Curzon, *see* Price, V. Curzon.

Cuthbertson, K. C., Henry, S. G. B., Mayes, D. G., and Savage, D. (1980) 'Modelling and forecasting the rate of exchange', International Economics Study Group, *Conference Proceedings* (University of Sussex).

Delgado, E. (1978) 'Institutional Evolution of the Central American Common Market and the Principle of Balanced Development', in W. R. Cline and E. Delgado, (eds), *Economic Integration in Central America* (Washington DC: Brookings Institution).

Demas, W. (1974a) *West Indian Nationhood and Caribbean Integration* (Barbados: CCC Publishing House).

Demas, W. (1974b) *Some Thoughts on the Caribbean Community* (Georgetown, Guyana: Caribbean Community Secretariat).

Demas, W. (1976) *Essays on Caribbean Integration and Development* (Mona, Jamaica: Institute of Social and Economic Research).

Demas, W. (1978) 'The Caribbean and the New International Economic Order', *Journal of Inter-American Studies and World Affairs*, vol. 10, no. 3, pp. 116–53.

Dell, S. (1966) *A Latin American Common Market?* (Oxford University Press).

Denison, E. F. (1967) *Why Growth Rates Differ: Post-war experience in Nine Western Countries* (assisted by J-P Poullier) (Washington, DC: Brookings Institution).

Deppler, M. C., and Ripley, D. M. (1978) 'The World trade model: merchandise trade', *IMF Staff Papers*, vol. 25, no. 1, March.

De Vries, B. A. (1977) 'Exports in the New World Environment: the Case of Latin America', *CEPAL Review*, vol. 3, pp. 112–17.

Dunning, J. H. (1980) 'Explaining the international direct investment position of countries: towards a dynamic or developmental approach', International Economics Study Group, *Conference Proceedings* (University of Sussex).

Durham, W. H. (1979) *Scarcity and Survival in Central America* (Stanford: Stanford University Press).

ECLA, *see* UN Economic Commission for Latin America.

EFTA Secretariat (1966) *Building EFTA: A Free Trade Area in Europe* (Geneva).

EFTA Secretariat (1968) *The Effects on Prices of Tariff Dismantling in EFTA* (Geneva).

EFTA Secretariat (1969) *The Effects of EFTA on the Economies of Member States* (Geneva).

EFTA Secretariat (1980a) *EFTA–Past and Future* (Geneva).

EFTA Secretariat (1980b) *The European Free Trade Association* (Geneva).

El-Agraa, A. M. (1979a) 'Common Markets in Developing Countries', in J. K. Bowers (ed.), *Inflation, Development and Integration: Essays in Honour of A. J. Brown* (Leeds University Press).

El-Agraa, A. M. (1979b) 'On Tariff Bargaining', *Bulletin of Economic Research*, vol. 31.

El-Agraa, A. M. (ed.) (1980) *The Economics of The European Community* (Oxford: Philip Allan).

El-Agraa, A. M., and Goodrich, P. S. (1980) 'Factor Mobility with specific reference to the Accounting Profession', Chapter 16 of A. M. El-Agraa (ed.), *The Economics of the European Community* (Oxford: Philip Allan).

El-Agraa, A. M., and Jones, A. J. (1981) *The Theory of Customs Unions* (Oxford: Philip Allan).

Emerson, M. (1979) 'The European Monetary System in the broader setting of the Community's economic and political development', in P. H. Trezie (ed.), *The European Monetary System: Its Promise and Prospects* (Washington, DC: Brookings Institution).

Farrell, T. (1977) 'Why CARICOM will fail: What can be done about it?', *Caribbean Contact*, July, vol. 5, no. 4, pp. 10–11.

Finch, E. A. (1973) *The Politics of Regional Integration: A Study of Uruguay's Decision to Join LAFTA*, Monograph No. 4, Centre for Latin American Studies, University of Liverpool, pp. 3, 36.

Fink, G. (1977) 'Measuring Integration: A Diagnostic Scale, Applied to EEC, CMEA, and East–West Trade, 1938–1975', *Forschungsberichte*, no. 42, August (Vienna: Wiener Institute für Internationale Wirtschaftsvergleiche).

Frank, C. (1978) 'The Demand for Labour in Manufacturing Industry in Central America', in W. R. Cline and E. Delgado (eds), *Economic Integration in Central America* (Washington DC: Brookings Institution).

Garland, J. and Marer, P. (1981) 'US Multinationals in Poland: Case Study of the International Harvester–BUMAR Cooperation in Construction Machinery', in *East European Economic Assessment*, a Compendium of Papers, submitted to the Joint Economic Committee, US Congress (Washington DC: US GPO).

Gehrels, F. (1956–7), 'Customs unions from a single country viewpoint', *Review of Economic Studies*, vol. 24.

Geiser, H., Alleyne, P., and Gajraj, C. (1976) *Legal Problems of Caribbean Integration: A Study on the Legal Problems of CARICOM* (Leyden: Sijthoff).

Ginsburgs, G. (forthcoming) 'Socialist International Economic Associations', in *Soviet and East European Law and the Scientific and Technical Revolution*.

Girvan, N. and Jefferson, O. (eds) (1971) *Readings in the Political Economy of the Caribbean*, (Mona, Jamaica: New World).

Girvan, N. (1977) 'Three Areas of Our Regional Crisis', *Caribbean Contact*, August, vol. 5., no. 5., p. 5.

Glezakos, C. (1973) 'Export Instability and Economic Growth: A Statistical Verification', *Economic Development and Cultural Change*, vol. 21.

Godwin, G., and Lake, Y. (1977) *The LDCs in Integration Schemes: The CARICOM Experience* (Antigua: ECCM Secretariat).

Grey, H. P. (1980) 'Towards a unified theory of international trade, international production, and direct foreign investment', International Economics Study Group, *Conference Proceedings* (University of Sussex).

Grey, H. P. (1981) 'Conditional Protection for 'Embattled' Industries: An Analysis', mimeo.

Grubel, H. C., and Lloyd, P. J. (1975) *Intra-industry Trade* (London: Macmillan).

Grundwald, J., Wionczek, M. S. and Carnoy, M. (1972) *Latin American*

Economic Integration and U.S. Policy (Washington DC: Brookings Institution).

Gwilliam, K. M. (1980) 'The transport policy', Chapter 8 of A. M. El-Agraa (ed.), *The Economics of the European Community* (Oxford: Philip Allan).

Haberler, G. (1964) 'Integration and growth in the world economy in historical perspective', *American Economic Review*, vol. 54.

Hall, K., and Blake, B. (1976) 'Major Developments in CARICOM 1975', in L. Manigat (ed.), *The Caribbean Yearbook of International Relations* (Leyden: Sijthoff) pp. 51–4.

Hall, K., and Blake, B. (1978) 'The Caribbean Community: Administrative and Institutional Aspects', *Journal of Common Market Studies*, vol. 16, no. 3, pp. 211–28.

Hall, K. (1979) 'Collective Self-Reliance: the Case of CARICOM', *IFDA Dossier*, no. 7.

Hansen, R. (1967) *Central America: Regional Integration and Economic Development* (Washington DC: National Planning Association).

Harberger, A. (1965) 'Survey of Literature on Cost Benefit Analysis for Industrial Project Evaluation', paper presented at the UN Inter-Regional Symposium in Industrial Project Evaluation, Prague.

Hazlewood, A. (1964) *Rail and Road in East Africa: Transport Co-ordination in Underdeveloped Countries* (Oxford: Blackwell).

Hazlewood, A. (1967) *African Integration and Disintegration* (Oxford University Press).

Hazlewood, A. (1975) *Economic Integration: the East African Experience* (London: Heinemann).

Hewett, E. (1974) *Foreign Trade Prices in the Council for Mutual Economic Assistance* (Cambridge University Press).

Holzman, F. (1974) *Foreign Trade Under Central Planning* (Cambridge, Mass.: Harvard University Press).

Houthakker, H. S., and Magee, S. P. (1969) 'Income and price elasticities in world trade', *Review of Economics and Statistics*, vol. 51.

Hu, Yao-Su (1979) 'German Agricultural Power: the impact on France and Britain', *The World Today*, vol. 35.

Hu, Yao-Su (1980) 'Energy Policy', Chapter 14 of A. M. El-Agraa (ed.), *The Economics of the European Community* (Oxford: Philip Allan).

Hufbauer, G. C. and Chilas, J. G. (1974) 'Specialization by Industrial Countries: Extent and Consequences', in H. Giersch (ed.), *The International Division of Labour: Problems and Perspectives* (Mohr: Tübingen).

IBRD (1980) *World Development Report* (Washington DC: The World Bank).

Ingram, J. C. (1973) 'The Case for European Monetary Integration', *Essays in International Finance*, April, no. 98 (Princeton University).

Instituto para la Integración de America Latina (INTAL), *El Proceso de Integración en América Latina*, annual.

Joel, C. (1971) 'Tax Incentives in Central American Development', *Economic Development and Cultural Change*, vol. 19.

Johnson, H. G. (1965) 'An economic theory of protectionism, tariff bargaining and the formation of Customs Unions', *Journal of Political Economy*, vol. 73.

Johnson, H. G. (1974) 'Trade diverting customs unions: a comment', *Economic Journal*, vol. 81.

Jones, A. J. (1979) 'The theory of economic integration', in J. K. Bowers (ed.), *Inflation, Development and Integration: Essays in Honour of A. J. Brown* (Leeds University Press).

Kaldor, N. (1971) 'The dynamics of European integration', in D. Evans (ed.), *Destiny or Delusion* (London: Gollancz).

Karnes, T. L. (1961) *The Failure of Union: Central America, 1824–1960* (Chapel Hill: University of North Carolina Press).

Kaser, M. (1967) *COMECON: Integration Problems of Planned Economies* (Oxford University Press).

Krause, L. B. (1968) *European Economic Integration and the Unites States* (Washington, DC: Brookings Institution).

Krauss, M. B. (1972) 'Recent developments in customs union theory: an interpretative survey', *Journal of Economic Literature*, vol. 10, p. 428.

Kreinin, M. E. (1961) 'The effects of tariff changes on the prices and volumes of imports', *American Economic Review*, vol. 51.

Kreinin, M. E. (1972) 'Effects of the EEC on imports of manufactures', *Economic Journal*, vol. 82.

Kreinin, M. E. (1973) 'The static effects of EEC enlargement on trade flows', *Southern Economic Journal*, vol. 39, no. 4, April, pp. 559–68.

Kreinin, M. E. (1979) 'Effects of European integration on trade flows in manufactures', European–American Seminar, University of Tilburg, June.

Lavigne, M. (1975) 'The Problem of the Multinational Socialist Enterprise', *The ACES Bulletin*, vol. XVIII: 1.

Lewis, V. (1976) 'Problems and Possibilities of the Caribbean Community', *Social Studies Education*, vol. 7, pp. 26–33.

Lipsey, R. G. (1957) 'The theory of customs unions, trade diversion and welfare', *Economica*, vol. 24, pp. 40–6.

Lipsey, R. G. (1960) 'The theory of customs unions: a general survey', *Economic Journal*, vol. 70.

Lizano, E. and Willmore, L. N. (1975) 'Second Thoughts on Central America: the Rosenthal Report', *Journal of Common Market Studies*, vol. 13.

Lysy, F. and Taylor, L. (1979) 'Vanishing Income Redistributions: Keynesian Clues About Model Surprises in the Short Run', *Journal of Development Economics*, vol. 6.

MacBean, A. (1966) *Export Instability and Economic Development* (New York: Allen and Unwin).

MacDougall, G. D. A. (1960) 'The Benefits and Costs of Private Investment From Abroad: A Theoretical Approach', *Economic Record*, vol. 36.

MacDougall Report (1977) *see* Commission of the European Communities (1977).

Machlup, F. (1977) *A History of Thought on Economic Integration* (London: Macmillan).

Machowski, H. (1977) 'International Economic Organizations within COMECON: Status, Problems, Prospects', in NATO Directorate of Economic Affairs, *COMECON: Progress and Prospects* (Brussels).

Marer, P. (1972) *Postwar Pricing and Price Patterns in Socialist Foreign Trade*, International Development Research Centre, Report 1 (Bloomington, Indiana).

Marer, P. (1976) 'Prospects for Integration in Eastern Europe: Council for

Mutual Economic Assistance', *International Organisation*, vol. 3, no. 4, reprinted in J. F. Triska and P. M. Cocks (eds), *Political Development in Eastern Europe* (New York: Praeger, 1977).

Marer, P. (1980) 'Western Multinational Corporations in Eastern Europe and CMEA Integration', in Z. Fallenbuchl and C. McMillan (eds), *Partners in East–West Economic Relations* (New York: Pergamon Press).

Marer, P. (1981) 'The Mechanism and Performance of Hungary's Foreign Trade, 1968–1979', in P. Hare, H. Radice and N. Swain (eds), *Hungary: A Decade of Reform* (London: Allen and Unwin).

Marer, P. and Montias, J. M. (1980) 'Theory and Measurement of East European Integration', in P. Marer and J. M. Montias (eds), *East European Integration and East–West Trade* (Bloomington: Indiana University Press).

Marer, P. and Montias, J. M. (1981) 'CMEA Integration: Theory and Practice', in *East European Economic Assessment* (Washington: Joint Economic Committee, Congress of the United States).

Marjolin Report (1975) *see* Commission of the European Communities (1975).

Mayes, D. G. (1971) *The Effects of Alternative Trade Groupings on the United Kingdom*, Ph.D. Thesis, University of Bristol.

Mayes, D. G. (1978) 'The effects of economic integration on trade', *Journal of Common Market Studies*, vol. 17, no. 1, pp. 1–25.

McClelland, D. H. (1972) *The Central American Common Market: Economic Growth and Choices for the Future* (New York: Praeger).

McIntyre, A. (1965) 'De-Colonialization and Trade Policy in the West Indies', in F. M. Andic and T. C. Matthews (eds), *The Caribbean Transition*, Institute of Caribbean Studies, Rio Piedras, Puerto Rico, pp. 189–212.

McIntyre, A. (1976a) *Evolution of the Process of Integration in the Caribbean* (Georgetown, Guyana: Caribbean Community Secretariat).

McIntyre, A. (1976b) *The Current Situation and Perspectives of CARICOM*, (Georgetown, Guyana: Caribbean Community Secretariat).

McIntyre, A. (1977) 'CARICOM – Setting the Records Straight', *Caribbean Contact*, July, vol. 5, no. 4, pp. 16–17.

McMillan, C. H. (1978) 'Some Thoughts on the Relationship Between Regional Integration in Eastern Europe and East–West Economic Relations', in F. Levcik (ed.), *International Economics: Comparisons and Interdependencies*, (Vienna: Springer Verlag).

Meade, J. E. (1955) *The Theory of Customs Unions* (Amsterdam: North-Holland).

Middle East Economic Survey (1968) vol. XI, no. 13, p. 2.

Milenky, E. S. (1973) *The Politics of Regional Organisation in Latin America*, (New York: Praeger).

Mingst, K. A. (1977/78) 'Regional sectoral economic integration: the case of OAPEC', *Journal of Common Market Studies*, vol. XVI.

Mitchell, C. (1967) 'The Role of Technocrats in Latin American Integration', *Inter-American Economic Affairs*, vol. 21, no. 1.

Mitrofanova, N. M. (1979) 'The Economic Nature of Contract Prices in Mutual Collaboration of CMEA Countries', *Izvestiia Akademii nauk SSSR*, translated in *Soviet and East European Trade*, vol. XV, no. 1, Spring, p. 9.

Monteforte Toledo, M. (1972) *Centro America: Subdesarrollo y Dependencia*, 2 vols., (Mexico City: Instituto de Investigaciones Sociales).

Montias, J. M. (1967) *Economic Development in Communist Rumania*, (Cambridge, Mass.: MIT Press).

Montias, J. M. (1969) 'Obstacles to Economic Integration of Eastern Europe', *Studies in Comparative Communism*, July–October.

Mordecai, J. (1968) *The West Indies: the Federal Negotiations* (London: Allen and Unwin).

Morgan, A. D. (1970) 'Income and price elasticities in world trade: a comment', *Manchester School*, vol. 38.

Morgenstern, K. (1978) 'The International Specialization of Production and its Concentration in CMEA Countries', *Voprosy ekonomiki*, no. 2, translated in *Soviet and East European Trade*, vol. xv, no. 1 Spring 1979.

Morris, C. N. (1980) 'The Common Agricultural Policy', *Fiscal Studies*, vol. 1, no. 2, March, pp. 17–35.

Mundell, R. A. (1967) 'Tariff preferences and the terms of trade', *Manchester School*, vol. 32.

Nevin, E. T. (1980) 'Regional Policy', Chapter 13 of A. M. El-Agraa (ed.), *The Economics of the European Community* (Oxford: Philip Allan).

Nugent, J. B. (1974) *Economic Integration in Central America* (Baltimore: Johns Hopkins University Press).

OECD (1979) 'The OECD international linkage model', *OECD Economic Outlook*, January.

Orcutt, G. H. (1950) 'Measurement of price elasticities in international trade', *Review of Economics and Statistics*, vol. 32.

Panić, M. (1980) 'Some longer term effects of short-run adjustment policies: behaviour of U.K. direct investment since the 1960s', International Economics Study Group, *Conference Proceedings* (University of Sussex).

Pécsi, K. (1977) *A KGST Termelési Integráció Közgazdasági Kérdései* (Economic Issues of CMEA's Production Integration), Közgazdasági es Jogi Könyvkiadó, Budapest. An English translation of a revised and updated edition will be published by M. E. Sharpe (New York: White Plains, 1981)

Petith, H. C. (1977) 'European integration and the terms of trade', *Economic Journal*, vol. 87.

Pinder, J. (1968) 'Positive and negative integration: some problems of economic union in the EEC', *The World Today*, vol. 24.

Pinder, J. (ed) (1971) *The Economics of Europe* (London: Knight).

Pollard, D. (1976) 'Institutional and Legal Aspects of the Caribbean Community', *Caribbean Studies*, vol. 14, no. 1, pp. 39–74.

Prest, A. R. (1979) 'Fiscal Policy', Chapter 4 of P. Coffey (ed.), *Economic Policies of the Common Market* (London: Macmillan).

Price, V. Curzon (1974) *The Essentials of Economic Integration* (London: Macmillan).

Proctor, J. (1956) 'Britain's Pro-Federation Policy in the Caribbean: An Inquiry into Motivation', *Canadian Journal of Economics and Political Science*, vol. 4.

Raddavero, B. C. (1978) 'La Promoción y el Desarrollo de Proyectos Multinacionales en América Latina', *Integración Latinoamericana*, Jan–Feb.

Raisman Report, Colonial Office (1961) *East Africa: Report of the Economic and Fiscal Commission*, Cmnd. 1279 (London: HMSO).

Ramsaran, R. (1978) 'CARICOM: the Integration Process in Crisis', *Journal of World Trade Laws*, vol. 12, no. 3, pp. 208–17.

Rapoport, A. (1978) 'Effective Protection Rates in Central America', Appendix K of W. R. Cline and E. Delgado (eds), *Economic Integration in Central America* (Washington DC: Brookings Institution).

Republic of Trinidad and Tobago (1979) *White Paper on CARICOM, 1973–78*, (Port-of-Spain: Government Printery).

Reynolds, C. and Leiva, G. (1978) 'Employment Problems of Export Economies in a Common Market: the Case of Central America', in W. R. Cline and E. Delgado (eds), *Economic Integration in Central America* (Washington DC: Brookings Institution).

Robson, P. (1968) *Economic Integration in Africa* (London: Allen and Unwin).

Robson, P. (ed.) (1972) *International Economic Integration* (Harmondsworth: Penguin).

Robson, P. (1980) *The Economics of International Integration*, (London: Allen and Unwin), p. 4.

Rosenthal, G. (1973) *The Role of Private Foreign Investment in the Development of the Central American Common Market*, mimeo, Guatemala.

Sackey, J. (1978) 'The Structure and Performance of CARICOM: Lessons for the Development of ECOWAS', *Canadian Journal of African Studies*, vol. 12, no. 2, pp. 259–77.

Scaperlanda, A. (1967) 'The EEC and US foreign investment: some empirical evidence', *Economic Journal*, March, vol. 77.

Schmitter, P. C. and Haas, E. B. (1964) *Mexico and Latin American Economic Integration*, Research Series no. 5, Institute of International Studies, University of California (Berkeley, California) p. 16.

Schweitzer, I. (1977) 'Some Particularities of Hungarian Machine Imports from the Soviet Union', *Acta Oeconomica*, 18:304.

Scitovsky, T. (1958) *Economic Theory and Western European Integration* (London: Allen and Unwin).

Shanks, M. (1977) *European Social Policy, Today and Tomorrow* (Oxford: Pergamon Press).

Shibata, H. (1971) 'The Theory of Economic Unions: comparative analysis of Customs Unions, Free Trade Areas and Tax Unions', in C. S. Shoup (ed.), *Fiscal Harmonisation in Common Markets* (Columbia University Press 1967), reproduced, amended, in P. Robson (ed.), *International Economic Integration* (Harmondsworth: Penguin).

SIECA (1973) *El Desarrollo Integrado de Centroamérica en la Presente Década: Bases y Propuestas para el Perfeccionamienro, y la Reestructuración del Mercado Comun Centroamericano*, 13 vols., Institute for Latin American Integration, Inter-American Development Bank (Buenos Aires).

Siri, G. (1978) 'Calculation of the Shadow Price of Foreign Exchange Based on the Central American Econometric Model', in W. R. Cline and E. Delgado (eds), *Economic Integration in Central America* (Washington DC: Brookings Institution).

Smith, Adam (1776) *An Enquiry Into the Nature and Causes of the Wealth of Nations* (Glasgow: Chapman).

Smith, A. J. (1977) 'The Council of Mutual Economic Assistance in 1977: new economic power, new political perspectives and some old and new problems', in US Congress Joint Economic Committee's *East European Economies Post-Helsinki*.

Soutar, G. (1977) 'Export Instability and Economic Growth', *Journal of Development Economics*, vol. 4.

Sowell, T. (1980) *Knowledge and Decisions* (New York: Basic Books).

Sumner, M. T., and Zis, G. (eds) (1982) *European Monetary Union* (London: Macmillan).

Sundelius, B., and Wiklund, C. (1979) 'The Nordic Community: the ugly duckling of regional cooperation', *Journal of Common Market Studies*, September, vol. XVIII, no. 1.

Swann, D. (1978) *The Economics of the Common Market* (Harmondsworth: Penguin).

Thomas, C. (1977) 'The Community is a big paper tiger', *Caribbean Contact*, July, vol. 5, no. 4, p. 15.

Thomas, C. (1979) 'Neo-Colonialism and Caribbean Integration', in B. Ince (ed.), *Contemporary International Relations of the Caribbean*, Institute of International Relations, U.W.I., St. Augustine, pp. 284–99.

Tinbergen, J. (1954) *International Economic Integration* (Amsterdam: Elsevier).

Trend, H. (1977) 'Economic Integration and Plan Coordination under COMECON', in K. Robert and J. F. Brown (eds), *Eastern Europe's Uncertain Future* (New York: Praeger).

UN Economic Commission for Latin America (1957) *Los Problemas Actuales del Comercio Interlatinoamericano*, E/CN. 12/423.

UN Economic Commission for Latin America (1962) *Multilateral Economic Cooperation in Latin America*, vol. 1, E/CN. 12/621.

UN Economic Commission for Europe (1971) 'Note on the Projection of the Matrices of International Trade', *Economic Bulletin for Europe*, vol. 22, no. 1.

Vaitsos, C. V. (1978) 'Crisis in Regional Economic Cooperation (Integration) among Developing Countries: A Survey', *World Development*, vol. 6, pp. 722–3.

van Brabant, J. M. (1980) *Socialist Economic Integration* (Cambridge University Press).

Vargas-Hidalgo, R. (1979) 'The Crisis of the Andean Pact: Lessons for Integration Among Developing Countries', *Journal of Common Market Studies*, vol. XVII, no. 3, March.

Verdoorn, P. J., and Schwartz, A. N. R. (1972) 'Two alternative estimates of the effects of EEC and EFTA on the pattern of trade', *European Economic Review*, vol. 3, pp. 291–335.

Viner, J. (1950) *The Customs Union Issue* (New York: Carnegie Endowment for International Peace).

Wallace, E. (1977) *The British Caribbean: From the Decline of Colonialism to the End of the Federation* (Toronto: University of Toronto Press).

Wallace, W. (1980) (ed.), *Britain In Europe* (London: Heinemann).

Werner Report (1970) *see* Commission of the European Communities (1970).

Wilford, W. T. (1970) 'Trade Creation in the Central American Common Market', *Western Economic Journal*, vol. 8.

Wilford, W. T. (1978) 'On Revenue Performance and Revenue-Income Stability in the Third World', *Economic Development and Cultural Change*, April.

Wilkie, J. W. and Reich, R. (1978, 1980) *Statistical Abstract of Latin America*, vols 19, 20 (Los Angeles: UCLA).

Williams, R. (1978) 'Economies of Scale Parameters for Central American

Manufacturing Industry', in W. R. Cline and E. Delgado (eds), *Economic Integration in Central America*, (Washington DC: Brookings Institution).

Willmore, L. N. (1975/6) 'Trade Creation, Trade Diversion and Effective Protection in the Central American Common Market', *Journal of Development Studies*, vol. 12, no. 4.

Willmore, L. N. (1976) 'Direct Foreign Investment in Central American Manufacturing', *World Development*, vol. 4.

Wionczek, M. S. (ed.) (1966) *Latin American Economic Integration* (New York: Praeger).

Wionczek, M. S. (1970) 'The Rise and the Decline of Latin American Economic Integration', *Journal of Common Market Studies*, vol. 9.

Wionczek, M. S. (1972) 'The Central American Common Market', in P. Robson (ed.), *International Economic Integration* (Harmondsworth: Penguin).

Yotopoulos, P. and Nugent, J. (1976) *The Economics of Development: Empirical Investigations* (New York: Harper and Row).

Author Index

Subject Index